MARCUS' KITCHEN

MARCUS' KITCHEN

My favourite recipes to inspire your home-cooking

Marcus Wareing

with Craig Johnston

Photography by Susan Bell

 HarperCollins*Publishers*

Contents

Introduction 9

Introduction

This is my most personal book yet, a collection of recipes we like to eat at home at different points during each week, depending on mood and occasion, but always focused on flavour. I hope they inspire you.

When we started discussing the ideas for this book we had no inkling of what was coming; as Covid-19 spread across the world and the UK, I was forced to close both of my restaurants as the first lockdown began. It was an unsettling time for everyone.

However, despite Covid and the trauma it brought to many, the changes to my life made the title Marcus' Kitchen take on a whole new meaning. For the first time in my almost 40-year working life I was at home all day, every day. Though it took some getting used to, I can honestly say I began to relish the routine: I enjoyed spending time with my family and creating new habits as I got to grips with the management of our home kitchen.

Food has always been a massive focus in our house, but in the past this was mostly restricted to weekends, when we were all home. Lockdown changed that; it became important every day. I know our family was very lucky – both Jane and I can cook and enjoy doing so, and we can afford the highest-quality ingredients. We shared the task and sometimes our children became involved. When the kids took over and cooked the entire meal it was a wonderful treat.

Our shopping habits changed, too: it suddenly became a once-a-week trip, which meant planning for the week ahead. This isn't a new skill – my mother shopped like this – but I have the feeling that before the pandemic it had become the norm for many of us to shop almost daily, buying ingredients based on what we felt like eating that night, rather than planning more and shopping less. I am a firm believer in thoughtful shopping, careful stock control and keen waste management. Not only does it involve less effort in the long run, but it keeps costs down. As a nation we waste so much food, which is bad for the environment as well as for our pockets.

The Wareing family meals are determined by the time available for cooking, the ingredients we have to hand, and the person at the hob. I've heard a lot of home cooks complain that they were stuck for ideas and getting bored of their usual dishes during the pandemic, most often when it was the same person doing the shopping and the daily cooking. If that sounds familiar, I hope this book will be useful to you. We have based this book on our family recipes and grouped them into different sections that are useful at different times of the week. The chapter titles are very much focused on the newly formed habits of our week.

TIGHT FOR TIME

Sometimes, a quick and easy meal is what's needed. I am adamant that being short of time should not lead to a compromise on flavour. A few of these dishes may take a little planning at the start of the day (such as the chocolate mousse, which needs to be in the fridge for a few hours), though the actual preparation and cooking is fairly fast. Of course, I am well aware that making these dishes is straightforward for me – initially you may be slower, as you read and learn the recipe – but I am sure they will become firm, speedy favourites. Try the Indonesian Raw Salad with Tofu on page 18 – the sauce is amazing.

MARKET GARDEN

I love my kitchen garden at Melfort House in Sussex. One of my favourite ways to cook is to see what's available in the garden then come up with a dish (I particularly love using the herbs we grow). If you don't grow your own, your local supermarket or greengrocer will stock seasonal British produce, which is usually a little less expensive than imported ingredients and definitely far tastier. This chapter includes recipes you can use through the year depending on the produce available, and ideas for making the most of bumper crops. The Braised Cabbage in a Warming Broth on page 64 is a delight each time we make it.

SIMPLY ESSENTIAL

As you get towards the end of the week and are running out of fresh ingredients, it's handy to have a well-stocked store cupboard. This chapter is a personal collection of my most-loved flavours, using ingredients that I always keep in my larder. The family's favourite and a real regular is the Pork Loin in Black Bean Sauce on page 102.

WEEKEND WONDERS

At the end of the working week, when we have a little more time on our hands, we like to make things that are more exciting and may take a bit more time and planning. On occasion over lockdown, we used a few of my restaurant suppliers to find some special ingredients and made some real 'wow' dishes. We started a list of 'best lockdown dinners' and a few appear in this chapter. The Baked Chilli Beef and Sweetcorn Cobbler on page 134, with its smoky flavours, is so good.

BAKING

I worked as a baker in Amsterdam early on in my career, and although I bake far less now, lockdown gave me the chance to pass on my skills to my daughter Jess. She has now taken on the mantel of home baker – it's her way of relaxing. This chapter features some delicious recipes: some are quick, others take a little more time. My advice is to follow the recipe carefully to ensure success – baking requires specific times and weights. A note about the bread recipes: they are all different and may use different yeast, different flour, and different techniques. Start with the Milk and Rosemary Loaves on page 150 – we love them (thank you, Chef Shauna).

WORTH THE WAIT

Working from home brought many challenges but it did reduce travel time and gave many the opportunity to spend more time in their kitchens, and to use cooking to relax and to learn new skills. All of these recipes take time, either through advance planning, cooking time or the level of technical skills required. They are all delicious and I'd be hard-pushed to pick a favourite, but the Rosemary and Malt-glazed Lamb Belly with Salsa Verde on page 194 is a winner.

SOMETHING SPECIAL

During lockdown we didn't get to entertain much – in fact we didn't entertain at all –but there are some fabulous dishes here which will be perfect as normal life resumes and we share a table with our loved ones. Some recipes are more involved than others – I would always advise practising first before serving to guests! The Rump Cap with Beef-fat Bearnaise and Potato Terrine on page 246 is a firm favourite with me and my sons.

KITCHEN FOUNDATIONS

This is full of useful recipes and hints, including some fantastic dressings. Some recipes in this book use lots of egg yolks so here you can find recipes to use the whites – I don't like waste!

Bringing the habits of the restaurant kitchen into the home

I first started working in a professional kitchen when I was 14 years old, so when I cook it's through instinct, knowledge, taste and years of experience. When I'm cooking at home, even though the dishes are different, I still use the same skills that I use at work.

Jane and our three children are always questioning, learning and watching as I cook. So far, we have Archie the breakfast chef, Jake the meat chef and Jessie on pastry and salads. I am determined that each of them will be able to cook well before they leave home, and my enforced time at home helped massively with the training.

As my colleague Craig Johnston and I pulled together the recipes for the book, it was so useful to have Jane (who isn't a professional chef) involved in the writing. She quizzed and queried and double-checked things with us as we went along, and asked the questions that you might also have, which led to us including plenty of hints and tips, which we hope will help you achieve the best results for each dish and assist you with your cooking generally.

A FEW HINTS BEFORE YOU START COOKING:
- First, read the recipe fully: do you have all the ingredients, do you have the kit, do you have the time?
- Just before you begin to cook, clear the kitchen! A tidy cook leads to an organised cook. The process of cooking will be more enjoyable, and you won't run out of utensils.
- Weigh and prep the ingredients as instructed in the recipe list. It makes it easier to cook if you have everything to hand and ready to use.

In this book we use medium free-range eggs, unsalted butter, whole milk (but semi-skimmed

can be substituted), and medium-sized fruit and vegetables – unless the recipe states otherwise. Also, we use Maldon salt when cooking, unless a recipe requires a finer salt, then it's usually table salt. You'll find most of the more specialist ingredients in supermarkets, but if you can't find them, look online.

Though we sometimes suggest alternative ingredients, ultimately the main recipe is what should be followed. Changing the ingredients will change the dish. The more experienced home cook will learn to adapt recipes to their own tastes – don't forget to make notes by the recipe if you change anything!

Spending time cooking with my family gave me a greater understanding of what the home cook experiences – the need to feed a family but also the desire to impress and learn. I hope that this collection of recipes will make your life easier but also inspire you to try different things, and perhaps even find a few new favourites that you return to time and time again.

As I write this in the summer of 2021, there is a feeling of positivity in the air. My restaurant Marcus at the Berkeley is open, and we can cook for friends and extended family in our homes again. If food was important before then it's vital now because it's bringing us back together. Cooking should be a pleasure, though sometimes it's simply a necessity. Make the most of your fridge, freezer and store cupboard, and try to reduce your shopping and waste – it might just give you more time to cook and enjoy the process! Hopefully this book offers a good mix of recipes that suit every need and every day of the week.

As we look forward, I feel that we have all learned something from the pandemic and hospitality and cooking – even shopping – may never be the same again. Happy cooking!

Tight for Time

Indonesian Raw Salad with Tofu

SERVES: 4
**PREP TIME: 20 MINUTES, PLUS
30 MINUTES SOAKING
COOKING TIME: 35 MINUTES**

4 eggs
150g mangetout
vegetable oil, for frying
150g firm tofu, cut into small cubes
100g bean sprouts
100g radishes, cut into quarters
1 small Chinese cabbage, shredded
1 small carrot, grated
½ cucumber, halved lengthways, seeds
    removed, and sliced
sea salt and freshly ground black pepper
1 lime, quartered, to serve

FOR THE DRESSING
30g dried shrimps, chopped
50ml vegetable oil
30g sliced pancetta, finely chopped
1 red onion, grated
2 garlic cloves, crushed
2 red chillies, finely chopped
1 tsp dried chilli flakes
100ml rice wine
2 tbsp kecap manis (sweet soy sauce)
2 tbsp oyster sauce
2 tbsp crunchy peanut butter

VARIATION

**The aim is to have crisp salad flavours,
so you could use almost anything, such
as cabbage (lightly blanched if you
prefer), fennel, tomatoes, green beans
and celery.**

If you are not a big fan of tofu, the way it is used in this raw salad will win you over as it did me. The salad is based on the Indonesian gado gado, a dish that we are becoming more familiar with here in the UK. The crisp vegetables work really well with the tofu, egg and spicy peanut dressing, which is similar to a satay dressing though a little looser. It is fresh and delicious and very hard to resist for lunch or a light dinner. You could serve it on a large platter and allow people to help themselves, or serve it in individual bowls.

1. First, put the dried shrimps for the dressing in a small heatproof bowl and cover with 100ml boiling water. Leave to soak for 30 minutes.

2. Heat the 50ml of vegetable oil for the dressing in a saucepan over medium heat, add the pancetta and cook for 2–3 minutes until crisp. Drain the shrimps and add them to the pan, reserving the soaking liquid for later. Cook the shrimp with the pancetta for 2–3 minutes until the shrimps begin to colour, then add the onion, garlic and fresh chillies and chilli flakes and sweat for 2–3 minutes until softened. Deglaze the pan with the rice wine and allow it to reduce by half, then add the remaining ingredients and mix until well combined. Remove from the heat. If the mix is too thick, loosen it with some of the reserved soaking liquid from the shrimps. The dressing should be thick but still pourable.

3. Bring a saucepan of salted water to the boil and cook the eggs for 6 minutes (or longer, depending on your preference). For the last minute of cooking, add the mangetout. Drain well and cool in iced water, then drain the mangetout and peel the eggs from their shells. Set aside.

4. Heat a splash of vegetable oil in a frying pan over medium heat, add the diced tofu and sauté for 8–10 minutes until golden. Drain well on kitchen paper and season with salt, and while it's draining, warm through the dressing.

5. To assemble the salad, combine the bean sprouts, radishes, Chinese cabbage, carrot, cucumber and the cooked mangetout then place a layer of the salad on each plate. Top with the crispy tofu and boiled eggs (which have been halved) and season with salt and pepper, then drizzle with the hot peanut dressing. Serve with a wedge of lime to squeeze over.

Beef Tartare with Piccalilli Dressing and Toast

SERVES: 2
PREP TIME: 30 MINUTES
COOKING TIME: 5 MINUTES

200g beef steak (fillet, sirloin or bavette)
2 thick slices of sourdough
50g beef dripping, melted
1 garlic clove, halved
2 egg yolks
sea salt and freshly ground black pepper

FOR THE PICCALILLI DRESSING

30g pickled silverskin onions, finely chopped
10g capers, roughly chopped
20g cornichons, sliced to match size of
     capers
½ bunch of chives, finely chopped
½ tsp English mustard
1 tsp wholegrain mustard
1 tsp American mustard
½ tsp ground turmeric
50ml extra virgin rapeseed oil
½ tsp Worcestershire sauce
Tabasco, to taste

* Make it perfect
The vinegar-based dressing will start
to cure the meat, so dressing and meat
should be combined just before serving.

   Fillet is ideal because it has no
additional fat so needs very little
preparation. Though it's more expensive,
you eat the weight that you buy (rather
than having to trim it of fat). Filet mignon,
the thinner end of the fillet, is a slightly
cheaper option: it has the same qualities
as regular fillet and it's ideal for chopping.
If you're using sirloin, you will need to
remove the layer of fat before chopping
the meat.

You typically find this classical French dish in brasseries, and when we had it on the menu at The Berkeley it was very popular. Traditionally it is served with capers, or silverskin onions, possibly with a raw egg yolk on top. Here the meat is mixed with a mustard-based sweet piccalilli dressing; piccalilli is a childhood favourite and here it slightly cures the meat and gives it a wonderful flavour. You could top the tartare with caviar to make it more decadent, if you like, though it is pretty special already. I recommend visiting your butcher to buy the best-quality meat; my preference for tartare is fillet as it is the leanest cut.

1. To prepare the tartare, finely chop the steak of your choice into small dice (or whatever size you prefer), discarding any fat. Once all the beef has been chopped, return it to the fridge in a bowl to keep it as cold as possible.

2. While the meat is in the fridge, make the piccalilli dressing by whisking all the ingredients together in a small bowl, adding a few drops of Tabasco (to your preference).

3. Preheat a griddle pan over medium heat.

4. Generously brush both sides of the sourdough with the beef dripping and season with salt and pepper. Place them in the hot griddle pan and toast for 2–3 minutes on each side until golden and crispy, trying not to move them between turns, so they develop brown char lines. Remove from the pan and rub both sides with the garlic.

5. To finish the beef tartare, mix enough of the dressing through the diced meat to coat every piece, taste the tartare and season with salt and pepper accordingly.

6. Divide the tartare between two serving plates, pressing it into the bottom of a large ring cutter, then remove the cutter and top the tartare with a raw egg yolk, seasoning the yolk with salt and pepper. Serve the tartare with the hot toast alongside.

Pan-fried Scallops with Celeriac and Chimichurri Slaw

SERVES: 4 AS A LIGHT LUNCH OR STARTER
PREP TIME: 20 MINUTES
COOKING TIME: 5 MINUTES

splash of olive oil
8 large scallops (coral removed and
    discarded), sliced through the middle (or
    use smaller scallops left whole)
25g unsalted butter
sea salt and freshly ground black pepper

FOR THE CHIMICHURRI
½ bunch of flat-leaf parsley
½ bunch of coriander
8 mint leaves
1 garlic clove, crushed
2 green chillies, deseeded and chopped
75ml olive oil
1 tbsp sherry vinegar

FOR THE SLAW
1 Granny Smith apple
½ small celeriac
2 tbsp Greek yoghurt
grated zest of 1 lime
1 tsp Dijon mustard

* Make it perfect
Scallops take very little time to cook, so it is important to know which went into the pan first. You can do this by placing the scallops around the pan in clock formation, starting at the top. Don't shake the pan as they cook, and only season them on the side in direct contact with the pan: as soon as you put salt on the flesh, it starts to draw out water, steaming the scallops rather than frying them, preventing them forming a flavourful caramelised crust. It's the same principle with steak.

Chimichurri, a South American spicy herb sauce, is a huge favourite in our house, though it is generally tasted with some trepidation as we all assess the chilli levels. I love pairing its freshness with these meaty scallops, by stirring it through a celeriac and apple slaw (a take on the classic celeriac remoulade). Chunky bread or grilled flatbread is a must, for mopping up the sauce.

1. First, make the chimichurri. Put all the ingredients in a small blender (including the herb stems as well as the leaves) and blitz until you have a smooth paste. Taste and season with salt if required.

2. To prepare the slaw, peel the apple and celeriac then cut them into thin slices (use a mandoline if you have one). Cut the slices into long, thin matchstick strips and place them in a mixing bowl. Add the yoghurt, lime zest, mustard and half of the prepared chimichurri, then mix until everything is well coated in the chimichurri and yoghurt. Season to taste with salt and pepper.

3. To cook the scallops, heat the olive oil in a large frying pan over medium-high heat. Season one side of the scallop with salt, then place it in the pan seasoned side down. Starting from the part of the pan furthest away from you, lay the scallops in a clockwise direction around the pan. Cook for 1½–2 minutes until caramelised, add the butter to the pan, season the uncooked side and then flip the scallops, starting with the first one you put in the pan and working in a clockwise direction to the last. Cook the scallops for a further 30 seconds–1 minute on the second side before quickly removing from the pan. You will know the scallop is cooked when it firms up and browns: avoid overcooking them as they can become rubbery. Remove in the same order you placed them in the pan, starting with the scallop at the top.

4. To serve, spoon piles of the dressed slaw in the centre of four plates, then place the scallop pieces evenly around. Drizzle the remaining chimichurri over the scallops for an extra chilli kick, if you like.

My Kedgeree

SERVES: 4, GENEROUSLY
PREP TIME: 40 MINUTES
COOKING TIME: 1 HOUR 10
MINUTES–1 HOUR 20 MINUTES

FOR THE SPLIT PEAS

200g yellow split peas, rinsed and drained
1 tsp ground turmeric
½ tsp salt

FOR THE RICE

300g basmati rice, rinsed and drained

FOR THE HADDOCK

500g undyed smoked haddock fillet
500ml milk
6 black peppercorns
2 bay leaves

This version of kedgeree makes a great brunch or a comforting supper on a cold night. My wife has always been a fan of kedgeree, and we both like this recipe with the addition of the split peas as it is a little creamier (historically the recipe always featured split peas – it seems that the peas have been lost over the years as it has become more Westernised). Kedgeree involves cooking various ingredients separately and then bringing them all together at the end. Start cooking the split peas about an hour before you start everything else – you don't want anything to chill completely before bringing it all together in the pan at the end.

1. First, cook the split peas. Put the peas in a large saucepan with the turmeric and add the salt and 1 litre of water. Cover and bring to the boil over medium heat, then reduce the heat to a simmer and cook the peas for 40–50 minutes, half covered with a lid, until soft. Remove from the heat, let them cool a little, and blitz with a stick blender (or in a blender) until smooth. Set aside.

2. Put the rice in a saucepan, cover with cold water (about 1.5cm above the rice level), cover and bring to the boil over medium heat. Once the water boils, allow it to simmer gently for 2–3 minutes. Switch off the heat, keeping the lid firmly on, and leave the pan on the hob so that the rice cooks with the residual heat (if your induction hob goes completely cold then you may need to leave the hob on a low setting – see page 100). The rice will steam and should be cooked after 10–15 minutes. It's okay if the grains still have a slight bite, as they are returned to the heat to cook further.

3. While the rice is cooking, cook the haddock. Place it skin side down in a large skillet or frying pan, so it sits in an even layer (cut the pieces in half if you need to). Pour over the milk and add the peppercorns and bay leaves to the pan. Cover and bring to the boil over medium heat then turn down the heat and simmer for 10 minutes, until the fish is just cooked through and flakes easily. Transfer the fish to a plate and strain the milk into a heatproof jug (retain the milk for later).

TO FINISH THE DISH

2 tbsp olive oil

1 white onion, finely chopped

1–2 green chillies, diced

6cm piece of fresh ginger, peeled and finely
    chopped

2 garlic cloves, finely chopped

2 tsp cumin seeds

sea salt and freshly ground black pepper

TO SERVE

4 eggs

small bunch of curly parsley, finely chopped

2 pieces of smoked salmon, cut into strips

VARIATIONS

**Leave out the haddock and salmon to
make the dish vegetarian, heating the
milk as above, with the pepper and
bay, and just excluding the fish.
If you prefer to serve the kedgeree with
a soft yolk, cook the eggs for 6 minutes
and serve them immediately to avoid
losing the runny yolk. Alternatively,
serve with soft poached eggs on top.**

4. To finish, heat the oil in the pan you used for the fish over medium heat, add the onion, chillies and ginger and cook for about 5 minutes until soft and starting to caramelise. Add the garlic and cumin seeds and cook for a further 2 minutes. Remove from the heat.

5. Cook the eggs in a pan of simmering water for 8 minutes, then cool immediately under cold running water, peel and quarter.

6. While the eggs are cooking, remove the fish from the skin – it should come away easily in large flakes.

7. Stir the cooked split peas into the spice mixture in the pan, add 4 ladles of the reserved milk and heat the mixture through, stirring to combine. Fold the cooked rice into the mixture and season well, then fold in the fish. If the mixture is too dry, add a little more of the reserved milk (you may end up needing to use it all). The consistency should be soft, like a risotto, and not dry or stodgy.

8. Check the seasoning, adding salt and pepper if needed, and serve on a plate or wide-based bowl with parsley on top and 4 egg quarters per portion. Drape the strips of smoked salmon over the top.

Peppered Sardines with a Green Olive Sauce

SERVES: 4
PREP TIME: 15 MINUTES
COOKING TIME: 5 MINUTES

8 fresh sardines, butterflied
olive oil
freshly picked oregano leaves, to serve
sliced fresh green almonds (optional)
sea salt

FOR THE PEPPER SEASONING

2 tbsp black peppercorns
1 tbsp pink peppercorns
½ tsp white peppercorns
1 tsp coriander seeds
2 tsp Maldon salt

FOR THE GREEN OLIVE SAUCE

200g fresh pitted green olives
200g warm (not hot) white chicken stock
50ml extra virgin olive oil
1 slice of white bread, crusts removed
1 garlic clove
juice of ½ lemon

VARIATION

Serve the sauce with other oily fish, such as mackerel or a fillet of salmon.

I love the Mediterranean feel to this dish: the olive-flavoured sauce perfectly complements the strong-flavoured fish with its oily and meaty texture. There are a variety of peppercorns used here, as each type brings its own flavour to the sauce. Fresh almonds, a seasonal treat in spring or early summer, are a delight with their soft, milky texture, but they can be left out if they're not available. When we are making the pepper seasoning (and any dried seasoning mixes) at home, we often make extra to keep for another time. If you want to do the same, keep them in old spice pots and tins, but remember to label them! Serve the sardines and sauce as they are with crunchy bread, or with boiled new potatoes.

1. To make the pepper seasoning, grind the spices and salt in a mortar with a pestle until finely ground.

2. Preheat the grill to its highest setting.

3. Make the green olive sauce in a high-speed blender. Put the pitted olives, chicken stock, olive oil, white bread and garlic in the blender and blitz on full speed for 2–3 minutes until smooth and glossy. Season the olive sauce with the lemon juice and then season with salt to taste.

4. To cook the sardines, drizzle them with olive oil on both sides and place on a grill tray or baking tray skin side up, then generously season the sardine skin with the pepper mix. Place under the hot grill and cook for 2–3 minutes until the skin is crisp and the fish is cooked through.

5. To serve, put a spoon of the green olive sauce on four large serving plates and spread it out slightly using the back of the spoon. Remove the peppered sardines from the grill and carefully place 2 sardines skin side up on top of the sauce. Garnish with a few freshly picked oregano leaves, almonds (if using) and finish with a drizzle of extra virgin olive oil. Serve the remaining green olive sauce on the side.

Chorizo and Sweetcorn Pancakes with Coriander Yoghurt

SERVES: 4
PREP TIME: 20 MINUTES
COOKING TIME: 15 MINUTES

175g self-raising flour
25g cornmeal or polenta
½ tsp salt
½ tsp sweet smoked paprika
150g buttermilk
3 eggs
100g tinned, drained sweetcorn
75g soft cooking chorizo, skins removed and sausage meat chopped into small pieces
vegetable oil, for frying

FOR THE CORIANDER YOGHURT
½ bunch of coriander
1 garlic clove
½ green chilli, chopped
pinch of salt
200g natural yoghurt
juice of ½ lemon

We always have some chorizo in the fridge, ready to liven up anything from salads to brown rice, but here it is used to make fabulous little pancakes using other store-cupboard ingredients. During the Covid lockdowns, with more people staying at home, 'What's for lunch?' became a common quandary and there was an increasing desire for something more exciting than sandwiches. These pancakes are easy to make and go down a treat with everyone.

1. First, make the coriander yoghurt. Place the coriander, garlic, green chilli and salt in a mortar and bash to a paste with a pestle. Transfer the paste to a bowl and stir through the yoghurt and lemon juice. Set aside.

2. Preheat the oven to a low setting (just hot enough to keep the pancakes warm).

3. Now make the pancake batter. Put the self-raising flour in a large bowl with the cornmeal, salt and smoked paprika. Mix until evenly combined.

4. In a separate jug, whisk the buttermilk with the eggs until smooth.

5. Make a well in the middle of the flour mixture then gradually pour the egg mixture into the dry ingredients, whisking slowly from the centre outwards until you have a smooth, thick batter. Once all the liquid has been added and incorporated, stir through the tinned sweetcorn and chopped chorizo.

6. Heat a large non-stick frying pan over medium heat. To cook the pancakes, drizzle a small amount of vegetable oil into the pan, then spoon in large dollops of the batter, leaving enough space between them for the pancakes to rise. Cook for 2–3 minutes on each side until cooked through and golden. Remove from the pan with a spatula and repeat until all the pancake batter has been used.

7. Keep the pancakes warm in the low oven.

8. Serve 2 hot pancakes per person, with a dollop of the coriander yoghurt on top. Any leftover pancakes can be frozen, separated with sheets of greaseproof paper.

Bresaola and Green Peppercorn Toasties

MAKES: 2 TOASTIES
PREP TIME: 5 MINUTES
COOKING TIME: 25 MINUTES

4 slices of sourdough
80g red Leicester cheese, grated
6–8 slices of bresaola
40g soft unsalted butter
sea salt and freshly ground black pepper

**FOR THE GREEN PEPPERCORN
BÉCHAMEL**
100ml milk
10g butter
1 tbsp plain flour
25ml brandy
1 tsp tomato purée
1 tsp brined green peppercorns, chopped
50g red Leicester cheese, grated
1 tbsp onion marmalade (page 116)

I do love a toastie and this one, reminiscent of steak with a peppercorn sauce, is right up there with the best. Thank you, Craig, for the inspired idea. Bresaola is air-dried salted beef, and to source the best I would head to an Italian deli. The toastie will work just as well with a slice of leftover roast beef, however. Green peppercorns are available online and in delis and most major supermarkets.

1. First, make the green peppercorn béchamel. Pour the milk into a small saucepan, place over low heat and slowly bring to simmering point (or warm it in a bowl in the microwave). Melt the butter in a second saucepan over medium heat, then add the flour and a pinch each of salt and pepper. Cook the flour for 1 minute, so it loses its raw flour flavour (being careful not to let it brown), then add the brandy and allow it to reduce quickly. Mix in the tomato purée then gradually add half of the warmed milk, whisking quickly to combine. Add the remaining milk and cook over low heat, stirring, for a further 5 minutes. Taste and adjust the seasoning if necessary.

2. Remove the béchamel from the heat and stir through the green peppercorns, the 50g grated cheese and onion marmalade until fully combined and the cheese has melted.

3. Preheat the oven to 200°C/180°C fan/gas 6 and line a baking tray with a silicone baking mat or baking parchment.

4. To assemble, divide the 80g grated cheese between two slices of sourdough then top with the bresaola. Spoon half the béchamel over each slice then top with the remaining two slices of sourdough.

5. Heat a frying pan over medium heat.

6. Spread half the softened butter on top of each sandwich and carefully transfer the sandwiches to the hot pan, buttered side down. Cook for 3–5 minutes, then brush the top of the sandwiches with the remaining butter. Gently flip them and cook for a further 3–5 minutes until golden brown.

7. Transfer the sandwiches to the lined baking tray and bake in the oven for 4–5 minutes to allow the cheese to melt and warm through.

Mushrooms on Toast with Bone Marrow and Red Wine Sauce

SERVES: 2
PREP TIME: 20 MINUTES
COOKING TIME: 25 MINUTES

500ml good-quality beef stock
1 tbsp olive oil, plus extra for drizzling
400g mixed mushrooms, sliced or quartered
2 shallots, roughly diced
3 garlic cloves, 2 thinly sliced and 1 cut in half
2 sprigs of thyme
50g butter
50ml brandy
100ml red wine
2 thick slices of sourdough
2 pieces of bone marrow, removed from the bone and diced
¼ bunch of flat-leaf parsley, leaves chopped
sea salt and freshly ground black pepper

The simplest things in cookery are often not actually as simple as they seem, and this elevated version of humble mushrooms on toast, enriched with beef stock, brandy, red wine and bone marrow, is a perfect example of this. Although this is a quick and easy recipe, it shouldn't be rushed – reducing the sauce properly enhances the flavours and creates a dish that could grace any restaurant menu. What's not to love about the ultimate mushrooms on toast? I see this as a wintry dish, but it doesn't need to be. You could, of course, leave out the bone marrow, but it does add a wonderful depth to the sauce.

1. Reduce the stock by half in a medium saucepan over medium heat, with the lid off. This will take about 10 minutes.

2. Meanwhile, heat a splash of the oil in a frying pan over high heat, add the mushrooms, a grind of pepper and a sprinkle of salt and cook for 3–5 minutes until lightly browned, then remove from the pan and set aside.

3. Add another splash of oil to the hot pan. Add the shallots, thinly sliced garlic and thyme, season with salt and pepper, and cook for about 5 minutes until lightly browned. Add the butter to the pan towards the end of the cooking time, then deglaze the pan with the brandy and allow it to almost entirely evaporate (you don't want it to burn). Add the red wine and simmer until reduced by half. Add the mushrooms and reduced beef stock, bring to a simmer and cook for 5–10 minutes until the mushrooms are coated in a lovely rich red wine sauce.

4. Preheat a griddle pan over medium heat. Generously drizzle both sides of the sourdough with olive oil, season with salt and pepper and toast on the hot griddle pan for 2–3 minutes on each side until golden and crisp. Try not to move the bread between turns – you want dark griddle lines. Remove from the pan and rub both sides with the halved garlic clove (this will give the bread a light garlic flavour).

5. Finish the sauce by stirring through the diced bone marrow and chopped parsley, and serve the mushrooms and sauce on the toasted sourdough.

Grilled Tuna with a Ponzu and Truffle Dressing

SERVES: 4
PREP TIME: 10 MINUTES
COOKING TIME: 5 MINUTES, PLUS RESTING

4 tuna loin steaks
1 tbsp vegetable oil
4 spring onions, trimmed and thinly sliced

FOR THE SHICHIMI SEASONING (FOR THE TUNA)
10g sea salt
40g black sesame seeds
20g ground ginger
2 sheets of dried seaweed
20g poppy seeds
30g cayenne pepper
grated zest of 1 orange

FOR THE PONZU AND TRUFFLE DRESSING
50ml truffle oil
30ml yuzu juice
50ml ponzu
50ml extra virgin olive oil
50ml soy sauce
2 tbsp truffle paste

VARIATION

Swap the tuna for beef fillet, just lightly searing it then slicing it as above.

I absolutely love the dressing in this dish – it has a light citrus flavour that works beautifully with tuna. It's so moreish we like to make extra and use it as a salad dressing too. Schichimi seasoning, or seven-spice Japanese seasoning, can be found in some supermarkets. Keep a jar in the cupboard to speed up this recipe or make extra and store it in an airtight container for another time. The truffle paste and oil may not be normal store-cupboard items but they are really important in this sauce. The oil would make a delicious addition to a mushroom soup, too, just drizzled over the top.

1. To make the shichimi seasoning, blitz all the spices and salt in a food processor or spice grinder (don't add the orange zest) to a fine powder. Transfer to a bowl and mix through the orange zest. Set aside.

2. To make the ponzu and truffle dressing, whisk all the ingredients together in a bowl. The dressing doesn't need any seasoning as the soy sauce is salty.

3. To cook the tuna, liberally season the tuna steaks with the shichimi seasoning. Heat a frying pan over high heat, add the vegetable oil and add the seasoned tuna steaks. Cook for 1 minute on each side to sear – the centre should still be pink, not grey – then remove from the pan and allow to rest for 2 minutes before carving each steak into 6 slices.

4. Divide some of the ponzu dressing among four serving bowls (putting the rest in a jug to serve alongside) and layer the sliced tuna on top. Top with the sliced spring onions and serve.

GET AHEAD
Make a large batch of shichimi seasoning (without the orange zest) and keep it in a sealed tin or jar. Add the orange zest just before using it.

Poached Salmon with Croutons and 'Grenobloise' Butter

SERVES: 4
PREP TIME: 10 MINUTES
COOKING TIME: 20 MINUTES

2 slices of white bread, crusts removed
4 x salmon fillet portions (120g each), skin removed
100g unsalted butter
50g lilliput capers
1 lemon, peel and pith removed, and cut into segments
sea salt

FOR THE POACHING STOCK
200ml white wine
750ml good-quality fish stock
1 bunch of parsley, leaves picked and chopped (keep these for the sauce), reserving the stalks
2 sprigs of thyme

VARIATIONS

Swap the salmon for sole fillets, or pair the butter with pan-fried skate wing.

This buttery sauce is a classic from Grenoble. I first learnt to make it at catering college some years ago but it is still popular in French brasseries. It is quick and easy to cook, which makes it a really useful addition to your kitchen repertoire. Though made from butter it has a tasty tang from the herbs, lemon and capers, which works well with the simplicity of poached salmon. Grilled fish would also work well. Serve with new potatoes and green vegetables.

1. First, prepare the croutons. Lightly roll the bread with a rolling pin to flatten, then cut into 1cm dice and set aside.

2. Now, prepare the poaching stock. Put the white wine, fish stock, parsley stalks and the sprigs of thyme in a saucepan and bring to the boil.

3. Lightly season the salmon fillet portions with salt, then place in a high-sided baking tray, skin side down. Once the stock has reached the boil, pour it over the salmon. Cover the tray tightly with foil and allow to sit for 10–12 minutes until the salmon flesh can flake apart.

4. Make the sauce while the salmon is gently cooking in the stock. Melt the butter in a frying pan over medium heat and cook for 2–3 minutes until foaming and beginning to turn a nut-brown colour. Add the diced bread and cook for 3–4 minutes until crisp and golden brown. Remove from the heat and stir through the capers, segmented lemon and chopped parsley then season to taste with salt (bear in mind that the brine from the capers is slightly salty).

5. Gently remove the salmon from the hot stock. Place a piece of salmon in the centre of each serving dish, then spoon a quarter of the croutons and butter onto each portion of fish.

Spiced and Roasted Aubergine

SERVES: 4
PREP TIME: 15–20 MINUTES
COOKING TIME: 1 HOUR

2 aubergines
4 garlic cloves, finely chopped
20g piece of fresh ginger, finely grated
1 tsp garam masala
1 tsp ground coriander
1 tsp sweet smoked paprika
½ tsp chilli powder
½ tsp ground turmeric
juice of 1 lemon
3 tbsp groundnut oil
175g natural yoghurt
500ml good-quality hot vegetable stock
150g cherry tomatoes, halved
sea salt and freshly ground black pepper

TO SERVE
½ red onion, thinly sliced
150g cherry tomatoes, halved
bunch of coriander, leaves and softer stalks
    chopped
100g crumbly cheese such as feta or
    Lancashire (optional)

I have lost count of the times we have had some aubergines in the fridge that were intended for a moussaka or aubergine parmigiana but we didn't quite manage to make the dish. This is a great way to use them up and is well worth a try. Roasted aubergine has a lovely taste, and the fresh toppings in this recipe work so well with it. It is really easy to make as it goes in the oven in one tray. Serve it on its own or with a green salad or just some crunchy bread.

1. Preheat the oven to 180°C/160°C fan/gas 4.

2. Cut the aubergines in half lengthways, through the stalks, and use a sharp knife to score the flesh in a criss-cross pattern, going as deep as you can into the flesh without piercing the skin, then place in a roasting tray, cut side up.

3. In a bowl, mix together the garlic, ginger, spices, half the lemon juice, 2 tablespoons of the oil, 2 tablespoons of the yoghurt and season with salt. Add a little water if required – it should be a runny paste.

4. Spread the paste evenly over the aubergine halves, paying particular attention to the criss-cross pattern, rubbing the seasoning in with the back of the spoon.

5. Pour the hot stock into the roasting tray, around rather than over the aubergines. You just need enough cover the base of your tray, so adjust accordingly. Place 150g of halved cherry tomatoes on the top of the aubergines, drizzle with the remaining oil and season with salt and pepper.

6. Place the roasting tray of aubergines in the oven and roast for 50 minutes–1 hour until the aubergines are very soft and almost gooey. While they cook, occasionally baste the tops with any juices in the tray.

7. Remove the aubergines from the oven and transfer to a serving platter.

8. Mix the remaining yoghurt and lemon juice together and drizzle the mixture over the top of the aubergines.

9. Top with the sliced onion, the remaining tomato halves and the chopped coriander, then finally scatter over the crumbled cheese (if using) and serve.

Lovage-baked Halibut with White Asparagus

SERVES: 4
PREP TIME: 15 MINUTES, PLUS
30 MINUTES CURING
COOKING TIME: 15 MINUTES

4 portions of halibut fillet, skin removed
12 spears of white asparagus
100ml white wine
sea salt

FOR THE CURE
60g caster sugar
40g Maldon salt or rock salt
grated zest of 1 lemon

FOR THE LOVAGE SALSA
1 bunch of chervil
1 bunch of lovage
20g anchovies in oil
½ garlic clove, crushed
40g capers
grated zest of 1 lemon
1 small shallot, finely diced
1½ tbsp honey
100ml extra virgin olive oil

VARIATION

Use green asparagus in place of the white, or even green beans or broccoli. Any white fish would work well, such as cod or pollock.

* Make it perfect
White asparagus has more body and is more fibrous with a slight bitter flavour that complements white fish. White asparagus season starts in May, and whether white or green, I only buy seasonal, local and more flavoursome English spears. I love to grate white truffle on top for a decadent treat.

White asparagus has a unique, delicate flavour. Generally more expensive than green, it's harvested before the tips emerge from the soil – before they see the light. Halibut is a firm fish which makes it a good choice for baking, though I have cured it slightly first to remove excess water. I love it here with the flavour of lovage; often compared to celery, it is actually part of the parsley family. Serve with a green salad.

1. First, lightly cure the halibut. Combine the cure ingredients in a bowl then, on a plate or small tray, cover both sides of the halibut with the mix. Allow to cure in the fridge for 15 minutes, then rinse under cold running water to remove any salt. Pat dry with kitchen paper and return to the fridge until required.

2. To prepare the asparagus, cut away any woody ends (about 2.5cm off each spear) then cut each piece in half lengthways. Prepare a bowl of iced water. Bring a saucepan of water to the boil, add a pinch of salt, then boil the asparagus for 1 minute 30 seconds. Remove and immediately transfer to the iced water. Once cool, drain and set aside.

3. Preheat the oven to 200°C/180°C fan/gas 6.

4. To make the lovage salsa, blitz the herbs, anchovies, garlic, capers and lemon zest to a smooth paste in a small food processor. Add the shallot, honey and oil and blitz again to a fairly smooth salsa (though still with a little texture). The salsa will be slightly sweet from the honey; adjust with salt to taste.

5. Cut a sheet of foil about 30cm square and lay a square of baking parchment of the same size on top. In the centre of the parchment lay 6 halves of asparagus and lightly season with salt, then place a portion of cured halibut on top, followed by a large spoonful of lovage salsa. Bring the sides of the foil together and seal at the top and one side. Before sealing the final side, pour in some white wine. Repeat to make 4 parcels.

6. Place all the parcels on a baking tray and cook in the oven for 10–15 minutes until the fish is cooked through and the asparagus is tender.

7. To serve, cut open the parcels and take to the table with the cooking liquor. Good with boiled, buttered new potatoes.

Café de Paris Mussels

SERVES: 6 AS A STARTER OR 4 AS A MEAL
PREP TIME: 20 MINUTES
COOKING TIME: 5 MINUTES

1.5kg fresh mussels
100ml white wine
4–6 sprigs of parsley
fresh bread, to serve

FOR THE BUTTER
150g soft unsalted butter
25g parsley, finely chopped
25g tarragon, finely chopped
2 banana shallots, finely diced
2 garlic cloves, grated
grated zest of 1 lemon (keep the lemon, halved, for squeezing)
50g tinned anchovies, finely chopped
30g capers, finely chopped
3 tbsp Worcestershire sauce
2 tsp curry powder
1 tsp wholegrain mustard
1 tsp Dijon mustard
1 tsp hot smoked paprika

VARIATIONS

Clams would be a great alternative to mussels. The butter sits well on a steak or any grilled meat or fish.

* Make it perfect
When you're cooking with wine remember that a poor wine will not improve with heat. Cook with a wine you would be pleased to drink. We keep the ends of bottles for cooking, including flat champagne or sparkling wine.

This dish makes for a very fast supper dish or a starter. The key to its success is proper preparation of the mussels – no one enjoys a mouthful of grit. Café de Paris butter is a classic French accompaniment for steak in French brasseries, though it also works really well here with mussels. Make extra butter and store it in the fridge, in a roll wrapped in greaseproof paper, for up to 5–7 days, slicing it when you need it. It can also be frozen (and there's no need to defrost it before using). Serve with freshly baked bread.

1. First, prepare the butter. Put all the ingredients in a large mixing bowl and stir until evenly combined. Refrigerate until required.

2. Now clean the mussels. Remove the beards (the fibres that sprout from the shell) by pulling them towards the hinged end of the mussel shell and pulling firmly, and wash the mussels thoroughly in a colander with cold running water to remove any grit, using a vegetable brush if you have one to scrub the shells. Discard any mussels that are damaged or are open and do not close when you tap them hard against a work surface. Set aside the clean mussels.

3. Preheat a large saucepan with a lid over medium-high heat until almost smoking. Once the pan is hot, remove the lid then, working fast, tip in the mussels followed by the white wine and the butter you have just prepared. Place the lid back on and lightly shake the pan then cook the mussels for 2–3 minutes, or until all the shells have opened. Discard any unopened mussels.

4. Remove from the heat and serve immediately. Divide the mussels between four or six serving bowls, being generous with the cooking liquor, then top with a sprig of parsley and squeeze over a little lemon juice. Serve with fresh bread.

SHORTCUT

Rather than finely chopping the ingredients for the butter, blitz them in a food processor.

Quinoa Salad with Cottage Cheese and Roasted Onions

SERVES: 2 AS A MAIN, 4 AS A SIDE
PREP TIME: 20 MINUTES, PLUS COOLING
COOKING TIME: 30 MINUTES

100g dried quinoa
1 tbsp extra virgin olive oil, plus extra for drizzling
2 onions, quartered (with skin on and root attached)
6 large kale leaves, stalks removed
1 tbsp sherry vinegar
1 punnet of mustard cress
¼ bunch of chervil, leaves picked (or curly parsley if you can't find chervil)
150g cottage cheese
seeds from ½ pomegranate (about 60g)
50g shelled unsalted pistachios
sea salt and freshly ground black pepper

FOR THE CINNAMON DRESSING
2 cloves
seeds from 2 green cardamom pods
1 tsp sumac
1 tsp ground cinnamon
75ml extra virgin olive oil
2 tbsp aged balsamic vinegar
1 tbsp pomegranate molasses

During the week Jane and I often eat a salad of grains, sometimes with meat or fish but often with cheese and whatever we find in the fridge, and this quinoa salad is a popular choice. The cinnamon, pomegranate and sumac give it a Middle Eastern influence, and it's great to use onion as a main ingredient rather than just a flavouring.

1. Put the quinoa in a saucepan and cover it with 300ml of water. Add 1 tablespoon of olive oil and a pinch of salt, place over medium heat and bring to the boil, then reduce the heat, cover and cook for 15–20 minutes until all the water has evaporated and the quinoa has doubled in size. Remove from the heat and leave to cool completely.

2. Dress the quartered onions generously with olive oil, then season with salt and pepper. Heat a griddle pan over high heat; once it's smoking add the onions and chargrill for 2 minutes on each side. Once charred, transfer to a mixing bowl and cover the bowl with clingfilm – this will encourage the onions to soften while cooling. Dress the trimmed kale leaves with olive oil, then season with salt and pepper. Cook on the hot griddle pan for 1 minute on each side until lightly charred. Once cooked, set aside and leave to cool.

3. Once the onions are cool, remove the skins and roots, then separate them into individual onion 'petals'. Place in a bowl and dress the onion petals with the sherry vinegar. Set aside.

4. To make the cinnamon dressing, lightly toast the whole spices in a small dry frying pan over low heat for 1 minute. Tip the toasted spices into a mortar and grind to a fine powder with a pestle. Mix all the ground spices with the extra virgin olive oil, balsamic vinegar and pomegranate molasses in a bowl or jar until you have an emulsified dressing.

5. To assemble the salad, create a bed of the cooked, cooled quinoa in a large serving dish. Next, create a layer of the charred kale and onion petals. Next, add a layer of the mustard cress and chervil leaves. Place dollops of the cottage cheese across the salad then scatter over the pomegranate seeds and pistachios. Lastly, finish the salad with a drizzle of the cinnamon dressing.

Calf's Liver with Mushroom and Brandy Sauce

SERVES: 2
PREP TIME: 25 MINUTES
COOKING TIME: 7–11 MINUTES

2 tbsp vegetable oil
2 tbsp plain flour
2 thick calf's liver slices (about 150g each)
25g unsalted butter
1 sprig of thyme
1 sprig of rosemary
sea salt and freshly ground black pepper

FOR THE MUSHROOM AND BRANDY SAUCE
25g unsalted butter
1 tbsp vegetable oil
1 shallot, finely diced
200g button mushrooms, thinly sliced
1 garlic clove, thinly sliced
50ml brandy
100ml white wine
1 tbsp Dijon mustard
1 tbsp wholegrain mustard
250g crème fraîche
¼ bunch of tarragon, leaves chopped

When my wife and I were first dating, almost 30 years ago now, as a young chef it was a treat to eat at Le Caprice and The Ivy. Calf's liver was always on the menu and was a popular choice. It appears on restaurant menus less often these days, but when cooked well it is just fabulous. Serve with a smooth potato mash or fries, and your vegetable of choice.

1. First, make the mushroom and brandy sauce. Melt the butter with the oil in a frying pan over medium heat, add the shallot, mushrooms and garlic with a little seasoning and fry gently for 5–8 minutes until softened, stirring every now and then. Add the brandy and wine and cook for a couple of minutes until reduced by half, then stir through the mustards, crème fraîche and tarragon. Remove from the heat and season to taste.

2. To cook the calf's liver, heat the vegetable oil in a large frying pan over medium-high heat.

3. Put the flour on a shallow tray, season well with salt and pepper, then add the liver and turn each piece in the flour to coat. Shake off any excess flour then place in the hot pan. Cook for 1–1½ minutes until lightly golden (depending on the thickness). Add the butter to the pan along with the herb sprigs and turn the liver slices, allowing the butter to melt and start to foam. Baste the liver in the foaming butter and cook for a further 1–1½ minutes until golden on both sides and still pink in the middle. Drain on kitchen paper to absorb any excess oil.

4. Divide some of the mushroom and brandy sauce between two serving plates, placing it the middle, then serve the pan-fried liver slices on top. Serve the remaining sauce alongside.

* *Make it perfect*
Liver is best served pink, so don't overcook it, as it becomes tough. Buy liver ready to cook, but if the membrane is still attached you need to remove it, otherwise it will tighten and the liver will curl as it cooks (and make it tough). The amount of oil for cooking might seem a lot, but it's correct. We need this much because the flour coating will burn if there isn't enough fat and the meat doesn't have its own.

Chocolate Mousse

MAKES: 8 SMALL PORTIONS
PREP TIME: 15 MINUTES
COOKING TIME: 5 MINUTES,
PLUS 15 MINUTES COOLING
AND 2–3 HOURS CHILLING

60g dark chocolate (70% cocoa solids or
    higher), broken into small pieces
40g runny honey
250ml double cream
1 tsp vanilla extract
2 eggs, separated

VARIATION

**If you like your chocolate desserts to
be richer in chocolate flavour, remove
100ml of the cream. It will make it more
bitter and a touch firmer.**

GET AHEAD
**The mousse can be made up to 2 days
before you want to serve it, but bear
in mind that the longer it stays in the
fridge, the firmer it will be.**

My daughter Jessie loves baking, and this year she has
become a little more adventurous, making desserts as well.
This mousse has been a hit in our house. It's really tasty and
is made without refined sugar, which is a bonus. Serve it
alone, or really go to town with the decoration. It works well
with raspberries, sliced banana and whipped cream, or even
with a quenelle of ice cream, and it's great served with coffee.
I like to serve it in sherry glasses. The higher the cocoa
content of chocolate, the less sugar it contains – 100 per
cent cocoa chocolate will have none. To lighten the flavour,
we add cream to the mix.

1. Put the chocolate pieces in a saucepan with the honey,
cream and vanilla extract. Warm over low heat until the
chocolate has completely melted, then stir well to combine
with the other ingredients.

2. Remove from the heat, pour into a clean bowl and allow
to cool slightly for about 10 minutes, stirring it occasionally
to help it cool a little faster. Lightly stir the egg yolks into the
chocolate mix.

3. In a separate clean and grease-free bowl, whisk the egg
whites until they form stiff peaks. Using a large metal spoon (to
avoid knocking the air out of the eggs), fold a quarter of the
whites into the chocolate mix. Once incorporated, you can add
the rest, again folding everything together gently.

4. Divide the mix among eight small glasses or ramekins and
chill for at least 2 hours, or until required.

5. Take it out of the fridge 20 minutes before you want to
serve, so it's not fridge-cold.

Market Garden

My Kitchen Garden Courgette Salad

SERVES: 6 AS A SIDE, 4 AS A LUNCH
PREP TIME: 20 MINUTES, PLUS 20 MINUTES MARINATING
COOKING TIME: 5 MINUTES

4 early-season, small courgettes (about 600g) (a variety of colours looks good)
homemade ricotta cheese (page 273) or 250g good-quality shop-bought
sea salt and freshly ground black pepper

FOR THE DRESSING
30ml lemon juice
grated zest of ½ lemon
4 garlic cloves, thinly sliced
150ml extra virgin olive oil
1 small red onion, finely diced
2 sprigs of tarragon, leaves finely chopped
3 sprigs of oregano, leaves finely chopped
2 small sprigs of chervil, leaves finely chopped
2 small sprigs of flat-leaf parsley, leaves finely chopped

TO SERVE
50g pine nuts, lightly toasted
picked baby mint and oregano leaves, to serve

I love this dish, as most of the ingredients grow in our kitchen garden – it's summer on a plate. Every summer we have a huge glut of courgettes, and this delightful recipe makes the most of their fresh flavour while they're young. It also uses herbs from the garden in a delicious dressing, and ricotta cheese, which you can buy or have a go at making yourself. You can vary the salad leaves depending on what you grow or can get hold of. Serve the salad simply with crusty bread for lunch, or as an accompaniment at a barbecue or with other cooked meat.

1. Combine all the dressing ingredients in a bowl and season to taste. It will be quite thick.

2. Thinly slice the courgettes at a slight angle to produce an oval shape. Put them in a bowl, add the dressing and leave to marinate for 20 minutes. This helps to soften them a little and add flavour.

3. To serve, spread the ricotta on the base of a flat serving plate. Using a slotted spoon, remove the courgette slices from the dressing and layer them on top of the cheese in a pile.

4. Drizzle the remaining dressing over the top of the courgettes. Sprinkle the pine nuts on the top of the pile and scatter with picked mint and oregano leaves.

Tempura Broccoli with Mint Salad and Blue Cheese Dressing

SERVES: 4 AS A STARTER
PREP TIME: 15 MINUTES
COOKING TIME: 10 MINUTES

4 spring onions, trimmed and thinly sliced
½ bunch of mint, leaves picked
extra virgin rapeseed oil, for drizzling
vegetable oil, for deep-frying
12 stems of Tenderstem broccoli, trimmed
    (ends removed)
1 lemon, for zesting

FOR THE BLUE CHEESE DRESSING
150g blue cheese
100g crème fraîche
1 tbsp Dijon mustard
1 tbsp white wine vinegar
50ml extra virgin rapeseed oil

FOR THE TEMPURA BATTER
200g gluten-free self-raising flour
1 tsp baking powder
½ tsp sea salt
160–180ml ice-cold sparkling water

* Make it perfect
Gluten-free flour makes a lovely, light batter and the sparkling water gives it lightness – make sure it is very cold to maximise bubbles.

Try to prepare everything, including the plates, before you make the batter and cook the broccoli. You want to eat them as soon as they are all cooked.

The oil will be quite clean and untainted, so you could keep it in the pan (cooled) for about 3 weeks and use it a couple of times to fry vegetables. Never put fat/oil down the drain. Always tip it into an old container you're happy to throw away and put it in the bin when cold.

Tempura dishes are a family favourite when we dine out, and it's easy to make your own at home. I am not normally a fan of blue cheese, but it works extremely well with the crunch of the batter and because it has been let down slightly to make a sauce it is less intense. Serve on one large platter or individually – it makes a great lunch with salad. The batter must be made at the last minute, just before frying.

1. To make the blue cheese dressing, put all the ingredients in a food processor and blitz until smooth. Taste and season if required (this depends on the strength of your chosen cheese).

2. Lightly dress the sliced spring onions and mint with a little drizzle of the rapeseed oil and set aside until ready to serve.

3. Pour oil into a deep pan or deep-fat fryer to a depth of about 5cm and place over medium heat. If using a deep-fat fryer or if you have a thermometer, heat the oil to 170°C. If not, check the oil is hot enough by dropping a cube of bread into the hot oil – it should turn golden and crisp in 1 minute.

4. While the oil heats, spread each plate with a few spoonfuls of the dressing, making a hollow in the centre.

5. To make the tempura batter, mix the flour, baking powder and salt in a bowl, make a well in the mixture, and pour in 160ml of the sparkling water, whisking continuously until you have a smooth batter with no lumps – it should be thick enough to coat the broccoli, so you may not need the extra 20ml.

6. Test to see if the oil is hot enough then lightly coat a couple of broccoli stems in the a batter, shaking off any excess. Gently lower them into the oil, so they start cooking before they sink (or they will stick to the bottom). Keep moving them with a slotted spoon and cook for 2–3 minutes until golden brown. Transfer to a wire rack placed over a tray, or sheets of kitchen paper, to remove any excess oil. Repeat for all the broccoli.

7. To assemble, stack 2–3 broccoli for each serving on top of the dressing. Scatter over the dressed mint leaves and spring onion, followed by a little freshly grated lemon zest.

GET AHEAD
The blue cheese dressing can be made up to 4 days ahead.

VARIATION

Try serving the tempura broccoli with Harissa Romesco Sauce (page 270) or chimichurri sauce, instead of the blue cheese dressing.

Chargrilled Asparagus with Sumac Salad Cream

**SERVES : 4 AS A STARTER OR LIGHT
LUNCH
PREP TIME: 15 MINUTES
COOKING TIME: 4–6 MINUTES**

2 bunches of asparagus, trimmed
    (500–750g)
olive oil
sea salt and freshly ground black pepper

FOR THE SUMAC SALAD CREAM
2 eggs
80ml white wine vinegar
20g plain flour
10g caster sugar
20g English mustard
pinch of cayenne pepper
½ tsp salt
200g mascarpone
grated zest and juice of 1 lemon
2 tsp sumac

TO SERVE
extra virgin olive oil, for drizzling
crusty bread (optional)
salad (optional)

VARIATION

**Drape slices of Parma ham or salami
over the top.**

I have been growing asparagus in our kitchen garden, but it's not quite ready for eating yet – it takes a couple of years to grow strong and big enough. I am hoping that next year we will have a small crop to try. Asparagus has a short season in the UK, so I really try to make the most of it when it arrives in April/May. We only ever buy British. Because the sumac dressing involves some effort, I always make plenty as we have done here, then store leftovers in the fridge, in an airtight container, for another day. It will keep for up to 5 days and is a perfect addition to a salad (or more asparagus!).

1. To make the salad cream, combine the eggs, vinegar, flour, sugar, mustard, cayenne and salt in a medium saucepan. Place over medium heat and cook for 5–6 minutes, whisking continuously, until the mixture has thickened. Remove from the heat and allow to cool for 5 minutes.

2. Once the mixture has cooled, transfer it to a food processor, add the mascarpone, lemon zest, juice and sumac and blitz until smooth. Adjust the seasoning if required.

3. Dress the asparagus with olive oil and season with salt and pepper. Heat a griddle pan over high heat, add the asparagus spears and cook for 3–4 minutes, shaking the pan every 30 seconds to ensure the asparagus is evenly charred.

4. Serve the chargrilled asparagus spears with a generous spoonful of the salad cream and dress with a drizzle of extra virgin olive oil, and some crusty bread and salad if you wish.

* Make it perfect
To prepare the asparagus, cut off the woody bottoms of the spears (you may need to remove about 2.5cm). You don't need to peel the spears for this recipe – the thicker the better for charring. If you have very thin asparagus spears you can marinate them and eat them raw.

Tomato and Fried Onion Salad

SERVES: 4 AS A SIDE DISH
PREP TIME: 30–35 MINUTES
COOKING TIME: 13 MINUTES

100ml extra virgin olive oil
2 red onions, thinly sliced
4 garlic cloves, thinly sliced
100g chorizo, finely diced
3 tbsp red wine vinegar
500g cherry tomatoes on the vine,
    halved, or quartered if larger, at room
    temperature
12–15 mini pickled gherkins or cornichons
    from a jar, drained
4 spring onions, trimmed and sliced into
    long strips
bunch of basil
2 sprigs of marjoram
sea salt and freshly ground black pepper

For those who live in a city, it's easy to get into the habit of choosing what you want for dinner then buying the ingredients to suit. However, I much prefer to be creative with what we have to hand – this is a skill I learnt when I worked in a resort in Upstate New York: making a four-course meal for paying guests from ingredients in the fridge was certainly challenging. This dish came about during the Covid-19 lockdown, from a handful of home-grown tomatoes, an array of garden herbs and a few store-cupboard flavours. I don't specify a type of chorizo here as I think it's very personal and you should use what you prefer. We always have some in the fridge to add to dishes just like this, and we buy the pre-chopped type. Find one you like and keep some in the fridge – I go for a medium-spiced one that's not too garlicky.

1. Heat the olive oil in a frying pan over medium heat (you don't want to be shy with the oil, as it's your dressing), add the onions and garlic to the oil and season well. Cook for about 10 minutes, reducing the heat a little if the onions and garlic are starting to crisp up or look as if they are cooking too quickly – they shouldn't take on colour or burn, so take your time.

2. Add the chorizo to the pan and cook for about 3 minutes. The mixture will turn orange as the fat is released from the chorizo, which is a good sign, and the onions should be softened. Add the red wine vinegar to the pan to deglaze, then remove the pan from the heat, set aside and allow to cool slightly.

3. Put the halved tomatoes in a bowl. Cut the gherkins in half lengthways and add them to the tomatoes. Pour the contents of the pan over the tomatoes and mix gently – the warm dressing will gently soften the tomatoes and infuse them with the flavours in the pan. Taste and season with salt and pepper if needed, and spoon the mix into a salad dish.

4. Finish the salad with the spring onions and some torn basil leaves and picked marjoram, and serve.

Whole Roasted Satay Cauliflower

**SERVES: 4 AS A MAIN,
6 AS A SIDE
PREP TIME: 15 MINUTES
COOKING TIME: 1 HOUR**

1 large cauliflower, outer leaves removed
   and stalk trimmed
50g toasted unsalted peanuts, chopped
¼ bunch of coriander, leaves and tender
   stems chopped

FOR THE SATAY MARINADE
3 garlic cloves, peeled
thumb-sized piece of fresh ginger, peeled
1 red onion, roughly chopped
1 tsp salt
1 tbsp ground cumin
1 tbsp ground coriander
1 tbsp ground turmeric
1 tbsp garam masala
½ tsp hot chilli powder (or to taste)
3 tbsp kecap manis (sweet soy sauce)
100g chunky peanut butter
1 x 400ml tin coconut milk
1 tbsp soy sauce
1 tbsp rice wine vinegar

VARIATION

**Swap the cauliflower for 4 chicken
breasts. Brown the breasts, then add to
a casserole dish and pour over the satay
marinade. Cook for 35–40 minutes until
cooked through, and serve with rice.**

GET AHEAD
**Make the satay marinade in advance.
It will keep for a couple of days in an
airtight container in the fridge.**

Cauliflower is a delicious and very versatile vegetable. We often roast it and serve as an accompaniment, but it's also great as a main dish in itself, served with brown rice (see page 272). Here, it keeps its shape and absorbs a delicious satay marinade, which you'll find yourself wanting to use for many other dishes, such as the chicken variation below.

1. Preheat the oven to 180°C/160°C fan/gas 4.

2. First, make the satay marinade. Put the garlic, ginger, onion and salt in a food processor and blitz to a coarse paste. Add the rest of the ingredients for the marinade and blitz until smooth.

3. Make sure the cauliflower can sit flat on its stalk, then place it in a large casserole dish. Pour the satay marinade over the cauliflower and cover the dish with the lid or foil. Place in the oven and bake for 1 hour, basting it regularly through the cooking.

4. Halfway through cooking, add 100ml water to ensure it doesn't dry out.

5. Once baked, the cauliflower should be soft. Check it by piercing it with a knife – there should be no resistance. If the cauliflower isn't quite ready, pop it back in the oven for 10 minutes and check again. To finish the cauliflower, sprinkle it with the chopped toasted peanuts and coriander and serve it from the pot (or transfer to a serving plate if you prefer, sprinkling it with the peanuts and coriander once it's on the plate).

Summer Pea Panzanella with Mint, Basil and Capers

SERVES: 4 FOR A LUNCH, LIGHT SUPPER OR AS A STARTER
PREP TIME: 40 MINUTES, PLUS SOAKING

200g piece of chunky stale bread such as ciabatta or sourdough, cut into 2cm pieces
100g raw garden peas
100g sugar snap peas, halved lengthways
extra virgin olive oil, for drizzling
½ bunch of mint, leaves picked
50g lilliput capers or non-pareil capers, preserved in brine
4 spring onions, trimmed and sliced
80–100g pea shoots, roughly chopped
sea salt and freshly ground black pepper
crème fraîche or sour cream, to serve (optional)

FOR THE PEA DRESSING
50g fresh podded peas
2 tbsp caper brine (from the jar of capers above)
½ bunch of basil
½ cucumber (about 140g), roughly chopped
1 garlic clove
juice of 1 lemon
50ml olive oil
1 tsp Dijon mustard
1 shallot, roughly chopped

This dish is based on the traditional Italian bread salad which is usually made with tomatoes and olive oil and, of course, stale bread. Here, instead of the tomatoes, we have other fabulous summer flavours of fresh peas and mint, with the zing of the capers (a simple swap for frozen peas means you can make it at any time of year). It is similar to the garden vegetable salad in *Marcus Everyday* but served as a salad rather than a soup. There is a natural marriage between lamb, pea and mint so this would be wonderful with roast lamb or barbecued lamb chops.

1. Combine all the ingredients for the pea dressing in a blender and blitz until smooth. Add a splash of water to loosen the dressing if necessary, and season to taste with pepper.

2. Place the chunks of stale bread in a shallow dish large enough to fit them in a single layer. Pour the pea dressing over the top and allow to sit for 20 minutes.

3. Mix the garden peas and sugar snap peas in a large bowl, dress with a glug of olive oil and season with a pinch each of salt and pepper. Add the soaked bread, picked mint, capers, spring onions and pea shoots to the dressed sugar snaps and peas and gently mix together. Serve immediately, with a dollop of crème fraîche or sour cream, and an extra drizzle of oil.

Peach, Radicchio and Smoked Almond Salad

SERVES: 4
PREP TIME: 15 MINUTES
COOKING TIME: 10 MINUTES

1 head of radicchio (about 250g)
2 ripe peaches, stones removed and flesh
  cut into thin wedges
handful of rocket (about 40g)
extra virgin rapeseed oil, for drizzling
1 tsp black onion seeds
sprig of coriander, leaves picked
sprig of mint, leaves picked
salt

FOR THE PICKLED RED ONION
50ml red wine vinegar
1 tsp yellow mustard seeds
2 tbsp honey
1 red onion, halved and thinly sliced

**FOR THE SMOKED ALMOND
DRESSING**
50g smoked almonds, lightly toasted
1 tbsp crème fraîche
2 tbsp white wine vinegar
75ml extra virgin rapeseed oil

GET AHEAD
**Make the dressing and pickle the onion
in advance. Remember, though, that the
longer the onion remains in the vinegar,
the softer and pinker it will become.
If you want a sharper tang, remove it
when it still has a crunch.**

I love this fresh, summery salad. Though it contains sweetness from the peach it also has the tang of red onion, the bitterness of salad leaves and a delicious creamy, nutty sauce. It works well served with a ham, or eaten alone with some chunky bread. The dressing works well for any salad, and the recipe here makes plenty, so you'll have enough to store in the fridge for another day.

1. First, prepare the pickled red onion. Bring the vinegar, mustard seeds, honey and 2 tablespoons of water to the boil in a saucepan with a pinch of salt. Meanwhile, layer the onion slices in a heatproof bowl. Once the liquor has reached boiling point, pour it over the onion, ensuring all slices are covered.

2. To make the smoked almond dressing, put all the ingredients in a small blender with 2 tablespoons of water and blitz until smooth. Season to taste with a touch of salt.

3. To assemble the salad, cut the base of the radicchio and separate the head into individual leaves. Dress the radicchio in a bowl with half of the smoked almond dressing (serving the rest alongside for people to help themselves), then arrange the dressed radicchio on a large serving platter. Drain the red onions and scatter them over the radicchio. Lightly dress the peaches and rocket in a bowl with a little rapeseed oil and season with a pinch of salt, then scatter them over the radicchio. Finish the salad by sprinkling over the onion seeds and the picked herbs.

Braised Cabbage in a Warming Broth

SERVES: 4
PREP TIME: 5 MINUTES
COOKING TIME: 35 MINUTES

1 hispi or spring cabbage, outer leaves removed
extra virgin olive oil, as required
1 medium white onion, thinly sliced
2 garlic cloves, crushed (skins on)
½ green chilli (optional)
2 sprigs of rosemary
1 small bunch of parsley
1 small bunch of oregano
300ml good-quality vegetable stock (or beef or chicken stock if you prefer)
2 tbsp light soy sauce
2 tbsp rice wine vinegar
sea salt and freshly ground black pepper

VARIATION

Break the cabbage into smaller pieces instead of quarters, add a little more stock to the casserole dish and cook some noodles separately while the cabbage is in the oven. Place the noodles in bowls then spoon some cabbage and cooking liquor over the top.

I love cabbage and I think it is a little undervalued. It has never been a vegetable that my children would choose to eat yet they love it when it's served like this. Braising cabbage is a delicious way to cook it – it can be served as an accompaniment for chicken, beef or lamb, or even as a main dish on a meat-free day because it keeps its shape as it cooks.

1. Preheat the oven to 180°C/160°C fan/gas 4.

2. Cut the cabbage lengthways into quarters, leaving the core intact. Wash the cabbage quarters if they are dirty but make sure they are dry before they go into the hot pan otherwise the oil will spit.

3. Heat a shallow cast-iron casserole dish over medium heat. When the pan is hot, coat the base with olive oil. Once the oil is hot place the four pieces of cabbage in the dish, flat side down. Season with salt and pepper and brown each side – this should take 8–10 minutes in total (4–5 minutes on each side). Once the cabbage colours, turn it over and brown the next side, adding more oil to the pan if needed. When all sides are browned, add the onion, garlic and chilli to the pan. Using tongs, manoeuvre the cabbage around the pan to allow the ingredients you've just added to start to cook. Add the herbs and cook slowly for 4–5 minutes over gentle heat then add the stock, soy sauce and vinegar. Soy sauce is salty, so check the flavour of the broth before adding salt – if it's under-seasoned, add more.

4. Put the lid on the casserole dish and cook in the hot oven for 20 minutes, until the cabbage is just tender all the way through.

Potato and Tunworth Cheesepot Pie

SERVES: 6
PREP TIME: 30 MINUTES, PLUS
30 MINUTES CHILLING
COOKING TIME: 1 HOUR 10
MINUTES

6 large floury potatoes (about 1.3kg), peeled
and cut into 1.5cm-thick slices
2 tbsp vegetable oil
200g shallots, sliced
2 garlic cloves, crushed
250g Tunworth cheese, cubed
75ml milk
300ml whipping cream
1 tbsp freshly chopped thyme leaves
sea salt and freshly ground black pepper

FOR THE SHORTCRUST PASTRY
235g plain flour, plus extra for dusting
125g cold unsalted butter, diced
½ tsp table salt
1 large egg, plus 2 large egg yolks
2 sprigs of thyme, leaves picked

VARIATION

**If your family prefers a milder cheese,
you could use Cheddar, a very light
goats' cheese or gouda, as it melts well.**

I have taken the classic English cheese and potato pie and adjusted it slightly. I am such a massive fan of Tunworth, a soft English cow's-milk cheese that's a little like camembert; we use it at the restaurant a lot. It's available in some supermarkets, at specialist cheese shops and delis and online, and it works really well with potato. This delicious pie is pure comfort food, and is so good for supper on a winter's night. It's great reheated the following day too, with or without the pastry. The cheese and potato mixture would work as an accompaniment for simple roast beef. You will need a 20cm circular baking dish. Serve the pie with a crisp green salad and vinaigrette.

1. To make the pastry, rub the flour, cold butter and salt together in a mixing bowl with your fingertips until the mixture resembles breadcrumbs and all the butter has been rubbed in, with no lumps remaining. (Alternatively, blitz in a food processor.) Stir in the whole egg and 1 of the egg yolks and mix to form a soft dough. Shape the dough into a ball, then flatten it slightly to form a disc and wrap it in clingfilm. Rest in the fridge for 30 minutes.

2. Dust a work surface lightly with flour, unwrap the pastry and roll it out into a 5mm-thick circle. Transfer it to a tray and chill in the fridge to rest again. The resting is important, as the pastry will relax and shrink back to its natural size.

3. Put the sliced potatoes in a saucepan, cover with water and add a pinch of salt, then place over medium heat and bring to the boil. Once boiling, reduce the heat to a low simmer and cook for 5–8 minutes, or until a knife can go through the potato slices but they're still firm. They will cook again in the oven, so they need to remain firm at this stage. Carefully drain the potatoes in a colander and allow to steam dry: they need to be really dry for the pie, as any excess water will dilute the sauce.

RECIPE CONTINUES OVER THE PAGE

Make it perfect

When boiling potatoes, always do so over medium heat. If you fiercely boil potatoes, the outsides will cook very quickly and the centres will not be cooked at the same speed, which means by the time the centres are cooked the outsides are overcooked, giving you mushy and over-wet boiled potatoes.

4. Heat the vegetable oil in a separate frying pan over low heat, add the sliced shallots and crushed garlic and sweat for 8–10 minutes until translucent. Add the diced Tunworth cheese and a ½ teaspoon of salt and cook over low heat for a further 10 minutes until the cheese breaks down and melts completely. Keep stirring the mixture to avoid it sticking to the bottom of the pan.

5. Meanwhile, in a separate saucepan, heat the milk, cream and chopped thyme until simmering (not boiling), then pour over the melted cheese mixture and mix until fully incorporated. The mixture should resemble a rich cheese sauce. If the sauce is thin, simmer it for 2–3 minutes to thicken it to a coating consistency.

6. Preheat the oven to 190°C/170°C fan/gas 5.

7. To assemble the pie, place a layer of the sliced potatoes in a 20cm circular baking dish and season with salt and pepper. Dress the potatoes with a generous layer of the cheese mixture and repeat the layers with the rest of the cheese and potatoes. Brush the edge of the dish with a little of the remaining egg yolk. Remove the rolled-out pastry from the fridge and lay it on top of the dish, allowing it to hang over the top. Neaten the edges of the pastry, leaving a slight edge as it will shrink a little as it cooks, then glaze the pastry with the egg yolk and sprinkle over the picked thyme leaves.

8. Bake in the oven for 30–35 minutes until the pastry is golden brown. Remove from the oven and serve immediately, while the pastry is crisp.

Madeira-caramelised Parsnips

SERVES: 6 AS A SIDE
PREP TIME: 15 MINUTES
COOKING TIME: 35 MINUTES

2 sprigs of thyme
1 sprig of rosemary
2 garlic cloves, halved
2 tbsp celery salt
500g parsnips, peeled and cut into large
    wedges
100g butter
100g honey
50ml sherry vinegar
100ml madeira
flaked sea salt and freshly ground black
    pepper

We often eat parsnips with roast chicken or pork, and cooking them with madeira, vinegar and honey is a fabulous way to bring out their natural flavour. In fact, these are so delicious I think I could eat a bowl of them on their own.

1. Bring a large saucepan of water to the boil over high heat and add the herbs, garlic and celery salt. Once the water is boiling, add the parsnips and cook for 4–5 minutes until they are just beginning to soften.

2. Drain in a colander and allow to steam dry. Once cool enough to handle, pick out any larger pieces of herb and also the garlic.

3. Heat a large frying pan over high heat, add the butter and cook until it is beginning to foam and turn nut brown in colour. Tip in the drained parsnips and sauté in the hot butter for 5–10 minutes until well coloured all over, shaking the pan every so often to ensure the parsnips colour evenly. Once coloured, drain in a colander to remove any excess butter.

4. Place the empty pan back over the high heat and add the honey. Cook the honey until it begins to caramelise and turn a deep amber colour, then deglaze with the vinegar and madeira and whisk to bring together as a thick syrup.

5. Put the parsnips back in the pan, toss them in the honey syrup and continue to cook over high heat for 2 minutes to allow the parsnips to become glazed in the sticky syrup. Finish with flakes of sea salt and freshly ground black pepper and serve.

Celeriac and Tahini Gratin

SERVES: 4
PREP TIME: 30 MINUTES
COOKING TIME: 1½ HOURS

butter, for greasing
800g floury potatoes, peeled
1 large celeriac, peeled
2 white onions, thinly sliced
4 sprigs of thyme, leaves picked
200g tahini
600ml good-quality vegetable stock,
    warmed
½ tsp fine sea salt
½ tsp ground white pepper
1 tsp garlic powder
handful of grated mature Cheddar cheese,
    to cover the top
freshly ground black pepper

GET AHEAD
**Cook the gratin the day before serving,
just until the vegetables are soft, then
finish it by just browning it in the oven
for 20 minutes with the cheese topping.**

This variation on dauphinoise potatoes includes gently mustardy celeriac and tahini, a sticky paste made from sesame seeds that's most often used in hummus. I found that cooking celeriac in a gratin was a great way to introduce my children to the vegetable, though I also love it fresh in a remoulade. Peeling celeriac takes a little dedication, but it's well worth the effort. A mandoline is a useful tool here, as it gives you lovely thin, uniform slices of potato and celeriac, which will then cook more evenly than if they are sliced by hand. You may even have a slicer on your food processor which would also help speed things up. The gratin works well alone as a vegetable dish, or serve it with a roast meat such as beef in a similar way to potato dauphinoise.

1. Preheat the oven to 180°C/160°C fan/gas 4 and grease a large casserole dish (about 26cm) with butter.

2. Using a mandoline or food processor with a slicer function, if you have one, thinly slice the potatoes and celeriac to a thickness of 1–2mm. The celeriac is tricky to handle due to its size and shape, so cut into half or quarters first for easy slicing.

3. Arrange a layer of sliced celeriac in the bottom of the greased baking dish and season with a little of the salt and pepper. Follow with a thin layer of sliced onion and picked thyme leaves, then a single layer of potatoes. Season again. Repeat the layering of vegetables and thyme until they have all been used, ensuring the final layer of potato is arranged neatly as this will be visible when you serve the dish.

4. Whisk the tahini and vegetable stock together in a jug until evenly combined, then mix through the seasonings of salt, pepper and garlic powder.

5. Pour the tahini mixture over the layered vegetables, allow it to sink in between the layers, then cover with foil. Bake the gratin in the oven for 1¼–1½ hours. To test if the gratin is cooked, insert a small knife into the centre – the potato and celeriac should be soft all the way through and the knife should meet no resistance. If necessary, cover with foil again and return to the oven for a further 15 minutes until soft (before adding the cheese). When the gratin is cooked, remove the foil, sprinkle evenly with grated cheese and return to the oven for 15 minutes to allow the top to colour before serving. It will be hot so can wait a few minutes.

Celery and Peanut Salad

SERVES: 4 AS A SIDE
PREP TIME: 20–30 MINUTES
COOKING TIME: 3–4 MINUTES

30g peanuts
juice of 2 limes
1 tsp caster sugar
1½ tbsp fish sauce
3 tbsp groundnut oil
1 red chilli, deseeded and finely chopped
    (or to taste)
2 celery hearts, trimmed, washed and dried
4 sprigs of Thai basil, leaves roughly
    chopped
4 sprigs of fresh mint, leaves picked and
    pulled
½ bunch of coriander, leaves roughly
    chopped
4 spring onions, trimmed and thinly sliced
sea salt and freshly ground black pepper
2 tbsp Greek yoghurt, to serve

My wife is a big fan of celery. There's always a lot of it in the fridge so it gets thrown into lots of different dishes but as it's so delicious I thought it was worthy of playing a starring role. The Asian flavours work really well here, it's very easy to make and very moreish too. It makes a great side at a barbecue.

1. Toast the nuts in a large dry frying pan over medium heat for 3–4 minutes until lightly golden, shaking the pan every now and then to stop the nuts from burning. Tip them onto a board and chop, then set aside.

2. In a small bowl, whisk together the lime juice and caster sugar until the sugar has dissolved, then add the fish sauce, oil and chilli. Mix, taste and season with salt and pepper, then set aside.

3. Peel the celery if you wish (though I don't think it's necessary), then cut into 1cm-thick diagonal slices. Toss the celery in the dressing in a bowl until coated, then transfer it to a serving bowl or platter and top with the toasted nuts, basil, mint, coriander and spring onions. Finally, top with the Greek yoghurt.

Poached Quince with Honey, Nuts and Crème Fraîche

SERVES: 4, WITH LEFTOVERS FOR BREAKFAST
PREP TIME: 20 MINUTES
COOKING TIME: 30–40 MINUTES

FOR THE POACHED QUINCE
4 quinces, peeled and halved
1 vanilla pod, split lengthways
2 bay leaves
1 cinnamon stick
130g caster sugar
100ml marsala wine
200ml sparkling wine
5 sprigs of lavender

FOR THE TOPPING
30g hazelnuts
30g walnuts
150–200g crème fraîche
runny honey, to taste
sprig of fresh lavender

VARIATION

To turn this into a breakfast dish, swap the crème fraîche for Greek yoghurt and the nuts for a crunchy granola.

Last year I was given a quince tree. It's a fabulous addition to our orchard, though it isn't quite mature enough to bear fruit. I do love cooking with quince. Quince is a hard fruit like an apple, with the shape of a pear. It is high in pectin, hence why it's often served as a paste with cheese; it requires cooking to soften its flesh. I have used marsala, a fortified wine in this recipe as I like its sweet and nutty flavour. When you come across it, grab a bottle as it's worth keeping some in your store cupboard.

1. Cut each peeled quince half into 6 wedges then carefully remove the core and any seeds from each wedge. Place in a large saucepan. Scrape the vanilla seeds from the pod and add them to the pan with the pod, then add the bay leaves, cinnamon stick, sugar, marsala wine, sparkling wine and lavender sprigs. Add enough water to cover the fruit, bring to the boil over medium heat, then reduce the heat, cover and simmer for about 30 minutes, adding more water if needed, to keep the fruit covered, until the quinces are soft but still retain their shape – how long they take to soften will depend on how ripe the fruit is.

2. Remove the quinces from the pan and set aside. Strain the cooking liquor and set aside. Leave both to cool.

3. To make the topping, toast the nuts in a dry frying pan over medium heat for a few minutes, until lightly golden, stirring frequently so they don't burn. Alternatively, put the nuts on a baking tray and toast in a 150°C/130°C fan/gas 2 oven for about 10 minutes until they colour lightly. Cool, then roughly chop.

4. To serve, put a layer of fruit in individual serving bowls. Pour some of the cooled cooking liquor into each bowl and add a spoonful of crème fraîche on top of the fruit. Use a spoon to drizzle some honey from side to side over the top of the crème fraîche. Finally, sprinkle with the chopped nuts and add a few lavender flowers pulled from the sprigs.

Baked Rhubarb with Ginger and Orange

SERVES: 4
PREP TIME: 10 MINUTES
COOKING TIME: 20–25 MINUTES

500g young rhubarb, cut into 5cm batons
grated zest and juice of 1 orange
75g caster sugar
2 pieces of stem ginger, thinly sliced
1 tbsp stem ginger syrup
vanilla ice cream, to serve

We use a lot of rhubarb in the restaurant, partly because we grow a lot in our kitchen garden. This recipe features young, early-season rhubarb which has slimmer stems and is less tough than later-season rhubarb. Rhubarb and ginger are perfect partners – the slight heat from the ginger complements the sharp rhubarb – and the orange brings sweetness to the dish. Serve with custard and shortbread biscuits, if you like, or simply some crème fraîche. It's delicious for breakfast with granola, too (see page 279).

1. Preheat the oven to 130°C/110°C fan/gas ¾.

2. Put the rhubarb in a casserole dish along with the rest of the ingredients and coat the rhubarb in the syrup mixture, making sure the rhubarb is spread out evenly.

3. Cover the dish with foil and bake in the oven for 20–25 minutes until the rhubarb is soft to touch but still holds its shape – how long this takes will depend on the thickness of the rhubarb. Remove from the oven and allow to cool a little.

4. Serve while still slightly warm, with a scoop of vanilla ice cream.

Apple Custard Pots with a Cashew Crumb

SERVES: 6
PREP TIME: 30 MINUTES, PLUS
MINIMUM 4 HOURS COOLING
COOKING TIME: 15 MINUTES

300g Baked Apple Sauce (page 264)
450ml double cream
6 eggs
120g caster sugar
1 Granny Smith apple

FOR THE CASHEW CRUMB
100g cashew nut butter
100g plain flour
¼ tsp salt
75g golden syrup (or maple syrup)

VARIATIONS

Try swapping the apple purée for another one made from hard fruits such as quince or pear.
Swap the cashew nut butter for another nut butter such as almond or hazelnut.
Use the crumb for topping other creamy, smooth desserts, or yoghurt. Or make it into balls for snacks (they'd be great dipped in melted chocolate).

This is a really easy dessert and it doesn't take very long to make, though it does require some planning as it needs a few hours to chill and you may have to make the apple sauce from scratch unless you have a frozen batch. It works perfectly as a midweek pudding: make the custard during the day, or the night before and it's ready for dinner. The custard pots keep well in the fridge for a few days (without the topping).

1. Combine the apple sauce and double cream in a saucepan and heat over medium heat for 3–5 minutes until it begins to simmer, then remove from the heat (don't use too fierce a heat as it will cause the mixture to split).

2. Whisk the eggs and the sugar together in a heatproof bowl until smooth, then pour in a third of the hot cream and apple mixture, whisking continuously and slowing down or stopping adding the cream for a moment if required, as you do not want to cook the eggs. Continue until all the apple mixture is incorporated into the egg mixture. It's important to stir well at this stage to ensure that all the sugar dissolves into the liquid.

3. Rinse out the pan, pour the custard mixture back into the pan and return to low heat. Cook the apple custard mix for 5–6 minutes, stirring constantly and gently with a spatula or spoon, until the first bubble rises to the surface as it approaches boiling point. To test if the custard is thick enough, coat the back of the spoon or spatula and run your finger through the mixture. If it's thick enough the line should remain. To be extra precise, check the mixture with a thermometer – it should reach exactly 82°C.

4. Remove the custard from the heat and, using a stick blender (making sure it's fully submerged in the liquid), blitz for 30 seconds to aerate the custard.

5. Divide the hot custard among six small serving pots, leave to cool, then transfer them to the fridge for 3–4 hours, preferably overnight, to allow them to chill and set.

6. Preheat the oven to 170°C/150°C fan/gas 4 and line a baking tray with a silicone baking mat or baking parchment.

7. To make the cashew crumb, combine all the ingredients in a bowl and, using your fingertips, rub together until you have a mixture that resembles breadcrumbs. Spread it out onto the lined baking tray and bake for 10–12 minutes, mixing the crumb halfway through to ensure it bakes evenly. Once it's golden brown, remove from the oven and leave to cool.

8. To serve, remove the set custard pots from the fridge and let them reach room temperature before covering the tops with a layer of the cashew crumb. Peel and dice the Granny Smith apple and scatter it over the top, then serve. (Don't be tempted to top them in advance, as the crumb will go soft and sink into the custard.)

Poached Figs with Honeycomb and Cinnamon

SERVES: 4
PREP TIME: ABOUT 1 HOUR
COOKING TIME: 25–30 MINUTES

I demonstrated this dish on *MasterChef: The Professionals* 2020 and this is one of my father-in-law, Guy's, favourite desserts. We have several fig trees at Melfort House which give us the most amazing crop every year. We make plenty of chutney with the figs, for the restaurant to serve with cheese, but this is always a wonderful way to use a fresh batch. Any leftover honeycomb will keep for up to a month in an airtight container. It's great on ice cream, or as a treat on its own.

8 fresh figs

FOR THE POACHING LIQUID
100ml ruby port
400ml red wine
4 star anise
1 cinnamon stick
½ lemon, sliced
2 tbsp caster sugar

FOR THE HONEYCOMB
a little vegetable or sunflower oil, for
    greasing
25g honey
38g liquid glucose
165g caster sugar
11g bicarbonate of soda

FOR THE CREAM
250ml double cream
½ vanilla pod
1 tbsp caster sugar

TO SERVE
ground cinnamon
basil micro cress or small basil leaves, picked

1. First, make the poaching liquid for the figs. Pour the ruby port and red wine into a large saucepan and add the star anise, cinnamon stick, lemon slices and sugar. Stir, bring to the boil over medium heat, then turn down the heat and simmer for 15 minutes to infuse the flavours.

2. Cut a 1cm-deep cross in the pointed end of each fig. Gently lower the figs into the simmering poaching liquor, cover with the lid and turn off the heat. Leave the figs in the liquid as it cools. This will gently infuse the flavours into the figs – you don't need to cook them as they are already soft.

3. When the figs are cold, strain the liquor into a small pan and set aside.

4. Now make the honeycomb. Line a large baking tray with a silicone baking mat or baking parchment and grease it lightly with the vegetable or sunflower oil.

5. Put the honey, liquid glucose, sugar and 30ml water into a wide, deep, heavy-based pan (the pan needs to be deep because when you add the bicarbonate of soda the mixture will bubble up). Place over medium heat and heat gently, without stirring, until it has a rich honey colour. It will continue to cook off the heat, so remove the pan as soon as you reach this stage, swirling to cool for a few seconds (the line between caramel and burnt sugar is fine, and burnt sugar will ruin the flavour). Add the bicarbonate of soda and carefully yet briskly whisk it in for just long enough to incorporate the powder into the caramel. It will bubble up and will be hot, so be careful not to splash yourself. As soon as the bicarbonate of soda is stirred in, immediately pour the liquid honeycomb into the lined baking tray and leave to cool.

6. When you are ready to serve, heat the pan of fig liquor over medium heat and reduce the liquid by about three-quarters, until it thickens to form a syrup – about 5 minutes. Take care not to reduce it too much, as it will thicken as it cools.

7. Combine the cream, the seeds from the vanilla pod and the sugar in a bowl and gently whisk to thick ribbon stage. Once it starts to thicken, slow down the whisking or it will be over-whipped (cream sets further once the whipping stops) – the cream should have some movement and not be firm.

8. Quarter or halve the poached figs and arrange them randomly on each plate (2 figs per serving), then drizzle the reduced syrup over the top. Break the cooled honeycomb into pieces and place on top of the cut figs. Put a spoonful of the cream on the side of the plate and, using a tea strainer, gently dust the top with ground cinnamon. Finish the dish with some basil micro cress or small basil leaves.

Simply
Essential

Dressed Crab with Bulgur Wheat and a Blood Orange and Chicory Salad

SERVES: 4 AS A STARTER OR LIGHT LUNCH
PREP TIME: 25 MINUTES
COOKING TIME: 5 MINUTES

200ml good-quality fish stock
100g bulgur wheat, rinsed and drained
400g picked white crab meat
2 blood oranges
2 heads of red chicory (about 140g)
salt
cayenne pepper, to serve

FOR THE MAYONNAISE
1 large egg yolk
1 tsp Dijon mustard
1 tbsp white wine vinegar
100ml extra virgin rapeseed oil, plus extra for dressing
100g crème fraîche
1 tbsp freshly chopped dill, plus extra sprigs to garnish
1 tbsp freshly chopped chervil, plus extra leaves to garnish
grated zest of 1 orange

Jane loves crab, and if we see it on a menu, I can guarantee she will order it. This is a delicious dish to enjoy at the weekend with a glass of rosé in the garden. Blood oranges have the most wonderful red flesh with a light orange flavour and hints of grapefruit, and are seasonal and only available usually from January to March. If you can't get them, navel oranges will make a good swap, or even use a mix of orange and grapefruit slices, which will take the recipe into summer. Homemade mayo is worth the effort – it has a beautiful, fresh richness that processed, shop-bought mayo will never have. If you don't grow or can't find chervil, use the smaller leaves of flat-leaf parsley mixed with tarragon to get a similar fragrant flavour, or use curly parsley.

1. Bring the fish stock to the boil in a medium saucepan with a pinch of salt. Once it reaches the boil, add the bulgur wheat and cook for 1 minute.

2. Cover with a lid then remove from the heat and allow the bulgur wheat to cool and absorb all the stock (this will take about 15 minutes), then fluff it up with a fork – it needs to be completely cold before you add it to the mayonnaise, as it will split the mayonnaise if warm.

3. While the bulgur wheat cools, make the mayonnaise. Whisk the egg yolk, Dijon mustard and vinegar in a bowl, then very slowly drizzle in the rapeseed oil, whisking continuously, until fully combined and emulsified. Stir in the crème fraîche, chopped herbs, orange zest and salt to taste.

4. Add the cold bulgur wheat and crab meat to the mayonnaise and fold everything together until the crab and the bulgur wheat are fully coated. Season to taste with salt and pepper.

RECIPE CONTINUES OVER THE PAGE

Make it perfect

When making mayonnaise, keeping the ingredients cool is essential for emulsification, so it helps if you make it over a bowl of ice. Whisk the egg and mustard vigorously for 2–3 minutes, then begin to incorporate the oil in a very slow and steady drizzle (the mixture will split if you add it too quickly), whisking all the time until the oil is all added and the mixture is thick. If you feel it's a little too thick, stir in a teaspoon of warm water.

If the mayonnaise splits, you can start again or add a teaspoon of boiling water to the mixture to bring it back together. Use a blender if you prefer (see page 267).

5. Cut the tops and bottoms off the blood oranges to sit them flat on a board. Next, with a sharp knife, carefully remove all the peel and pith from the oranges by cutting down from the top of each fruit in sections. Once peeled, cut each orange into 6 circular slices. You should have 12 slices.

6. Cut the bottom 2cm of root off the chicory heads and separate into individual leaves. Wash and dry if required. Dress the sliced oranges and chicory leaves in a bowl with a little extra virgin rapeseed oil and a pinch of salt.

7. On one of your serving plates, press a quarter of the dressed crab mixture flat inside a round ring mould or cutter about 9cm in diameter and 3–5cm high. Carefully lift the mould off the plate while pressing the mix down. Repeat with the remaining three plates and mixture.

8. Arrange a small pile of orange and chicory salad on the side of the crab stacks and garnish with picked dill sprigs and chervil leaves. Finish with a twist of black pepper on the crab and the salad, and a light dusting of cayenne pepper in the crab if you wish.

Baked Eggs and Creamed Spinach with Nutmeg and Parmesan

SERVES: 4–6
PREP TIME: 40 MINUTES
COOKING TIME: 25 MINUTES

200ml milk
50g unsalted butter
2 tbsp plain flour
2 tsp Dijon mustard
120g crème fraîche
½ nutmeg, for grating
1 tbsp olive oil, plus extra for drizzling
2 shallots, finely diced
300g baby leaf spinach, washed
6 eggs
20g Parmesan cheese
sea salt and freshly ground black pepper

VARIATIONS

Add chopped chorizo to the shallots as they cook, to add some spicy heat to the mix.
To make the sauce cheesy, add a handful of grated Cheddar to the béchamel, along with the crème fraîche.

TIP

To wash spinach thoroughly, fill a clean sink with water, add the spinach and allow the leaves to float – the grit, etc. will sink to the bottom. Drain well.

We use a huge number of eggs in our house, mostly for breakfast or for baking. This baked egg dish makes a delicious brunch or even a quick supper – it's so easy. Serve with crunchy bread or toast (a little bacon on the side would be good, too). We have the majority of these ingredients in the cupboard all the time, which makes it an easy dish to pull together. We often have spinach, too, which we use in salads and smoothies.

1. Preheat the oven to 190°C/170°C fan/gas 5.

2. First, make the béchamel. Pour the milk into a small saucepan and slowly bring to a simmer over low heat.

3. In a second saucepan, melt 25g of the butter over medium heat, then add the flour and a pinch each of salt and pepper. Cook the flour and butter for 1 minute, being careful not to let it brown as this will add a burnt flavour to the sauce (start again if this happens). Gradually add half of the warmed milk, whisking quickly to combine, then stir in the remaining milk. Cook over low heat for a further 2 minutes until it has thickened to a smooth gloop. Stir through the mustard and crème fraîche then grate in all the nutmeg. Remove from the heat, taste and adjust the seasoning if necessary.

4. Heat the olive oil in a small frying pan over medium heat, add the remaining butter, then add the diced shallots, season with a pinch of salt and sweat for 2–3 minutes until softened. Add the baby spinach and cook for about 2 minutes until completely wilted, stirring every now and then.

5. Spoon the wilted spinach and shallot mixture and any juices into the béchamel sauce and fold together. Transfer to an ovenproof dish (roughly 20cm) and use the back of a spoon to make six dips in the creamed spinach. Crack an egg into each dip, finely grate the Parmesan all over the eggs and drizzle with olive oil.

6. Place the dish in the oven and bake for 10–20 minutes until the egg whites are just set and the yolks are still soft (or done to your liking). Serve immediately.

Sausage and Chorizo Casserole

SERVES: 4
PREP TIME: 10 MINUTES
COOKING TIME 1 HOUR 15 MINUTES

2 tbsp vegetable oil
8 good-quality sausages
200g cooking chorizo, diced
1 leek, rinsed and sliced
1 carrot, diced
2 garlic cloves, sliced
2 sprigs of rosemary, needles picked and chopped
300g Puy lentils, washed and well drained
1 tsp hot smoked paprika
50ml sherry vinegar
150ml white wine
450ml good-quality chicken stock
500g passata
1 x 400g tin butter beans, drained
½ bunch of flat-leaf parsley, chopped
extra virgin olive oil, for drizzling
sea salt and freshly ground black pepper

In *Marcus Everyday* there is a lovely recipe for haddock served with lentils. It has long been a family favourite of ours, especially throughout lockdown. This slight variation came about from cooking the lentils with other things we had in the fridge, such as sausages. I have put this into the Simply Essential chapter as most of the ingredients are store-cupboard supplies. We always keep diced chorizo in the fridge with a variety of vegetables, and lentils and passata are a store-cupboard must. Serve with crusty bread and butter and a simple green salad.

1. Preheat the oven to 200°C/180°C fan/gas 6.

2. Heat the vegetable oil in a large, shallow casserole dish over medium heat, then add the sausages and fry until golden brown on all sides (the browning is for the appearance – they don't need to be cooked through). Remove from the dish and set aside for later.

3. Add the diced chorizo to the dish and cook for 2–3 minutes until the fat has rendered out and the chorizo is beginning to brown. Add the leek, carrot, garlic and rosemary and cook over medium heat for 3–4 minutes until softened (don't worry about the excess oil from the chorizo – it has a wonderful flavour). Add the lentils, season with salt and the smoked paprika, cook for 30 seconds, then deglaze the dish with the sherry vinegar. Once the vinegar has become sticky in the pan, pour in the white wine and allow it to reduce by half.

4. After it has reduced, add 350ml of the stock, the passata and butter beans and return the browned sausages to the dish. Bring to the boil then cover with a lid or foil and transfer to the oven for 45 minutes.

5. Check the casserole halfway through cooking, adding the remaining stock if it's drying out. After 45 minutes the lentils should be soft and the sausages cooked through. Cook the casserole for a little longer if the lentils are not yet soft.

6. To finish, remove from the oven, remove the lid or foil and stir through the chopped parsley. Drizzle with olive oil and adjust the seasoning with salt and pepper if necessary.

Red Lentil Hummus with Curry-roasted Carrots, Pickled Mustard Seeds and Sultanas

SERVES: 4 AS A STARTER OR LIGHT LUNCH
PREP TIME: 10 MINUTES
COOKING TIME: 35–45 MINUTES

10 large baby bunched carrots, washed and
   tops removed
3 tbsp vegetable oil
1 tbsp curry powder
2 star anise
4 green cardamom pods, lightly crushed
sea salt and freshly ground black pepper
extra virgin rapeseed oil, for drizzling
1 small bunch of coriander, leaves and stalks
   finely chopped, to serve

FOR THE PICKLED MUSTARD SEEDS AND SULTANAS
2 tbsp black mustard seeds
40g sultanas
100ml white wine vinegar
60g soft brown sugar
pinch of salt

My family all love hummus, mostly homemade, but sometimes bought from our local deli. This is a slightly different take on the normal chickpea hummus, as it starts with a base of lentils. I like to serve this as a light lunch, though it would work equally well as a canapé before dinner for friends. Here it is served with curried carrots, but it could also be served with flatbreads or a variety of raw vegetables. The pickled seeds and sultanas make a tasty addition to many dishes, such as couscous or a salad. Double up the mix and keep in the fridge in an airtight container until required.

1. First, pickle the seeds and sultanas. Toast the black mustard seeds in a small frying pan over medium heat for 1–2 minutes, being careful not to let them burn. Transfer to a small heatproof mixing bowl and add the sultanas.

2. Back in the same pan, add the white wine vinegar, brown sugar and 30ml water along with the salt, then gradually bring to the boil. Pour the liquor over the toasted seeds and sultanas, cover with clingfilm and allow them to soak up the pickle until cool.

3. To make the hummus, heat the vegetable oil in a saucepan over medium heat, add the garlic and sweat until softened, then add the ground cumin and turmeric. Cook the spices in the oil for 30 seconds, stirring them to ensure they don't catch and burn, then add the dried lentils and cook them in the spice mix for 1 minute, stirring to coat. Season with salt and pepper, pour in the vegetable stock and bring to the boil over medium heat. Reduce the heat to a simmer and cook, covered, for 10–15 minutes until the lentils are soft and all the stock has been absorbed, stirring occasionally to avoid the lentils sticking to the bottom of the pan. Add a little more stock if the lentils are not soft once all the stock has evaporated. Overcooked is better than undercooked in the case of lentils.

FOR THE HUMMUS
2 tbsp vegetable oil
5 garlic cloves, crushed
2 tsp ground cumin
1 tsp ground turmeric
400g dried red lentils, washed and drained
800ml good-quality vegetable stock
50g tahini
grated zest and juice of ½ lemon

VARIATIONS

Cauliflower works well with the curry flavourings as a substitute for carrots. For a pre-dinner snack, serve the hummus with raw vegetables or flatbread (page 274).

GET AHEAD
You can make the hummus up to 5 days ahead and keep it in the fridge in a sealed container.

4. Once the lentils have absorbed all the stock, the mixture will have thickened and dried up a little and the lentils will have started to break down. Place the cooked lentils in a food processor with the tahini and lemon zest and juice and blitz until smooth. (If the hummus does not become smooth it means the lentils were undercooked.) Taste and season with salt and pepper as required, place a layer of clingfilm on the surface of the hummus and leave to cool.

5. Meanwhile, preheat the oven to 200°C/180°C fan/gas 6.

6. Cut the carrots in half lengthways, transfer them to a large baking tray, coat with the oil, curry powder and whole spices, and season with salt and pepper. Cook in the oven for 10–15 minutes until golden, turning them halfway through the cooking time to ensure they are all are coated and cooked evenly. You want them to take on colour yet remain crunchy.

7. To assemble the dish, place a good dollop (about 1 tablespoon) of hummus on each of four plates and create a hollow in the centre with the back of a spoon. Place the curried carrots in the middle of each portion (5 per plate), then – using a slotted spoon – dribble the pickled seeds and sultanas over the carrots. Finish by sprinkling over finely chopped coriander and drizzling over some rapeseed oil.

Rarebit-style Curried, Smoked Haddock

SERVES: 4
PREP TIME: 10 MINUTES
COOKING TIME: 25 MINUTES

200g smoked haddock fillet
250ml milk
15g unsalted butter
1 tbsp plain flour
1 tsp curry powder
100ml Indian Pale Ale
1 tsp English mustard
1 tbsp Worcestershire sauce
200g extra-mature Cheddar cheese
2 egg yolks
4 thick slices of sourdough bread
1 red chilli, deseeded and thinly sliced
2 spring onions, trimmed and thinly sliced

VARIATION

Swap the haddock for hot-smoked poached salmon (you won't need to poach the salmon before assembling the rarebit).

This is a variation on a usual rarebit, combining curry flavours and smoked haddock in a creamy sauce. Béchamel is usually made with flour, butter and milk; here, the milk is replaced with ale, which gives the dish a slightly bitter taste. If you prefer not to use a hoppy ale, you could replace it with a lighter one or use the milk from poaching the fish. Serve as a weekend lunch or easy weeknight supper alongside a green salad dressed with vinaigrette, to cut through the creaminess.

1. First, poach the smoked haddock. Place the fillet, skin side down, in a wide saucepan and cover with the milk. Place over medium heat and bring to the boil, then reduce to a simmer and poach the fish for 4–5 minutes until the flesh flakes easily. Remove from the heat and allow the fish to cool in the milk, then carefully remove from the pan, remove the skin and any bones and flake into small pieces. Retain the milk for now, in case you need to add some to the sauce.

2. To make the rarebit sauce, melt the butter in a saucepan over medium heat, and once it starts to foam stir in the flour and curry powder. Cook for 1–2 minutes, then add half the ale and whisk until smooth. Add the remaining ale along with the mustard and Worcestershire sauce and whisk to a thick sauce.

3. Remove the pan from the heat and tip in the grated cheese. Whisk into the sauce until melted and fully incorporated, then add the egg yolks and beat them into the cheese sauce.

4. Preheat the grill and toast the sourdough lightly on both sides.

5. To finish the rarebit mixture, fold the chilli, spring onions and poached haddock through the cheese sauce.

6. Put the toasted sourdough on a baking tray and spoon the rarebit mixture on top of each piece, spreading it out flat until it almost reaches the edges. (Don't worry if some slips over the edge, it will just bubble up deliciously!) Cook under the hot grill until bubbling and nicely golden, keeping a constant eye on the rarebits as they will colour quickly.

7. Serve immediately, while still hot.

Zhoug-spiced Tofu and Spinach Filo Rolls

SERVES: 4 AS A STARTER OR LIGHT LUNCH (2 ROLLS EACH)
PREP TIME: 25 MINUTES, PLUS COOLING
COOKING TIME: 35 MINUTES

4 tbsp extra virgin olive oil
200g firm tofu, finely chopped
150g spinach
1 x 270g pack of filo pastry (about 7 sheets)
sea salt and freshly ground black pepper

FOR THE ZHOUG PASTE
½ bunch of coriander
½ bunch of flat-leaf parsley
2 green chillies, chopped
1 tsp ground cumin
½ tsp ground cardamom
2 garlic cloves
2 tbsp extra virgin olive oil
½ tsp fine salt
2 egg yolks

VARIATIONS

Make sausage-meat filo rolls. Season about 500g sausage meat with salt and pepper and add the zhoug paste. Put the sausage mix in a piping bag and pipe along the edge of the filo sheets before rolling. Or replace the tofu with 200g feta cheese chopped into small chunks and added to the spinach above, after the cooking stage.

These meat-free rolls of spiced tofu and spinach wrapped in the light crunch of the filo pastry are really tasty. Zhoug paste has chilli heat but also wonderful warming Middle Eastern flavours of cumin and coriander which enhance the tofu. You can serve them hot or cold, and they are great with a green salad and simple vinaigrette. Tofu tends to have a reasonable fridge life so it's a really useful ingredient to have at the ready.

1. First, make the zhoug paste. Put the coriander, parsley and chillies in a food processor and blitz until roughly chopped. Scrape down the sides of the bowl and add the rest of the paste ingredients, then blitz again until smooth.

2. To make the filling, heat 2 tablespoons of the olive oil in a large frying pan over high heat, then add the chopped tofu and cook for 3–4 minutes until lightly coloured. Add the spinach and cook for a further 2 minutes, until the spinach has started to wilt. Remove the pan from the heat and transfer the filling to a bowl. Place in the fridge to allow the filling to cool completely.

3. Once the filling is cool, combine it with the zhoug paste until evenly mixed, and adjust the seasoning with salt and pepper to taste.

4. Preheat the oven to 170°C/150°C fan/gas 4 and line a baking tray with a silicone baking mat or baking parchment.

5. Lay one sheet of pastry on a work surface (keeping the remaining sheets moist and pliable by covering them with sheets of damp kitchen paper) and brush it liberally with some of the remaining olive oil. Repeat this step, building up to three layers of pastry in total.

6. Spoon half of the mix across the length of the layered pastry, then roll it up as tightly as you can in the pastry, like a large cigar. Repeat with three more pastry sheets to use up the remaining filling. (If you have a spare sheet at the end, make a little parcel from it with a spoon of the filling and bake it as a cook's treat.)

7. Cut each cigar into 4 pieces with a serrated knife. Brush them with oil and transfer them to the lined baking tray, then bake for 20–25 minutes until crisp and golden brown.

8. Remove from the oven, allow to cool for 5 minutes, then serve.

Garlic and Anchovy Tagliatelle

SERVES: 4
PREP TIME: 10 MINUTES
COOKING TIME: 15 MINUTES

50ml olive oil
4 garlic cloves, any green germ removed,
    and the rest thinly sliced
25g jarred or tinned anchovy fillets, in oil
200ml single cream
100ml milk
300g dried tagliatelle
1 heaped tbsp dried breadcrumbs
finely grated zest of 1 lemon and juice of ½
sea salt and freshly ground black pepper
extra virgin olive oil, for drizzling

Styled after bagna càuda, a hot Italian sauce made with garlic and anchovies that's traditionally served with crudités, this dish serves it with ribbons of tagliatelle pasta instead. The sauce and pasta are really delicious together, especially with a twist of ground black pepper on top. You can, of course, make your own pasta, but there are plenty of great dried pasta options available to keep in your store cupboard for a quick supper. Top the tagliatelle with some grated Parmesan cheese, if you like, and serve with asparagus or green salad.

1. Heat the 50ml of olive oil in a frying pan over low heat. Add the sliced garlic and sweat gently for 3–4 minutes, making sure the garlic doesn't take on any colour. Add the anchovy fillets and cook for a further 2 minutes until the fillets start to break apart.

2. Add the cream and milk to the pan and simmer for 5–10 minutes until the garlic is completely soft.

3. Bring a large saucepan of salted water to the boil and cook the pasta according to the packet instructions, until al dente.

4. While the pasta is cooking, transfer the garlic and anchovy cream to a blender or food processor with the breadcrumbs and lemon juice and blitz until smooth. Taste and add more lemon juice if needed.

5. Once the pasta is cooked, drain and return it to the pan. Pour over the garlic cream and mix well.

6. To serve, divide the pasta among serving bowls, top with a little of the finely grated lemon zest and a drizzle of extra virgin olive oil and a twist of ground black pepper, if you like.

Beef and Pine Nut Kibbeh Traybake with Sweet Beetroot Chutney

MAKES : 9 SQUARES
PREP TIME: 1 HOUR, PLUS
COOLING TIME
COOKING TIME: 1 HOUR

Lebanese kibbeh are a wonderful combination of spices, ground meat, bulgur wheat and pine nuts. Usually, they are formed into a meatball with a filling. They are quite tricky to shape, so here we have a simpler variation – a delicious layered traybake.

100g fine or medium bulgur wheat, rinsed
and well drained
3 tbsp olive oil
500g minced beef
2 small onions (about 300g), coarsely grated
1½ tsp ground allspice
2 tsp ground cumin
1 tsp hot smoked paprika
1 tbsp freshly chopped mint
75g pine nuts, lightly toasted
sea salt and freshly ground black pepper

**FOR THE SWEET BEETROOT
CHUTNEY**
100g demerara sugar
150ml red wine vinegar
about 3 medium raw beetroot, peeled and
coarsely grated (wear gloves to avoid
staining your hands)
1 cooking apple (about 300g), peeled and
coarsely grated
1 cinnamon stick
2 tbsp redcurrant jelly
150ml apple juice

GET AHEAD
**You can make the chutney up to 5
days in advance, storing it in a sealed
jar in the fridge (the chutney will keep
longer if the jar is sterilised), and make
extra if you wish – it's delicious as an
accompaniment for mature Cheddar
cheese or cold meats, or roast pork.**

VARIATION
**The traybake would also work well
with the Roasted Garlic and Buttermilk
Dressing on page 268.**

1. First, make the chutney. Put the sugar in a medium heavy-based saucepan over medium-high heat and cook until the sugar dissolves and caramelises, tilting the pan every now and then to ensure the sugar cooks evenly (don't stir). Once the sugar is golden amber, deglaze the pan with the vinegar and allow it to reduce by half, then add the remaining ingredients along with a pinch each of salt and pepper. Cook over low-medium heat for 20–25 minutes until the mixture has a loose chutney consistency. It will look like there is a lot of liquid about halfway through cooking, but don't worry as this reduces and will gradually evaporate. Turn off the heat and leave to cool completely.

2. Preheat the oven to 190°C/170°C fan/gas 5 and lightly grease a 20cm non-stick square baking tray with oil.

3. Put the drained bulgur wheat in a heatproof bowl with a pinch of salt. Pour over 100ml boiling water, shake the bowl gently to level out the bulgur and ensure it's covered by the water, then cover with a pan lid and set aside for about 20 minutes for the bulgur to absorb the liquid and cool completely.

4. While the bulgur wheat is soaking, prepare the kibbeh filling (this will be the middle layer of the traybake). Heat 2 tablespoons of the olive oil in a frying pan over high heat. Add 200g of the minced beef (the rest is used later) and season with a pinch of salt and pepper. Cook for 3–4 minutes until well browned, breaking it up with a wooden spoon so there are no large lumps. Add half of the grated onion and cook for a further 4–5 minutes until the onion starts to soften and take on a little colour. Add ½ teaspoon of the allspice, 1 teaspoon of the ground cumin and all the paprika, along with a splash of water. Season well with salt and pepper and toast the spices for 30 seconds, then transfer the spiced mince to a mixing bowl to cool. Once cool, mix through the chopped mint and toasted pine nuts.

5. To make the kibbeh mix, which will form the top and bottom layer of the traybake, combine the soaked bulgur wheat with the remaining beef, spices and grated onion in a large mixing bowl. Season with a pinch each of salt and pepper and mix well, until the mixture has a dough-like consistency. Halve the mixture.

6. Add half the kibbeh mix to the greased tray and press it down into an even layer. Evenly scatter the kibbeh filling over the base. Press the remaining kibbeh mix evenly over the filling to sandwich the filling between the two layers of bulgur wheat.

7. Brush the traybake with the remaining olive oil and use a small knife to cut the bake into 9 equal squares. This will make it easier to portion once cooked. Bake in the hot oven for 15–20 minutes until golden brown.

8. Serve the warm kibbeh traybake with the cooled beetroot chutney.

Hoisin Duck Broth with Chicken Dumplings

SERVES: 4
PREP TIME: 35 MINUTES
COOKING TIME: 1½ HOURS

500g duck bones, chopped
1 tbsp vegetable oil, plus extra for greasing
2 onions, roughly chopped
1 carrot, roughly chopped
2 garlic cloves, peeled
1 thumb-sized piece of fresh ginger, peeled and chopped
1 red chilli, cut in half
1.5 litres good-quality chicken stock
3 tbsp hoisin sauce
3 tbsp dark soy sauce
handful of coriander stalks
sea salt

FOR THE CHICKEN DUMPLINGS

250g chicken mince
1 tbsp rice flour
1 tsp cornflour
1 egg white
1 tsp salt
¼ bunch of coriander, leaves and tender stalks roughly chopped
¼ bunch of chives, roughly chopped
2 garlic cloves, crushed
2 spring onions, trimmed and thinly sliced
½ tsp Chinese five-spice powder

TO SERVE

a few coriander leaves
a few dried chilli flakes (optional)
2 spring onions, trimmed and sliced at an angle

GET AHEAD

Make the chicken dumplings and/or the broth in advance and freeze until required. Defrost and cook as above.

Hoisin is a well-known Chinese sauce often served as a dipping sauce with Peking duck. This dish recreates those same flavours as a hearty, warm broth, served with tasty chicken dumplings. Leftover broth would work with noodles for a quick lunch, too. And best of all, most of the ingredients will store in your cupboard or freezer. My family loves a broth like this – the hotter the better for my sons. Your butcher should be able to supply you with duck bones, but if you have trouble getting them, use chicken bones.

1. Preheat the oven to 200°C/180°C fan/gas 6.

2. Chill a food processor bowl and blade in the fridge. This is important, or the chicken will start to cook when blending.

3. Arrange the duck bones in a roasting tray in a single layer. Roast in the oven for 25–30 minutes until golden brown.

4. While the bones are roasting, heat the oil in a large saucepan over high heat, add the onions, carrot, garlic, ginger and chilli and cook for 5–10 minutes until all are well coloured. Cover with the stock and bring to the boil. Once boiling, add the roasted bones (drained of the roasting fat), the hoisin and soy sauces and coriander stalks. Lower the heat and simmer, half-covered with a lid, for 45 minutes to infuse all the flavours.

5. While the stock is simmering, make the dumpling mixture. Put the mince, rice flour, cornflour, egg white and salt in the cold food processor bowl fitted with the cold blade and blitz for 30 seconds to bring it all together as a thick paste. Transfer to a mixing bowl and stir through the remaining ingredients.

6. Grease your hands with a little oil then take a teaspoon of the dumpling mix in your palms and roll it into a smooth ball. Place on a lightly greased plate and repeat until you have about 20 balls. Place in the fridge to firm up for 30 minutes.

7. After 45 minutes, strain the stock through a fine-mesh sieve into a clean saucepan. Return to low heat and simmer.

8. To cook the dumplings, gently place them in the hot broth, cover the pan and poach for 5– 8 minutes until cooked through. Serve immediately in bowls, piping hot, sprinkled with coriander leaves, chilli flakes (if using) and spring onions.

VARIATION

You could make a pork broth, using pork bones instead of duck bones, but bear in mind it will contain more fat.

Thai Baked Coconut Rice

SERVES: 4
PREP TIME: 15 MINUTES
COOKING TIME: 30–45 MINUTES

350g white or brown long-grain or basmati
  rice, rinsed and drained
1 x 400ml tin coconut milk
300ml good-quality vegetable stock

FOR THE THAI GREEN PASTE
1 bunch of basil
1 bunch of coriander
1 small green chilli (or to taste)
4 garlic cloves, peeled
1 thumb-sized piece of fresh ginger, peeled
1 shallot, roughly chopped
2 sticks of lemongrass, roughly chopped
  (any tough outer layers discarded)
3 makrut lime leaves
2 tbsp fish sauce
grated zest and juice of 2 limes
1 tsp sea salt

We eat a lot of rice in our house, buying it in large 5kg bags at a time (it's cheaper to buy in bulk) and loving its many forms. Cooking it with different flavours adds interest to this great staple that most people have in their store cupboards, and this fuss-free dish makes a flavourful meal in itself, though it can also be served as a side with pan-fried prawns or chicken and some green vegetables. Cooking rice in the oven is an easy way to deliver evenly cooked, fluffy rice. The addition of the coconut milk gives the dish a creamy texture, and the Thai green paste lifts the rice with the slight heat from the chilli and the fragrant flavours of the lime, coriander and basil.

1. Preheat the oven to 190°C/170°C fan/gas 5.

2. To make the Thai green paste, blitz all the ingredients in a food processor until smooth.

3. Combine the rice and the freshly made paste in a bowl and mix until all the grains are evenly coated.

4. Transfer the rice to a roasting tray with the coconut milk and stock. Mix well, then cover the tray tightly with foil. Place in the oven and bake for 30–35 minutes until the rice is cooked and fluffy (brown rice will take longer than white, perhaps up to 45 minutes). Remove from the oven and transfer to a serving dish. If you prefer, you can use a casserole dish to cook the rice.

Pork Loin in Black Bean Sauce

SERVES: 4
PREP TIME: 20 MINUTES
COOKING TIME: 12–13 MINUTES

1 tbsp vegetable oil

3 good-quality boneless pork loin chops (about 500g in total), rind removed but fat left on, cut into 2.5cm chunks

2 tbsp groundnut oil

1 small green pepper, deseeded and cut into 2.5cm chunks

1 small red pepper, deseeded and cut into 2.5cm chunks

1 medium onion, peeled, halved and cut into 8 wedges

150g chestnut mushrooms, halved (large ones quartered)

4 garlic cloves, thinly sliced

75g black bean sauce or black bean rayu (a fermented black bean relish), or to taste

2 tbsp kecap manis (sweet soy sauce)

1 tbsp shop-bought satay sauce (or use the satay sauce on page 58)

sea salt

steamed brown or white rice, to serve (page 272)

We don't order many takeaways, preferring to cook or dine out; however, the one fallback we have is our local Chinese delivery service. You can guarantee we always order something with black bean sauce – it's my childhood favourite. Here I have created my own version using pork loin, though of course it would work with any offcuts of beef or chicken that you have in the freezer. If you keep jars of black bean sauce, soy sauce, kecap manis and satay sauce in your cupboard, this makes a quick and easy supper. If you prefer lean pork, use pork fillet instead of pork loin chops. I have found that you get best results by using a wok, and you can even buy them for induction hobs nowadays, so it's well worth investing in one.

1. Make sure you have all the ingredients prepared and to hand, then heat the vegetable oil in a wok or a large-based pan over high heat until almost smoking. Add a third of the pork, season with salt and sauté for about 1½ minutes until golden brown on all sides. Transfer to a bowl and sauté the remaining pork in two more batches until golden. Spoon the fat from the pan into a bowl and set aside (the pork fat has lots of flavour).

2. Heat the groundnut oil in the wok or pan over high heat, add the veg and garlic and sauté for 4–5 minutes, just until they are cooked through. You don't need them to take on colour particularly – they should still have a bite and retain their shape.

3. While the vegetables are cooking, stir the black bean sauce (or relish), kecap manis and satay sauce together in a bowl.

4. Once the vegetables are cooked, add the meat, fat and any rested juices to the pan and cook for just long enough to warm through the meat. Add some of the sauce mixture and toss everything together to coat the vegetables. Reduce the heat a little and toss the pork, vegetables and sauce for 2–3 minutes, before adding the rest of the sauce to heat through.

5. Serve immediately, with steamed rice.

Gruyère-crusted Cod with Creamed Lentils

SERVES: 4
PREP TIME: 20 MINUTES
COOKING TIME: 35 MINUTES

75g panko breadcrumbs
85g Gruyère cheese, grated, plus extra to
  serve
60g unsalted butter, melted and cooled
1 tsp freshly chopped thyme leaves
4 x 120–150g cod portions (skin removed)
2 tbsp Dijon mustard
sea salt and freshly ground black pepper

FOR THE LENTILS
2 tbsp olive oil
1 onion, finely diced
2 garlic cloves, thinly sliced
200g Puy lentils, rinsed and drained
100ml white wine
500ml good-quality vegetable stock
100g button mushrooms, thinly sliced
100g crème fraîche
juice of ½ lemon
¼ bunch of flat-leaf parsley, chopped

My kids are huge fans of the haddock and lentil dish that appeared in my last book, *Marcus Everyday,* so to take advantage of their new love for lentils I have come up with a variation on the theme, and I'm pleased to say my guys love this one, too (though they do leave the mushrooms!). It reminds me of a turbot dish with a herby cheese topping, a dish created a very long time ago when I first opened Restaurant Pétrus in London. Serve this with a green salad dressed with vinaigrette, to help cut through the creamy lentils and cheese.

1. Preheat the oven to 190°C/170°C fan/gas 5 and line a baking tray with baking parchment.

2. For the lentils, heat the olive oil in a large saucepan over medium heat, then add the chopped onion and garlic and cook for 10 minutes until softened. Add the lentils and cook for 30 seconds, stirring to coat them with the oil in the pan. Deglaze the pan with the white wine and allow it to evaporate completely, then cover the lentils with the vegetable stock and season with salt. Bring to the boil, then reduce to low heat and simmer uncovered for 20–25 minutes until softened and most of the stock has been absorbed. If the stock has evaporated but the lentils are not soft, add more liquid and continue to cook until the lentils are tender.

3. Meanwhile, make the Gruyère topping. Blitz the breadcrumbs and grated Gruyère cheese in a food processor for 30 seconds, then add the cooled butter and chopped thyme and blitz again until the mixture has a crumb-like texture.

4. To prepare the cod, lightly season both sides with salt and pepper, then place evenly spaced apart on the lined baking tray. Brush the top of the fish generously with the mustard using a pastry brush, then sprinkle over the cheesy breadcrumb topping (the mustard will help the topping stick to the fish).

VARIATION

Swap the cod for fillets of another white fish, such as hake, pollock or haddock.

5. Bake the cod in the oven for 10–12 minutes until the fish is cooked and the cheese topping is golden. To check if the fish is cooked, insert a small knife or skewer – it should go through easily, without tension.

6. Add the sliced mushrooms and crème fraîche to the lentil pan and cook for 2–3 minutes to soften the mushrooms. Remove from the heat and stir in the lemon juice and chopped parsley. Season with salt if required.

7. To serve, ladle a portion of lentils into serving bowls. Finely grate some Gruyère cheese over the top generously then, using a palette knife, carefully lift the Gruyère-crusted cod from the baking tray and place it on top of the creamy lentils.

Panettone Bread and Butter Pudding with Marmalade Custard

SERVES: 6
PREP TIME: 35 MINUTES, PLUS
30 MINUTES SOAKING
COOKING TIME: 50 MINUTES

750g panettone, cut into thick slices
50g butter, melted
50g dark chocolate, roughly chopped
50g sultanas
500ml double cream
5 eggs
100g caster sugar

FOR THE MARMALADE CUSTARD
300ml milk
300ml double cream
6 egg yolks (see tip)
100g caster sugar
2 tbsp fine-cut marmalade
grated zest of 1 orange
50ml Grand Marnier or orange liqueur
   (optional)

TIP
Leftover egg whites can be frozen in an ice-cube tray to make individual portions. Transfer, once frozen, to a freezable container or bag, then take the whites out as needed and defrost to use in meringues, sponges or cocktails (page 277).

Perhaps we should call this 'January pudding' as panettone is best known as an Italian bread served around Christmas time. I love using leftover panettone to make a bread and butter pudding, as it already contains some fruit. It is quite a rich and decadent dessert, especially with the added custard, so it's not for the faint-hearted. The addition of the alcohol is optional – it works well with or without.

1. Brush one side of each slice of panettone with the melted butter.

2. Arrange half of the buttered panettone in a single layer buttered side up in a medium casserole dish, then sprinkle over the dark chocolate and sultanas. Arrange the second half of the sliced panettone as the final layer.

3. Pour the double cream into a small saucepan and slowly bring to the boil over medium heat, removing it before it reaches boiling point. Whisk the eggs and sugar together in a heatproof bowl until smooth, then pour in a third of the hot cream, whisking continuously and slowing down or stopping adding the cream for a moment if required, as you do not want to cook the eggs. Continue until all the cream is incorporated into the egg mixture.

4. Pour the cream mixture evenly over the layered panettone and allow the liquid to soak into the bread for 30 minutes.

5. Preheat the oven to 160°C/140°C fan/gas 3.

6. Place the casserole dish in a larger roasting tray that has been slightly filled with water – the water should come about three-quarters of the way up the casserole dish (no less than halfway). Cooking the pudding in a water bath (bain marie) like this helps it to cook through as the top browns.

7. Place the tray containing the casserole dish in the oven and bake for 30–35 minutes until the top of the pudding is golden brown and the centre has set firm.

RECIPE CONTINUES OVER THE PAGE

SHORTCUT
Swap the marmalade custard for good-quality shop-bought custard or cream.

8. While the pudding is in the oven, make the marmalade custard. Combine the milk and cream in a saucepan and slowly bring to the boil over medium heat.

9. Whisk the egg yolks and sugar together in a heatproof bowl until smooth. Once the cream and milk mixture has almost reached boiling point, slowly pour a third of it into the eggs, whisking continuously and slowing down or stopping adding the hot cream for a moment if required, as you do not want to cook the eggs. Continue until all the hot cream mixture is incorporated into the egg mixture. It's important to stir well at this stage to ensure that all the sugar dissolves into the liquid.

10. Rinse out the pan, pour the custard mixture back into it and return to a low heat. Cook the custard for 4–5 minutes, stirring constantly and gently with a spatula or spoon, until the first bubble rises to the surface as it starts to approach boiling point. You will know the custard is thick enough when you test it with the spoon or spatula – coat the back of the spoon or spatula and run your finger down through the mixture. If it's thick enough the line you've made should remain. Keep stirring so that it doesn't catch on the bottom of the pan and burn. To be extra precise, check the mixture with a thermometer – it should reach exactly 82°C. Take care not to boil the custard as the egg yolks will scramble. Once the custard is cooked, remove from the heat and whisk through the marmalade, orange zest and orange liqueur (if using).

11. To serve, divide the bread and butter pudding among serving bowls, then ladle over the hot marmalade custard.

Jessie's Digestive's

MAKES: ABOUT 24 BISCUITS
PREP TIME: 30 MINUTES, PLUS
30 MINUTES CHILLING
COOKING TIME: 15–20 MINUTES

200g rolled jumbo or instant oats
200g spelt flour, plus extra for dusting
1 tsp baking powder
200g cold unsalted butter, cubed
150g maple syrup

* Make it perfect
Leave them in the freezer for as long as you can, even overnight. The butter sets which makes it much easier to shape before cooking.

Our youngest child, Jess, spends a lot of time baking. She finds it restful and therapeutic, and it gives her the chance to try different things while knowing exactly what she is eating – she often alters recipes, swapping white flour for brown, or reduces the sugar. She sometimes drizzles a little melted dark chocolate over these for a change. This recipe was inspired by one of Davina McCall's. Serve with a cup of tea as a sweet treat, spread them with peanut butter and top with a slice of banana, or serve with cheese and apple.

1. Put the oats in the bowl of a food processor and blitz, making sure they are not too finely ground as larger pieces of oats add to the texture of the biscuit.

2. Put all the oats in a mixing bowl with the flour and baking powder, then add the butter and use your fingertips to rub the butter into the oats and flour until the mixture resembles fine breadcrumbs. Stir the syrup into the dry ingredients then knead with your hands to make a dough.

3. Shape the dough into a ball, then flatten it slightly to form a disc and wrap in clingfilm. Chill in the fridge for 30 minutes.

4. Preheat the oven to 190°C/170°C fan/gas 5 and line 2 large baking trays with a silicone baking mat or baking parchment.

5. Remove the dough from the fridge, unwrap it and cut it in half (working with half of the dough at a time makes it easier to handle and prevents it getting too warm).

6. Dust a large board or work surface with flour, and roll out half the dough to a thickness of 5mm. Using a round 7cm cutter (about the size of a digestive biscuit), cut out 8 biscuits. Re-roll the remaining dough (avoid overworking it) and cut 4 more biscuits. Repeat with the other half of the dough.

7. Place the biscuits on the lined trays, leaving space between them. Bake in the oven for 15–20 minutes. You will know they are ready when they are still soft in the centre but the edges are golden. Swap the trays round halfway through to ensure all the biscuits are baking evenly.

8. Remove from the oven and transfer the biscuits to a wire rack to cool, then store in an airtight container. They will keep for up to 1 week.

Sticky Toffee Carrot Cake

SERVES: 8
PREP TIME: 15 MINUTES, PLUS COOLING
COOKING TIME: 50 MINUTES

crème fraîche or vanilla ice cream, to serve

FOR THE SPONGE
100g pitted dates, chopped
50g sultanas
150g carrots, grated
1 Earl Grey tea bag
½ tsp ground cinnamon
½ tsp mixed spice
200ml boiling water
1 tsp bicarbonate of soda
50g soft unsalted butter
150g golden caster sugar
2 eggs (at room temperature), beaten
150g self-raising flour

FOR THE CARROT CARAMEL SAUCE
200g demerara sugar
100g unsalted butter, cubed
200g carrot juice
200ml double cream
pinch of sea salt

A combination of two classic puddings. The carrot cake and sticky toffee pudding together create something unique and really delicious. Carrot juice can be bought from the supermarket, in the fridge section or in a long-life carton. Keep a couple of cartons in your store cupboard so you can easily make this tasty cake. It's important that the caramel ingredients are at room temperature before you start to make the sauce. You will need a 23cm square baking tin.

1. Preheat the oven to 175°C/155°C fan/gas 4 and line a 23cm square baking tin with baking parchment.

2. Put the dates, sultanas, grated carrots, tea bag and spices in a large saucepan. Cover with the boiling water, then place over medium heat and bring to the boil. Remove from the heat once it reaches boiling point and remove the tea bag. Whisk in the bicarbonate of soda until fully dissolved (this must be off the heat or the bicarbonate of soda will create a volcanic effect).

3. Beat the butter with the caster sugar in a large mixing bowl for 2–3 minutes until pale and fluffy, by hand with a wooden spoon or using an electric whisk or stand mixer, then gradually add the beaten eggs, mixing until fully incorporated (add a small spoon of the measured flour when adding the egg if the mixture looks like it's curdling). Sift in the flour and gently fold through to a smooth batter. Gently fold the cooked date and carrot mixture through the batter until fully combined.

4. Transfer the batter to the baking tin and bake in the oven for 25–30 minutes until golden brown. When cooked, a knife inserted into the middle of the cake should come out clean.

5. Remove from the oven and allow to cool slightly in the tin before transferring it to a serving plate.

6. To make the carrot caramel sauce, put the sugar in a large saucepan over medium heat and heat for 3–5 minutes until it has dissolved and you have an evenly golden caramel. Reduce the heat to low and add the butter bit by bit, whisking until smooth – be very careful not to splash yourself with the caramel. Add the carrot juice, cream and salt and increase the heat to medium. Bring the sauce back to the boil and cook for 5–8 minutes until you have a thickened, rich caramel sauce.

7. Portion the warm cake into bowls, generously cover with the sauce and add a big spoonful of crème fraîche or ice cream.

Weekend Wonders

Caramelised Onion Potato Rosti with Duck Egg and Caper Vinaigrette

SERVES: 4
PREP TIME: 30 MINUTES, PLUS
15 MINUTES COOLING
COOKING TIME: 25 MINUTES

100g butter
2 tbsp vegetable oil
2 white onions, thinly sliced
3 large red-skinned potatoes, peeled
3 sprigs of thyme, leaves picked
1 tsp onion powder
1 tbsp cornflour
4 duck eggs
sea salt and freshly ground black pepper

FOR THE VINAIGRETTE
30g capers, chopped
30ml sherry vinegar
1 tbsp Dijon mustard
100ml extra virgin olive oil
¼ bunch of chives, chopped
juice of ¼ lemon

* Make it perfect

People sometimes go a little wrong with rostis because they stick to the pan or fall apart, and this can be off-putting. The key to success when cooking rosti is to remove as much water from the potato as possible – don't worry if it browns, it will be cooked. Look after it as it cooks, adding more butter if it is looking a little dry, and don't have the heat too high. Once you get it right, they look stunning and are really satisfying to make.

What's not to love about a crunchy potato rosti and a rich, delicious fried egg. This is a perfect brunch dish for the weekend or even a weekday supper as it's very quick and easy to make, and the duck eggs have a wonderful colour (though you could use hen's eggs if you prefer, perhaps two per portion). The vinaigrette is quite punchy but it works really well with the rich egg. Add some simple salad leaves for lunch.

1. Melt half the butter with half the oil in a medium saucepan over high heat and cook until it has a nut-brown colour. Add the sliced onions and cook for 3–5 minutes until golden brown, then remove from the heat and allow to cool for 15 minutes.

2. Coarsely grate the potatoes into a large mixing bowl and add ½ teaspoon of salt. Mix and leave for 10 minutes (the salt will draw the moisture out of the potatoes), then tip the potatoes into a clean tea towel or muslin cloth, bring the corners together to form a ball and squeeze as much moisture out as you can. The more you remove the better, as then the potatoes hold together and won't steam instead of frying.

3. Transfer the potato to a clean mixing bowl, add the thyme leaves, onion powder, cornflour, caramelised onions and their cooking butter, and mix to break up any lumps of cornflour.

4. Heat a 20cm non-stick frying pan over medium heat, add the remaining tablespoon of oil, then add all the rosti mixture, pressing it flat to fill the base of the pan. Cook for 4–5 minutes until golden brown on the underside, then flip it over carefully – with a large fish slice or remove the pan from the heat, invert it over a large plate, then return the rosti to the pan raw side down. Cook on the other side for 4–5 minutes until golden brown and tender right through. Remove from the pan and allow it to rest for a few minutes before cutting into quarters.

5. Melt the remaining butter in the frying pan and, once hot, crack in the duck eggs. Season and cook to your liking.

6. To make the vinaigrette, whisk together all the ingredients in a jug or bowl, adjusting the seasoning as required.

7. Serve each duck egg with a quarter of the rosti and the vinaigrette on the side to drizzle.

Tarte Flambée with Red Onion Marmalade, Goats' Cheese and Thyme

SERVES: 4 AS A LIGHT LUNCH
PREP TIME: 30 MINUTES, PLUS CHILLING
COOKING TIME: 30–35 MINUTES

150g rindless goats' cheese (I prefer a mild one such as Chavroux)
1 tbsp freshly chopped thyme leaves
extra virgin olive oil, for drizzling

FOR THE DOUGH
175g plain flour, plus extra for dusting
¼ tsp table salt
½ tsp dried thyme
½ tsp onion powder
3 tbsp extra virgin olive oil

FOR THE RED ONION MARMALADE
200g red onions, thinly sliced
½ tsp salt
75ml ruby port
75ml red wine
75ml red wine vinegar
20g demerara sugar
40g redcurrant jelly
pinch of ground cinnamon

TIP
We have a wood-fired pizza oven in the garden. This is a great alternative to the usual pizza.

This is based on a traditional Alsace dish, normally topped with ham and goats' cheese. We have varied it slightly here by topping with a delicious rich onion marmalade to complement the cheese. Serve the tart with a green salad and vinaigrette, to cut through the richness of the topping. If you like, make a larger batch of the marmalade, so you can keep some back to serve as a chutney, cold with cheese.

1. To make the marmalade, put the sliced onions, salt, ruby port, red wine and vinegar in a saucepan over medium heat. Bring to a simmer and cook for 8–10 minutes until all the liquid has evaporated. Next, add the sugar, redcurrant jelly and cinnamon, then cook over low heat for 3–4 minutes to a jam-like consistency. Remove from the heat and leave to cool.

2. To make the dough, combine the flour, salt, thyme and onion powder in a bowl, then add 100ml cold water and the olive oil and bring everything together with a blunt knife or spoon to form a dough. Transfer to a floured work surface and knead for 3–5 minutes until you have a smooth dough. Alternatively, make the dough in a stand mixer fitted with the dough hook. Shape the dough into a ball, then flatten it slightly to form a disc and wrap in clingfilm. Rest in the fridge for 30 minutes.

3. Preheat the oven to 220°C/200°C fan/gas 7.

4. Dust a work surface lightly with flour and roll out the pastry into a 30 x 20cm rectangle. Transfer to a floured baking tray.

5. To assemble the tarte, spread the cooled onion marmalade over the dough, leaving a 1cm border clear around the edge. Crumble the goats' cheese over the marmalade, sprinkle with the thyme and drizzle with olive oil. Bake in the oven for 18–20 minutes until the base is crisp and the cheese has started to caramelise. Remove from the oven and serve immediately.

Spicy Chicken and Mango Salad

SERVES: 4
PREP TIME: 30 MINUTES
COOKING TIME: 5 MINUTES

1 tbsp vegetable oil
400g chicken mince
1 green (unripe) mango, peeled
½ small mooli, peeled
2 carrots (about 180g), peeled
4 spring onions, trimmed and thinly sliced
   at an angle
½ bunch of mint, leaves picked
75g toasted unsalted peanuts, lightly
   crushed
sea salt and freshly ground black pepper

FOR THE DRESSING
2 garlic cloves
2–3 green bird's eye chillies
2 tbsp palm sugar
juice of 4 limes
2 tbsp fish sauce
1 tsp shrimp paste

My three teenage children all love Asian flavours and lots of chilli. Usually, Asian dishes use sliced chicken meat, but this variation using chicken mince works well – it's just as tasty. We like to eat the delicious mixture spooned into iceberg lettuce leaves, or wrapped in a Chinese pancake, and they make a great lunchtime snack (we often make double the quantities as it's very popular). You could serve it in wraps or a simple corn taco, if you prefer. Mooli (also called daikon) is a large white radish and you can often find it in large supermarkets, but if you can't get hold of it, you could use celeriac as an alternative, or smaller radishes, although it will take longer to prepare them.

1. Heat the vegetable oil in a frying pan over high heat, add the chicken mince and season with salt and pepper. Cook for 3–5 minutes until it starts to brown, breaking the clumps of mince into small pieces as it cooks. Once cooked through, transfer to a plate lined with kitchen paper and leave to cool completely.

2. To make the dressing, grind the garlic, chillies and palm sugar in a mortar with a pestle until they form a smooth paste. Add the remaining ingredients and stir until evenly combined.

3. For the salad, thinly slice the mango, mooli and carrots using a mandoline, a sharp knife or a slicing attachment on a food processor. Take a stack of the slices and slice into thin matchsticks.

4. To assemble the salad, combine the prepared mooli, carrot and mango in a mixing bowl with the spring onions and cooked chicken mince. Pour over the dressing and toss to coat all the ingredients. Check the seasoning and add salt to taste.

5. To serve, transfer the salad to a serving dish and scatter with the freshly picked mint leaves, then the toasted peanuts.

Crayfish Vietnamese-style Sandwich

SERVES: 2
PREP TIME: 25–30 MINUTES
COOKING TIME: 5 MINUTES

2 small/medium baguettes or 1 long
   baguette cut in two
1–2 tsp vegetable oil
150g peeled and cooked crayfish tails,
   drained on kitchen paper
small handful of picked coriander leaves
sea salt and freshly ground black pepper

FOR THE CUCUMBER PICKLE

50ml rice wine vinegar
30g caster sugar
¼ cucumber, sliced in half lengthways, seeds
   removed and thinly sliced
1–2 green chillies, deseeded and thinly
   sliced

FOR THE NUOC CHAM DRESSING

¼ bunch of coriander, leaves and tender
   stalks chopped
¼ bunch of mint, leaves chopped
grated zest and juice of 1 lime
2 spring onions, trimmed and finely chopped
1 garlic clove, crushed
1 tbsp fish sauce
1 tsp–1 tbsp sambal oelek (spicy Asian chilli
   sauce), to taste
½ tsp honey

FOR THE SRIRACHA MAYONNAISE

2 egg yolks
1 tsp Dijon mustard
1 tbsp rice vinegar
200ml vegetable oil
1–4 tbsp sriracha

This sandwich is based on the French-Vietnamese bánh mì. It is a real luxury: the combination of the delicate flesh of crayfish tails and the delicious Vietnamese flavourings seems to cover every taste sensation, from sweet and hot to sour and salty. The herbs and cucumber pickle give it a really fresh feel and the mayonnaise is just delicious. Make extra mayo and dressing to eat with other things; they will keep for 4–5 days in the fridge, in a sealed container.

1. First, make the cucumber pickle. Put the rice wine vinegar, sugar and a pinch of salt in a saucepan, bring to the boil over high heat and simmer to dissolve the sugar. Put the cucumber and chilli in a heatproof bowl and toss together, then pour the hot syrup over the top. Set aside and leave to cool.

2. To make the nuoc cham dressing, put all the ingredients in a bowl and mix together. Adjust the seasoning to taste.

3. To make the sriracha mayonnaise, combine the egg yolks, mustard and vinegar in a bowl. Very slowly pour in the oil, whisking continuously, until fully combined and emulsified, then whisk through the sriracha and season to taste with salt (see my Make it Perfect tips for mayo on page 267).

4. Cut the baguettes (or halved baguette) in half to open them out and toast both sides under a hot grill or on a griddle pan.

5. Heat the oil in a large frying pan over high heat. Once it's really hot, add the crayfish, season with salt and pepper, then sauté for 1–2 minutes until lightly coloured and hot throughout. Remove from the pan and toss in a bowl with the dressing.

6. To assemble the sandwiches, spread the inside of the baguettes with the sriracha mayonnaise, then top with the dressed crayfish tails. Drain the cucumber pickle and place on top of the crayfish. Finish with freshly picked coriander leaves.

TIP
I have seen sambal oelek in my local supermarket (in the specialist ingredients section) and online, or you can make your own: blitz 2 red chillies, 2cm piece of peeled ginger, 1 tsp caster sugar, ½ stick of lemongrass, a pinch of sea salt and the zest and juice of lime in a small food processor, then add enough vinegar to make a paste, blitzing it again. Store in the fridge in a sealed jar and use as a dip or condiment.

VARIATION

Swap the crayfish for the same weight of cooked, peeled tiger prawns.

Smoked Mackerel with Taramasalata and Potato Salad

SERVES: 4
PREP TIME: 20–30 MINUTES
COOKING TIME: 17–23 MINUTES

4 boneless hot-smoked mackerel fillets
extra virgin rapeseed oil, for drizzling
sea salt and freshly ground black pepper
salad cress or snipped chives, to serve

FOR THE POTATO SALAD
300g new potatoes
1 tbsp extra virgin rapeseed oil
1 tbsp crème fraîche
½ bunch of dill, chopped

FOR THE TARAMASALATA
150g smoked cod's roe, membrane removed
1 slice of white bread, crusts removed
   (about 35g)
2 garlic cloves, crushed
50ml cold water
200ml vegetable oil
juice of ½ lemon
pinch of hot smoked paprika

Mackerel and potato are a great match: the earthy potato and the oily fish complement each other so well. Taramasalata is traditionally a Greek dip but it reminds me of a canapé we used to serve at Marcus Wareing at The Berkeley a few years ago. Serve it with some crunchy bread to mop up the delicious flavours on the plate. It's great for lunch or a light supper.

1. First, cook the potatoes for the salad. Bring a pan of salted water to the boil over medium heat, carefully add the potatoes to the pan and bring to the boil once again. Reduce the heat to a simmer and cook for 15–20 minutes, or until soft.

2. To make the taramasalata, put the cod's roe in a food processor with the bread and garlic. Blitz to a smooth paste, then – with the motor running – drizzle in the water and oil simultaneously until emulsified, scraping down the bowl every now and then, until the mixture has a mayonnaise-like texture.

3. Transfer to a bowl and season with lemon juice and salt to taste, stirring together until smooth. If the taramasalata is too thick, add a spoonful of cold water to loosen.

4. Just before the potatoes have finished cooking, preheat the grill to hot. Prepare the mackerel by placing all the fillets on a tray skin side up. Season the skin with salt and pepper and drizzle with rapeseed oil, then place under the hot grill and cook for 2–3 minutes until the skin crisps up.

5. When the potatoes are cooked, drain in a colander and allow to cool a little and air-dry.

6. Whisk the oil and crème fraîche for the potatoes in a bowl.

7. While the potatoes are still slightly warm (not hot), break each one in half and add it to the crème fraîche with the dill. Dress the potatoes, folding them into the sauce, being careful not to break them, and adjust the seasoning with a little salt.

8. Assemble on individual plates, placing a large spoonful of taramasalata to the left, creating a little well in the centre with the back of the spoon. Fill this with rapeseed oil and sprinkle over the smoked paprika. Opposite this, make a small pile of potato salad and sprinkle over some salad cress or chives. Finally, lay the crispy-skinned mackerel on the potato salad.

Sweet and Spicy Halloumi with Aubergine Yoghurt

SERVES: 4
PREP TIME: 30 MINUTES
COOKING TIME: 45–50 MINUTES

2 aubergines
2 tbsp Greek yoghurt
1 tbsp freshly chopped marjoram
juice of 1 lemon
2 tbsp olive oil, plus extra for drizzling
250g halloumi, cut widthways into thin slices
2 tbsp runny honey
2 tbsp red wine vinegar
sea salt and freshly ground black pepper
handful of wild rocket, to serve

FOR THE ZA'ATAR SPICE MIX
2 tbsp cumin seeds
2 tbsp sesame seeds
2 tbsp dried oregano
2 tbsp sumac
1 tbsp dried chilli flakes

SHORTCUT
Use shop-bought za'atar mix.

My eldest son is a huge fan of halloumi and it's such an easy addition to a salad or sandwich. He is particularly keen on this recipe as the Greek cheese is seasoned with za'atar, a wonderful Middle Eastern dry seasoning mix which is slightly fragrant with a hint of chilli heat. The softened aubergine combined with yoghurt offers a fabulous cooling contrast to the spiced cheese. Serve with crunchy bread and make extra spice mix if you like – it keeps well in an airtight jar or tin, and makes a wonderful seasoning for meat, too.

1. Preheat the oven to 200°C/180°C fan/gas 6.

2. Prick the aubergines all over with a fork and place in a baking dish. Roast in the oven for 40–45 minutes until softened. Remove from the oven and allow to cool for 20–30 minutes.

3. To make the za'atar spice mix, put all the ingredients in a dry frying pan and toast over low heat for 1–2 minutes. Once toasted, transfer to a mortar and grind with a pestle or grind in a spice grinder or small food processor until finely ground.

4. Transfer the aubergines to a board and slice them in half lengthways. Scoop out the flesh, discard the skins and chop the flesh until it forms a smooth, chunky pulp. Transfer the aubergine to a bowl, add the yoghurt, marjoram and half the lemon juice and mix to combine. Season to taste.

5. For the halloumi, heat half the oil in a frying pan over medium heat. Add half the halloumi and fry for 1–2 minutes on each side, then drizzle with half the honey and cook for 5 minutes, until the honey starts to caramelise and the halloumi is golden. Give the pan a gentle shake to glaze the cheese in the syrup, transfer to a plate and repeat with the remaining oil, halloumi and honey. Once all the halloumi has been cooked, pour the red wine vinegar into the pan with the rest of the lemon juice. Stir to release flavour from the base of the pan and make a dressing, then remove from the heat. Season the halloumi with the spice mix and a pinch of salt.

6. To serve, spread the aubergine yoghurt in a large serving platter, then, using the back of a spoon, create a well in the centre. Fill the well with halloumi slices and drizzle over the syrupy dressing. Top with rocket and a drizzle of olive oil.

'Nduja and Feta Ravioli

**SERVES: 4 AS A STARTER
(3 RAVIOLI EACH)
PREP TIME: 25 MINUTES
COOKING TIME: 2 MINUTES**

24 wonton sheets (wrappers)
plain flour, for dusting
1 egg yolk, beaten
1 red chilli, deseeded and sliced
extra virgin olive oil, for drizzling
2 sprigs of oregano

**FOR THE 'NDUJA AND FETA
FILLING**
75g feta cheese
100g 'nduja, at room temperature
25g mascarpone
2 tsp freshly chopped oregano

VARIATION

**To make vegetarian wonton, replace the
'nduja with roasted butternut squash,
mashed and cooled, then added to the
feta mix.**

'Nduja, a spreadable Italian spicy pork product, works well as a pasta filling due to its texture. I have been making ravioli for years at work, where pasta-making is a therapeutic exercise in a busy kitchen; however, I rarely make pasta at home. Wonton sheets or wrappers are a very handy alternative to fresh pasta. Made from flour, egg and water, they can be bought in Asian supermarkets. Using a piping bag for placing the filling on the ravioli is ideal for neatness, but not essential.

1. Start by making the filling. Crumble the feta cheese into a bowl then add the 'nduja, mascarpone and oregano and mix to combine until it has the texture of smooth cream cheese. Transfer the filling to a piping bag fitted with a medium plain nozzle, if using (if you are using a disposable piping bag, just cut the tip – a nozzle isn't required).

2. To assemble the ravioli, spread 12 wonton sheets out on a lightly floured work surface. Divide the filling evenly between the 12 sheets, using the piping bag or a teaspoon and being careful to keep the mixture tight in the centre. Lightly brush the edges of the wonton sheets with a little egg yolk. Place a second wonton sheet over the filling and seal the two sheets by pressing the edges together with your thumb, being careful to remove any excess air in the process. Once all the ravioli are sealed, use a pair of scissors or a round cookie cutter to trim the edges of the wonton sheets to make the ravioli circular.

3. Bring a saucepan of salted water to the boil. Drop the ravioli into the boiling water, reduce the heat slightly to just below boiling point, and cook the ravioli for 2 minutes. Remove the ravioli from the water as gently as you can using a slotted spoon as they will be delicate once cooked.

4. To serve, divide the ravioli among four plates and finish with the sliced chilli, a generous drizzle of olive oil and, finally, tear over the oregano leaves.

Sea Bream Ceviche and Seaweed Tacos

SERVES: 4
PREP TIME: 25 MINUTES
COOKING TIME: 15 MINUTES

FOR THE SEA BREAM CEVICHE
1 tbsp rice wine vinegar
juice of ½ lemon
1 tsp sesame oil
1 tbsp light soy sauce
½ tsp wasabi paste
2 sea bream fillets, skinned and thinly sliced
½ avocado, peeled and cut into small dice
2 spring onions, trimmed and thinly sliced
1 red chilli, deseeded and thinly sliced
6 small radishes, finely diced
bonito flakes, to serve

FOR THE SEAWEED TACOS
vegetable oil, for deep-frying
4 nori sheets
2 large egg whites
140g gluten-free self-raising flour
120–150ml ice-cold sparkling water

* *Make it perfect*
The goal is to create a light, crispy batter. A low-protein or gluten-free flour will help achieve this. As will the addition of bubbles in the fizzy water. The cold water makes the batter a little thicker so it coats the nori.

My children adore anything that they can eat with their fingers, and the addition of the Asian flavours makes this a big hit in our house. We always have nori sheets in the cupboard as my daughter often makes sushi for us all. This is great fun to make, though it takes a little practice to perfect the shaping of the nori shells. The combination of crispy seaweed works so well with the spicy, silky fish that's a little like sushi.

1. Start by preparing the marinade for the fish. Combine the vinegar, lemon juice, sesame oil, soy sauce and wasabi paste in a mixing bowl and whisk well to dissolve the wasabi paste.

2. Pour enough vegetable oil into a deep saucepan or deep-fat fryer to come up to about 5cm and place over medium heat. If using a deep-fat fryer or if you have a thermometer, heat the oil to 180°C. If not, to check the oil is at the right temperature, drop a 2–3cm cube of bread into the hot oil – it should turn golden and crisp in 30 seconds.

3. Cut each nori sheet into a circular shape 15–20cm in diameter using scissors.

4. Whisk the egg whites, flour and sparkling water together in a mixing bowl to make a smooth, runny batter.

5. Quickly dip a nori sheet in the batter to coat, then immediately drop the coated nori sheet gently into the hot oil. Fry for 1–2 minutes until lightly golden, then flip and fry the other side for another 30 seconds. Remove from the oil with a pair of tongs and drain on a wire rack placed over a baking tray. While it's still hot, use the pair of tongs to gently fold the battered sheet in half to form a taco shell shape. If oil collects inside the taco, pat dry with kitchen paper. Fry and shape the remaining nori sheets, one at a time.

6. Towards the end of frying, add the sliced bream fillets to the marinade and marinate for 10 minutes. Add the avocado, spring onions, chilli and radishes to the marinated fish after 10 minutes and mix them in to coat them in the dressing.

7. To serve, fill the prepared 'taco' shells with the ceviche mix and top with a few bonito flakes.

Venison and Pickled Red Cabbage Bao Buns with Mustard Mayo

MAKES: 16 BAOS (SERVES 6–8 FOR LUNCH/DINNER)
PREP TIME: 1 HOUR, PLUS 1 HOUR 25 MINUTES RISING AND PROVING
COOKING TIME: 20 MINUTES

a small bunch of coriander, to serve

FOR THE BAO BUNS
5g fast-action dried yeast (page 275)
220ml tepid water
500g plain flour, plus extra for dusting
1 tbsp milk powder
1 tbsp caster sugar
1 tsp baking powder
vegetable oil, for greasing

FOR THE QUICK-PICKLED CABBAGE
¼ small red cabbage, thinly sliced
50ml red wine vinegar
50g caster sugar
50g sriracha (hot chilli sauce), or to taste

GET AHEAD
Prepare and cook the buns in advance. They will keep for up to 3–4 days in an airtight container in the fridge, or can be frozen (defrost fully before using). The cabbage can be pickled, and – once cooled – kept in the fridge for up to 2 weeks.

Bao buns, a steamed bun from Chinese cuisine, are light and very easy to make, and it's worth getting everyone involved for speed. The venison filling here works so well with the juniper berries – juniper and venison is a classic combination – and the creamy mayo and crunchy cabbage. These buns are normally filled with pulled pork or minced prawns, so for a change I love this cut of meat. Photographed overleaf.

1. First, make the bao bun dough. Mix the dried yeast into the tepid water in a jug. Combine the plain flour, milk powder, sugar and baking powder in a bowl. Make a well in the centre of the mixture and pour in the liquid, then begin to mix, from the centre outwards, until a dough forms and the mixture leaves the sides of the bowl. (You may find you need to add a splash more water.)

2. Turn the dough out onto a lightly floured work surface and knead it for 8–10 minutes until smooth. Transfer the dough to a clean mixing bowl, cover with clingfilm and allow to rise for 45 minutes in a warm place.

3. Once the dough has risen, turn it out onto a lightly floured work surface and knock it back, then divide it into 16 pieces and roll each one into a ball.

4. Use a rolling pin to roll out each ball into a 3–4mm-thick oval shape. Brush the top of each piece of dough with a little oil, then fold the oiled sides together into half to make a half-moon shape. Place each folded piece of dough onto an individual piece of baking parchment, cover loosely with a sheet of clingfilm and allow to prove for 30–40 minutes until doubled in size.

5. While the bao are proving, prepare the cabbage. Put the sliced cabbage in a heatproof bowl. Bring the vinegar, sugar and sriracha to the boil in a saucepan, then pour the mixture over the cabbage. Cover the bowl tightly with clingfilm and leave to cool completely.

6. Place a large steaming basket (bamboo or metal) over a pan of boiling water over medium-high heat. Fill the basket with a layer of bao buns, leaving enough space between them

FOR THE MUSTARD MAYO
2 egg yolks
1 tbsp wholegrain mustard
1 tbsp white wine vinegar
200ml vegetable oil

FOR THE VENISON
10g black peppercorns
10g juniper berries
10g sea salt
2 venison loin steaks (about 150g each), at
    room temperature
1 tbsp vegetable oil
20g butter

VARIATION

Swap the venison for sirloin steak and omit the juniper (keeping the ground pepper). Cook in the same way as the venison above.

to allow them to rise. Cover and steam for 8–10 minutes until the buns are spongy to touch, then transfer to a sheet of greaseproof paper to rest. Repeat with more buns until they are all cooked.

7. To make the mustard mayonnaise, combine the egg yolks, mustard and vinegar in a bowl, then very slowly pour in the oil, whisking continuously, until the oil is fully incorporated and the mixture is emulsified. Season to taste with salt, then set aside, covered in clingfilm (see page 267 for Make it Perfect mayonnaise tips).

8. To prepare the venison, grind the spices with the salt to a fine powder in a mortar with a pestle. Generously season the venison steaks with the spice mix. Heat 1 tablespoon of vegetable oil in a frying pan over high heat, add the steaks and let them colour for 2 minutes before turning them, adding the butter and basting them while they cook for a further 1½ minutes. Remove from the pan and allow to rest for 5 minutes.

9. To serve the bao buns, carve each venison steak into 8 slices. Fill the freshly steamed buns with a spoonful of the pickled cabbage, a dollop of the mustard mayonnaise and, finally, a slice of the spiced venison. Top with a few coriander leaves.

★ Make it perfect
When you're cooking steaks, a few rules apply:
- Cook them over high heat.
- Make sure meat is at room temperature before cooking. We don't tend to cook steaks all the way through, they are seared on the outside (especially if eaten rare) and the middle is pink. If straight from the fridge, the inside will still be cold.
- Don't season the meat until it goes into the pan and only season the side going into the pan first. If you season the top side as well it will start to cure the meat and draw out the water, and when you turn it over in the pan it will spit.
- Once it's cooked, rest the meat. It helps it to relax, the juices won't run onto the plate and it gets the best from the meat as it will be more tender.

Baked Chilli Beef with Sweetcorn Cobbler

SERVES: 6
PREP TIME: 1 HOUR
COOKING TIME: 2 HOURS

4 tbsp olive oil
500g minced beef
2 red onions, diced
2 garlic cloves, crushed
2 tsp ground cumin
1 tsp chilli powder (or to taste)
2 tsp hot smoked paprika
2 tbsp tomato purée
150g jarred piquillo peppers or marinated
   red peppers in brine, chopped
1 litre hot good-quality beef stock
1 tbsp Worcestershire sauce
1 tbsp Marmite
250g tomato passata
1 x 400g tin red kidney beans, drained
sea salt and freshly ground black pepper

GET AHEAD
**Make a large batch of chilli in advance
and freeze it, then defrost, add the
cobbler balls and the extra stock and
pop in the oven to bake the cobbler
topping.**

Chilli con carne is a staple meal in my house. Jane often makes a large batch, then serves portions of it with different accompaniments on another day or freezes it to make an easy freezer dinner for another time. This chilli is cooked in the oven rather than on the hob and is finished with a sweetcorn cobbler topping which has a texture like the suet dumplings my mother used to make with stew. I know Marmite is a love/hate product, but I really value it as a flavouring in savoury dishes: it gives the sauce an extra dimension and added depth. The peppers and smoked paprika are a real wow, too – we use hot smoked paprika to give the chilli another spicy punch. Serve the chilli family style, with a dollop of sour cream and some freshly squeezed lime and a green salad on the side, if you like. I guarantee this will become a go-to recipe. See photograph on previous page.

1. Heat 2 tablespoons of the olive oil in a large saucepan or casserole dish over high heat (the pan or dish should be wide enough to fry the meat in an even layer and fit the 18 cobbler balls on top). Add the minced beef and cook for 8–10 minutes until well browned, using the back of a spoon to break up the mince. Don't rush this part – the browning process adds flavour to the dish.

2. Transfer the cooked mince and juices to a bowl and set aside.

3. Heat the remaining 2 tablespoons of the olive oil in the saucepan or casserole over medium heat, add the onions and garlic and sweat for 5 minutes until softened. Next, add the ground cumin, chilli powder and smoked paprika and toast the spices for 1 minute. Stir through the tomato purée and chopped piquillo peppers and cook for a further 3–4 minutes to start to break down the peppers. Add 500ml of the stock and the remaining ingredients to the pan or dish, along with the cooked mince. Bring to the boil, then reduce to a simmer and cook for 30–40 minutes until the liquid has reduced and you have a rich ragout.

4. Preheat the oven to 180°C/160°C fan/gas 4.

FOR THE SWEETCORN COBBLER

155g wholemeal self-raising flour, plus extra
for dusting
25g polenta
pinch of salt
80g cold unsalted butter, cubed
1 egg, beaten
2 green chillies, finely chopped
2 sprigs of oregano, leaves chopped
1 x 165g tin of sweetcorn, not drained

TO SERVE

sour cream
wedges of lime
green salad (optional)

5. While the chilli is cooking, make the cobbler. Combine the self-raising flour, polenta and salt in a mixing bowl and whisk to evenly combine. Use your fingertips to rub the cubed butter into the flour mix until the mixture resembles fine breadcrumbs, then add the egg, chopped chillies, oregano leaves and tinned sweetcorn, including the liquid from the tin. Mix until the mixture comes together to form a soft dough. Divide the dough into 18 pieces and roll into balls with floured hands. It'll be quite sticky. Transfer the balls to a clean plate.

6. Once the chilli has reduced, if you're using a saucepan transfer the mixture to an ovenproof casserole dish, add the remaining beef stock and stir well. Taste and season with salt and pepper if needed. Place the casserole dish over low heat and bring to a simmer again.

7. Top the chilli with the cobbler balls, flattening them slightly in the palms of your hands before you do so, and leaving a little space between each one (they will expand in the oven). Place the cobbler-topped chilli in the oven and bake for about 25 minutes until golden and crisp. Remove from the oven and serve with sour cream, lime wedges and a green salad, if you like.

* Make it perfect

By cooking the meat and the vegetables separately you maximise the flavour in the dish. The ingredients all cook at different speeds, so putting them into the pan together doesn't get the most from them. Cooking them carefully and allowing them to colour adds depth of flavour to the dish – this is true for any minced-meat dish such as Bolognese or shepherd's pie, and dishes made with other cuts of meat.

Korean-style Fried Monkfish with Sesame Pickles

SERVES: 4
PREP TIME: 30 MINUTES,
PLUS MINIMUM 2½ HOURS
MARINATING AND PICKLING
COOKING TIME: 15 MINUTES

1 tbsp buttermilk
½ tsp salt
thumb-sized piece of fresh ginger, peeled
   and finely grated
500g monkfish fillet, cut into 8 equal pieces
vegetable oil, for deep-frying
75g cornflour
2 tbsp white sesame seeds, toasted
2 spring onions, trimmed and sliced at an
   angle

FOR THE SESAME PICKLES
200ml rice wine vinegar
2 tbsp toasted sesame oil
3 tbsp honey
½ tsp salt
10 radishes, halved
1 carrot, peeled and thinly sliced
½ cucumber, deseeded and cut into batons
   (peel on)

FOR THE KOREAN-STYLE GLAZE
4 tbsp gochujang paste
2 tbsp light soy sauce
3 tbsp honey
2 tbsp rice wine vinegar
1 garlic clove, crushed
1 tbsp toasted sesame oil

GET AHEAD
Make the Korean-style glaze ahead of
time and reheat before serving.
The sesame pickles can be made up to a
day ahead and stored in the fridge until
needed.

I like spicy dishes and the gochujang paste used here has a special flavour – it can be hot and spicy, but also salty and almost smoky. I imagine Korean cuisine involves a lot of tasty street food that can easily be eaten with one hand, like this monkfish, a meaty white fish with a gochujang glaze.

1. First, make the sesame pickling liquor for the vegetables. Put the rice wine vinegar, sesame oil, honey and salt in a saucepan with 75ml of water and bring to the boil.

2. Separate the vegetables in three heatproof bowls then divide the hot pickle liquor between them. Cover with clingfilm, pressing it onto the surface of the liquor. Cool completely, then store in the fridge for at least 30 minutes. Separating the vegetables ensures they retain their natural colours.

3. Mix the buttermilk, salt and ginger in a bowl, add the fish, cover with clingfilm and marinate in the fridge for 2 hours.

4. While the monkfish is marinating, make the Korean-style glaze. Combine all the ingredients in a small saucepan, place over medium heat and bring to the boil, then reduce for 1 minute to a loose jam consistency. Remove from the heat.

5. Pour enough oil in a deep-fat fryer or a large, deep saucepan to come up to 5cm. If using a deep-fat fryer or if you have a thermometer, heat the oil to 170°C. If not, to check the temperature, drop a 2–3cm cube of bread into the hot oil – it should turn golden and crisp in 30 seconds. Remember the heat will drop each time you add things to the oil so keep an eye on the temperature through the cooking process.

6. Remove the monkfish from the fridge, discard any excess marinade, then dredge each piece into the cornflour and dust off any excess. Gently drop the monkfish pieces into the hot oil and fry for 3–4 minutes until golden and crispy.

7. Use a slotted spoon to transfer the fish to kitchen paper to drain any excess oil, then place in a mixing bowl and drizzle over the glaze. Mix until all the fish is coated in the glaze, then sprinkle with the toasted sesame seeds and spring onions.

8. Serve the glazed monkfish with the sesame pickles.

White Chocolate and Ras el Hanout Fudge

MAKES: A TRAY OF ABOUT 64 SQUARES
PREP TIME: 15 MINUTES, PLUS COOLING AND WHISKING
COOKING TIME: 20–25 MINUTES, PLUS 2–3 HOURS CHILLING

340g caster sugar
120g liquid glucose
120g unsalted butter, plus a little extra for greasing
150ml double cream
150ml whipping cream
50g good-quality white chocolate, broken into pieces
1 tbsp icing sugar
2 tsp ras el hanout
pinch of sea salt

I love fudge, and can't help but have a piece if I see it. Ras el hanout is a North African spice mix with a fragrant undertone which works really well with the sweet white chocolate and gives the fudge a spicy warmth. Serve the fudge in small pieces (it's pretty rich) with coffee after a meal or make as a gift. You will need a 20cm square baking tin.

1. Grease a 20cm square baking tin and line the base and sides with baking parchment.

2. Combine the sugar, glucose, butter and both creams in a large heavy-based saucepan. Place over low heat and cook very gently for 3–4 minutes, stirring, to allow the butter to melt and the mixture to become smooth. Increase the heat very slightly and slowly bring to the boil. Continue to cook on a steady heat for 15–17 minutes, stirring it regularly to prevent it catching and burning on the bottom of the pan, as it gradually reduces and thickens, changing in colour from creamy and milky to a pale golden toffee colour the closer it comes to turning into fudge. The level will start to drop in the pan. If you have a sugar thermometer, the fudge is ready when it reaches 118°C.

3. Once cooked, remove from the heat and add the remaining ingredients. Beat well with a wooden spoon until smooth, leave for 5 minutes and the top will start to set. Beat the mixture again until smooth; repeat these steps twice more. Eventually the mixture will thicken as it is cooling down. On the second and third time of beating, you'll notice it has become very thick around the edge of the pan so you'll need to beat this into the middle of the mixture. By the third beating, the mixture will be holding its shape more and will look fudgy, and you'll see the base of the pan, too. Transfer the fudge to the lined baking tin and press it flat, then put into the fridge for 2–3 hours to set completely.

4. Once set, cut into bite-size pieces.

5. The fudge will keep in an airtight container for up to 2 weeks in a cool place (in the fridge if you want to keep it for longer). Remove from the fridge a while before eating, as it's best not eaten fridge-cold.

Coffee and Bourbon Babas With Whipped Mascarpone

MAKES: 12
**PREP TIME: 45 MINUTES, PLUS
1½ HOURS RESTING**
COOKING TIME: 30 MINUTES

280g strong white bread flour
¼ tsp table salt
4 eggs, plus 4 egg yolks (see Tip on page
  106)
2 tbsp lukewarm water
1 tbsp runny honey
6g fresh yeast or 3g dried active yeast (not
  instant, fast-action or easy bake) (see
  page 275)
100g soft unsalted butter, cubed
vegetable oil, for greasing
cocoa powder, for dusting

FOR THE COFFEE SYRUP
400g golden caster sugar
1 vanilla pod, split in half lengthways and
  seeds scraped out
500ml freshly brewed coffee
100ml bourbon
100ml marsala wine

This French classic of small dry cakes made with yeast and soaked in a syrup made with a strong-flavoured alcohol takes me back to when I was working at Guy Savoy in Paris. This recipe uses a muffin tray instead of the traditional rum baba moulds, so it's a little simpler to make, though of course you could use traditional moulds if you have them.

1. Put the flour, salt, eggs and egg yolks in the bowl of a stand mixer fitted with the dough hook.

2. In a jug, mix the lukewarm water and honey, then add the dried yeast or crumble in the fresh yeast and stir to activate it. Leave for 5 minutes.

3. Make a well in the centre of the flour mixture and pour in the liquid. Mix on medium speed for up to 10 minutes until the ingredients come together to form an elastic dough that starts to come cleanly away from the sides of the bowl, then add the cubed butter bit by bit and mix until it is fully incorporated into the dough.

4. Transfer the dough to a clean bowl lightly greased with a little oil. Cover the bowl with clingfilm and allow to rest at room temperature for 30 minutes.

5. Use a pastry brush to grease the holes of a deep 12-hole muffin tray. Using a spoon, divide the dough evenly among the holes. Tap the tray on a work surface until the dough has flattened, then cover the tray with a piece of lightly greased clingfilm and allow the dough to rise at room temperature for up to 1 hour, until it reaches the top of the holes before cooking.

6. Preheat the oven to 180°C/160°C fan/gas 4.

7. Once the dough has fully risen, remove the clingfilm, place the tray in the oven and bake for 20–25 minutes until evenly golden brown. Remove from the oven and allow to cool for 10–15 minutes in the muffin tray.

FOR THE WHIPPED MASCARPONE

100ml double cream
100g crème fraîche
100g mascarpone

TIP

Vanilla pods are expensive – they can and should be used more than once. Even if the seeds have been removed you can still use the pod. Remove it from the cooled syrup and either dry it out and retain for future use or pop it into some caster sugar to create vanilla sugar (which you could use in this recipe in place of the caster sugar and vanilla pod in ingredients).

8. While the babas are baking, make the coffee syrup. Put the sugar and vanilla (seeds and pod) in a large saucepan and cover with 300ml water. Place over medium heat and slowly bring to the boil until all the sugar has dissolved. Remove from the heat and add the brewed coffee, bourbon and marsala wine. Allow to cool until lukewarm.

9. Once the syrup has cooled a little but is still warm, place the baked babas in it and allow to soak for 5–10 minutes, turning them every few minutes so that they absorb the coffee syrup evenly. You could do this in the pan if it has a large enough base for them all to soak together, or in a wide, shallow dish. Once the babas are evenly soaked in syrup, carefully transfer them to a wire rack (with a tray or greaseproof paper underneath to catch the drips) and allow any excess syrup to drain away.

10. To make the whipped mascarpone, combine all the ingredients in a mixing bowl and whisk with an electric handheld whisk until thickened (it should be thick enough to hold its shape when spooned onto the baba).

11. To serve, slice a baba in half down the middle and place two halves in each serving bowl. Spoon over a dollop of the whipped mascarpone and lightly dust with a little cocoa powder. Pour the excess coffee syrup over the babas if you wish, for an extra coffee kick.

Lemon Meringue Shortbread

MAKES: ABOUT 15 SLICES
PREP TIME: ABOUT 30 MINUTES
COOKING TIME: ABOUT 1 HOUR

FOR THE SHORTBREAD
200g soft unsalted butter
90g caster sugar
240g plain flour
grated zest of 1 lemon

FOR THE LEMON CURD
juice of 4 lemons
2 tsp agar agar flakes
200g caster sugar
1 tbsp cornflour
115g cold unsalted butter, cubed
3 eggs

FOR THE MERINGUE
75g caster sugar
75g icing sugar
2 egg whites

My mum used to make the most incredible lemon meringue pies when I was growing up, and this is my version. It has the same lemon curd and crunchy meringue, but instead of a pastry case it has the delightful simplicity of buttery shortbread. Agar agar flakes are a plant-based substitute for gelatine made from an algae, and they help the curd set. Serve with a cup of tea and a napkin – it can be messy!

1. Preheat the oven to 160°C/140°C fan/gas 3 and line the base and sides of a 35 x 24cm loose-bottomed rectangular cake tin or 26cm round cake tin with baking parchment.

2. To make the shortbread, beat the butter and sugar in a bowl with an electric whisk or wooden spoon until smooth. Add the flour and lemon zest and stir through, then work the mixture until the dough forms a smooth paste. Transfer the shortbread mix to the lined tin and press it down evenly into all corners, using the back of a spoon, until it is flat and even all over. Bake in the oven for 20–25 minutes until lightly golden all over.

3. While the shortbread is baking, make the lemon curd. Combine the lemon juice, agar agar flakes and sugar in a saucepan. Stir together, then slowly simmer over low heat for 5–10 minutes until the sugar and agar agar flakes have dissolved. Mix the cornflour with 1–2 teaspoons of water to make a thick paste, add this to the lemon syrup mixture and whisk in. Increase the heat and cook the mixture for 2–3 minutes, whisking continuously until it thickens (this will ensure the mixture doesn't taste of raw flour, so taste it before adding the butter – be careful as it will be hot!). Remove the pan from the heat and gradually whisk in the cold cubed butter until smooth. The butter enriches the sauce and mellows the lemon.

4. Lightly beat the eggs in a mixing bowl, then pour over one-third of the lemon mixture and whisk together. Stir through the remaining two-thirds of the lemon mix.

5. Once the shortbread is baked, remove from the oven and reduce the oven temperature to 140°C/120°C fan/gas 1.

RECIPE CONTINUES OVER THE PAGE

6. Once the oven has cooled to its lower temperature, pour the lemon curd mixture over the shortbread and spread it out to cover the base. Place the tin back in the oven and bake for 10–15 minutes, until the curd is beginning to set but still has a slight wobble.

7. While the curd is baking, make the meringue. Mix together the sugars in a small bowl until evenly combined. Using an electric mixer or a stand mixer fitted with the whisk attachment, whisk the egg whites in a spotlessly clean grease-free bowl until soft peaks form. Gradually add the sugar to the egg whites, one spoonful at a time, whisking continuously for about 10 minutes until all the sugar has dissolved and the meringue is smooth and thick – you should be able to upturn the bowl without the meringue falling out.

8. Once the lemon curd layer has begun to set, remove from the oven and spoon the meringue mixture over the top. Gently spread the meringue out evenly with the back of a spoon. Return the tin to the oven and bake for a further 10–15 minutes until the meringue forms a thin crust and colours slightly. Remove from the oven and leave to cool completely.

9. Once cool, carefully remove the dessert from the tin and cut it into 15 even slices.

Rice Pudding Cake with Cinnamon Frosting and a Crispy Crunch

SERVES: 10 (MAKES 1 LOAF)
PREP TIME: 30 MINUTES
COOKING TIME: 1 HOUR, PLUS 15 MINUTES COOLING

115g puffed rice cereal
175g self-raising flour
½ tsp table salt
1 tsp baking powder
175g caster sugar
3 eggs
2 tsp vanilla bean paste
90g unsalted butter, melted and slightly cooled
1 x 400g tin Ambrosia rice pudding

FOR THE CRISPY CRUNCH
85g caster sugar
50g puffed rice cereal

FOR THE CINNAMON FROSTING
150g soft unsalted butter
200g icing sugar
1½ tsp ground cinnamon
2 tbsp sour cream

SHORTCUT
Leave out the frosting and crispy crunch and serve the cake as it is if you are short of time, or serve with just a blob of crème fraîche.

This cake is a really easy dessert to throw together. Although I've never been a massive fan of tinned rice pudding, my wife loves it with a spoonful of jam so we always have some in the cupboard. I like it here as it adds moisture and a rich creaminess to the cake. The cake, without the crunch and icing, is great toasted under the grill the next day.

1. Preheat the oven to 170°C/150°C fan/gas 4. Line the base and sides of a 900g loaf tin and baking tray with baking parchment.

2. Blitz the 115g of puffed rice cereal to a fine powder in a food processor for 1–2 minutes, then transfer to a large mixing bowl along with the flour, salt, baking powder and caster sugar and mix together with a spoon or whisk until well combined.

3. Blitz the eggs, vanilla bean paste, butter and rice pudding in the food processor for 1 minute to break up the rice pudding. Pour the wet mix into the dry ingredients and whisk to a smooth batter.

4. Pour the cake batter into the lined loaf tin, then transfer to the oven and bake for 40–50 minutes until golden brown.

5. While the cake is in the oven, make the crispy crunch. Put the caster sugar in a medium saucepan over medium heat. Cook the sugar until it reaches a light amber caramel, without stirring, then remove from the heat (to prevent the sugar cooking any further) and add the puffed rice cereal. Stir until all the rice is coated in the caramel, then tip out onto the lined baking tray, spread out and leave to cool completely.

6. To make the cinnamon frosting, beat the butter in a large mixing bowl. Add half the icing sugar and mix until smooth. Add the remaining icing sugar with the cinnamon and sour cream and beat until you have a smooth and creamy frosting. Transfer to a piping bag fitted with a plain nozzle.

7. To check if the cake is ready, insert a knife into the centre – it should come out clean. Remove from the oven and cool for 10–15 minutes. Transfer to a wire rack to cool completely.

8. To finish, pipe the frosting in a zigzag pattern over the top (or spread it over with a spatula), then break the caramelised rice into small clusters and stick on top of the frosting.

Baking

Easy Grain Batch-bake Bread

**MAKES: 4 SMALL ROLLS AND
2 LARGER LOAVES
PREP TIME: 30 MINUTES, PLUS
30 MINUTES PROVING
COOKING TIME: 30 MINUTES**

12g dried active yeast (not instant, fast-
    action or easy bake) or 24g crumbled
    fresh yeast (page 275)
300ml lukewarm water
350g plain flour, plus extra for dusting
125g malted grain bread flour
heaped ½ tbsp fine sea salt
2 tbsp runny honey
1 tbsp malt extract
1 egg, beaten
10–15g rolled oats, for sprinkling
vegetable oil, for greasing

* Make it perfect
Don't skimp on the kneading time, as
you need to stretch the gluten in the
flour. Equally, don't go over time as it
will become tight.

This recipe makes a batch of delicious bread rolls and
a couple of loaves. The rolls work particularly well for
breakfast with lashings of butter and a spoonful of jam. You
then have a couple of loaves for the rest of the week.

1. Dissolve the fresh or dried yeast in a jug or heatproof bowl
with 150ml of the lukewarm water. Leave it for about 2 minutes,
then whisk the mixture to ensure all the yeast has dissolved.

2. Combine both flours with the salt, honey, malt extract and
the remaining 150ml lukewarm water in the bowl of a stand
mixer fitted with the dough hook. Add the yeast liquid and mix
for about 10 minutes until you have a smooth, elastic dough
that leaves the sides of the bowl.

3. Alternatively, to make the dough by hand, use a blunt knife
or spoon to combine the flour mixture with the yeast mixture,
then use your hands to form a dough that comes clean away
from the sides of the bowl.

4. Tip the dough out onto a lightly floured surface and knead
for about 10 minutes until smooth and elastic.

5. Dust the work surface with flour and roll the dough into a
large sausage. Cut away 4 rolls weighing about 65g each, and
split the remaining dough to make 2 loaves. You can shape the
dough for the loaves as you prefer: round or loaf-shaped.

6. Brush each roll and loaf with beaten egg, sprinkle with oats
and dust lightly with flour. Gently score a thin, shallow line
down the middle of each using a sharp knife.

7. Preheat the oven to 220°C/200°C fan/gas 7 and put two
baking trays in the oven to heat up.

8. Place the dough on the hot trays (loaves on one, rolls on
another), leaving enough room for them all to rise, cover
loosely with a layer of lightly greased clingfilm and leave
somewhere warm to prove for about 30 minutes.

9. After proving, remove the clingfilm and bake the rolls for
about 15 minutes. The loaves should take about 25 minutes.

10. When cooked, the rolls and loaves will be a golden brown,
and should sound hollow when tapped on the base. Eat warm,
or leave to cool fully before storing. They will keep for several
days in an airtight container.

Milk and Rosemary Loaves

MAKES: 12 SMALL LOAVES
**PREP TIME: ABOUT 1 HOUR,
PLUS 1½ HOURS RISING AND
20 MINUTES PROVING
COOKING TIME: ABOUT 25
MINUTES**

FOR THE WATER ROUX (DAY 1)
40g strong bread flour, sifted
200ml water

FOR THE DOUGH (DAY 2)
580g strong bread flour
50g caster sugar
25g table salt
10g fast-action dried yeast or easy-bake
  yeast (page 275)
10g dried milk powder
260ml milk, at room temperature
1 egg
water roux (above)
50g soft unsalted butter
1 sprig of rosemary, needles picked and
  finely chopped
vegetable oil, for greasing

FOR THE GLAZE
1 egg yolk
1 tbsp milk

FOR SPRINKLING
Maldon salt flakes
nigella (kalonji) seeds
onion seeds

**FOR THE ROSEMARY AND GARLIC
BUTTER**
75–100g unsalted butter
3 sprigs of rosemary
3 garlic cloves, peeled and crushed

We serve this delicious bread with burrata at Marcus, thank you for the recipe, Shauna. It takes two days to prepare, so don't try to rush it. The loaves look fantastic and it would be a great bread to serve to guests. The bread is made using a water roux method, which involves making a pre-starter the day before, which is then added to the dry bread mix. This gives the yeast a boost and makes the bread light and fluffy by retaining moisture. This recipe provides two methods for baking the loaves – freeform, and in mini ring moulds as we do at the restaurant. If you prefer, you can make half the mixture into small individual loaves and the rest into one large loaf – just double the cooking time for the large loaf.

DAY 1
Make the water roux. Put the flour in a saucepan over medium heat, then slowly add the water, beating with a wooden spoon or spatula, until all the water is added and the mixture has a gummy consistency. Transfer to a container using a spatula and chill in the fridge overnight.

DAY 2
1. Combine all the dry ingredients in the bowl of a stand mixer fitted with the paddle attachment. With the mixer on the lowest speed, gradually pour in the milk, then add the egg and, finally, the day-old roux (using it straight from the fridge is fine). Once just combined, add the soft butter and the chopped rosemary and mix on low speed for 10 minutes until the dough is soft and elastic. Scrape down the sides of the bowl every now and then to redistribute the dough, and increase the speed slightly for the last 2 minutes.

2. Grease a large mixing bowl with oil, add the dough to the bowl, lightly cover with greased clingfilm and leave in a warm place to rise for 1½ hours, or until it has doubled in size.

3. Preheat the oven to 180°C/160°C fan/gas 4 and line two baking sheets with baking parchment.

RECIPE CONTINUES OVER THE PAGE

GET AHEAD
Bake the loaves ahead of time, freeze, then defrost fully and reheat slightly in a hot oven before serving.

4. Divide the risen dough into 12 even-sized pieces, each weighing about 100g.

5. Take one piece of dough and divide it into 4 x 25g balls. If you're forming the rolls freehand, position 3 x 25g balls together in a triangle shape, then place a fourth ball on top to make a pyramid – they will rise together as they cook and become one loaf. Transfer to one of the lined baking sheets and continue until you've used up all the dough and made 12 mini loaves. Alternatively, place 12 x greased 10cm ring moulds on the lined baking sheets and put 4 balls into each ring (or if you've only got a few moulds, make a mixture of the two).

6. Cover loosely with greased clingfilm and leave to prove in a warm place for 20 minutes.

7. Whisk the egg yolk and milk for the glaze and, once the loaves have risen, brush them with the glaze. Sprinkle each loaf with some Maldon salt, nigella and onion seeds, place in the oven and bake for 20–25 minutes until golden on top. Lift one and tap the bottom – it should sound hollow.

8. While the rolls are baking, make the rosemary and garlic butter. Melt the butter in a small saucepan over low heat and cook until it becomes nut brown. Add the rosemary sprigs and crushed garlic, take off the heat and allow to cool slightly.

9. Remove the baking sheets from the oven and leave the rolls on the sheets. Brush the tops with the rosemary-and-garlic-scented butter (leaving the moulds on, if using). Once the loaves have cooled slightly, you can remove them from the moulds (if using). Leave to cool, then serve.

Bacon and Onion Brioche

MAKES: 1 LOAF
PREP TIME: 30 MINUTES, PLUS
1¾ HOURS RISING AND PROVING
COOKING TIME: 35 MINUTES

vegetable oil, for frying and greasing
150g unsmoked streaky bacon, cut into
    small bite-size pieces
250g strong bread flour, sifted, plus extra
    for dusting
7g sachet fast-action dried yeast or 23g
    crumbled fresh yeast (page 275)
3 eggs, plus 2 egg yolks
1½ tsp table salt
25g caster sugar
150g soft unsalted butter, cubed
50g shop-bought crispy fried onions

Bread is a weakness of mine; I absolutely love it. I am also rather fond of bacon, so this is a perfect combination for me. Baking doesn't really lend itself to shortcuts, but the shop-bought crispy fried onions in this loaf work well: as they are dry, they are better than home-cooked onions, which would be moist and result in a wet and greasy dough. They are a useful addition to the store cupboard, too, for scattering over a curry or a salad. This brioche is delicious with butter or a soft cheese. Alternatively, try it sliced and toasted, with a fried egg on top, for breakfast. You will need a non-stick 900g loaf tin.

1. Line a plate with kitchen paper. Heat a little oil in a frying pan over medium heat, add the chopped bacon and cook for about 5 minutes until golden and crispy (make sure it doesn't burn). Use a slotted spoon to transfer the bacon to the lined plate to absorb excess oil, and leave to cool.

2. To make the dough, combine the flour, dried yeast or crumbled fresh yeast and the 3 eggs in the bowl of a stand mixer fitted with the dough hook. Mix on medium speed for 8–10 minutes until you have a soft, smooth dough that leaves the sides of the bowl. Add the salt and sugar, set the mixer to slow speed, then gradually add the butter, cube by cube, mixing for about 3 minutes until the butter has been fully incorporated into the dough. You may need to scrape down the sides of the bowl as the dough will be very soft.

3. Alternatively, to make the dough by hand, mix the flour, dried yeast or crumbled fresh yeast, and whole eggs together in a large bowl until a dough has formed, then tip out onto a lightly floured work surface and knead for 10–12 minutes until smooth. Add the salt, sugar and a couple of cubes of butter to the dough and continue to knead until the salt and sugar no longer feel grainy, then keep adding the butter a few cubes at a time and work the dough until all the butter is incorporated (this can take up to 15 minutes). Don't be alarmed if the dough is sticky – it will come together! You may find a dough scraper useful to help you keep the dough from sticking too firmly to your work surface, rather than adding extra flour.

* *Make it perfect*
Ensure all the ingredients are at room temperature before you begin, to aid the yeast as it works its magic.

If you want to make two loaves, don't double the recipe quantities, as a large quantity of dough would be difficult to manage. Instead, make two separate loaves (using two 900g tins).

4. Transfer the dough to a clean mixing bowl, cover the bowl with clingfilm and allow to rise in a warm place for 45 minutes.

5. Once the crispy bacon has cooled, chop it to a fine-crumbed texture using a large knife and set aside.

6. Cut a piece of clingfilm large enough to cover the top of a 900g loaf tin. Lightly but thoroughly grease the tin on the bottom and the sides with a little oil and grease one side of the clingfilm. Set both aside.

7. Once the dough has risen, turn it onto a floured work surface (dust your hands with flour, too, as it's a sticky dough). Add the bacon bits to the dough, followed by the crispy onions, and knead them through until evenly dispersed. Gently shape the dough into a rugby-ball-shaped loaf and press it into the prepared tin. Cover the dough loosely with the greased clingfilm (it should not be tight-fitting, as the dough needs room to rise) and leave in a warm place. Prove for a further 45 minutes to 1 hour, until it has doubled in size.

8. While the dough is proving, preheat the oven to 180°C/160°C fan/gas 4.

9. Lightly beat the two remaining egg yolks with a little splash of water to make an egg wash.

10. Once the loaf has proved, remove the clingfilm and gently brush the top of the loaf with the egg wash, being careful not to knock out any air from the dough. Place the dough in the middle of the hot oven and bake for 30 minutes until golden brown.

11. Remove from the oven and allow to cool in the tin for 10 minutes before transferring to a wire rack to cool completely.

Roasted Onion Tarte Tatin with Cheddar Mascarpone

SERVES: 4–6
PREP TIME: 45 MINUTES
COOKING TIME: 55 MINUTES

1 x 300g block of all-butter puff pastry
plain flour, for dusting
100g unsalted butter, cubed
5 medium onions, halved from top to
   bottom (skin on and root attached)
75g caster sugar
1 tbsp sherry vinegar
2 tbsp Worcestershire sauce
2 star anise
2 sprigs of thyme
sea salt and freshly ground black pepper

FOR THE CHEDDAR MASCARPONE
150g mature Cheddar cheese, grated
100g mascarpone

We often make a sweet tarte tatin at the restaurant to use up a glut of apples or pears. This savoury variation is made with onions, but the principle is the same. We tend to keep blocks of pastry in the freezer at home, and we always have a large bowl of onions, so this makes a very easy and tasty store-cupboard lunch or supper. Bear in mind that generously seasoning everything is important in this dish, to complement the strong onion flavour and the sweet caramel.

1. Roll the puff pastry out on a lightly floured work surface to a thickness of 3–4mm, then use a roughly 24cm diameter plate as a template to cut the pastry into a circle – it will need to cover the onions in the frying pan. Place the pastry disc in the fridge to chill until needed.

2. Place a large 20–22cm ovenproof frying pan over high heat, add 25g of the butter and, once it begins to foam, place the onions in the pan flat side down and season with salt and pepper. Cook for 4–5 minutes until the flat surfaces of the onions are well roasted and almost beginning to char. Remove from the pan and leave to cool. Once cooled, remove any dry layers of onion and discard. Keeping a small piece of root attached, slice each of the onion halves into two pieces.

3. Preheat the oven to 190°C/170°C fan/gas 5.

4. Clean the frying pan, removing any remaining butter, then place it over medium heat. Once hot, add the caster sugar and cook slowly for 5 minutes, swirling it gently in the pan if necessary to encourage it to melt evenly, but not stirring, until you have a deep amber caramel. Just before the caramel begins to smoke, turn off the heat, then deglaze the pan with the vinegar and Worcestershire sauce. Keep stirring gently until the caramel comes together. Once the liquids are incorporated into the caramel, add the remaining cubed butter and whisk until emulsified. You may find it easier to add the butter in small batches to keep the caramel from splitting. Allow the caramel to set for 5 minutes.

RECIPE CONTINUES OVER THE PAGE

VARIATION

Use a different strength of Cheddar cheese or another hard cheese, such as blue cheese or hard goats' cheese.

5. Once the caramel has set, place the star anise and sprigs of thyme evenly around the caramel. Arrange the onion quarters in a circle around the edge of the pan, on top of the caramel, then in the centre of the pan in the same pattern. Ensure you keep the onion quarters as close together as possible as they will shrink slightly during the cooking time.

6. Remove the puff pastry disc from the fridge and place it over the arranged onions, using a spoon to tuck the pastry in and around the inside edges of the frying pan. Make six tiny cuts evenly over the top of the pastry – this will allow any steam to escape while the tarte is baking.

7. Bake in the oven for 35–40 minutes until the pastry has evenly risen and is golden brown. Remove from the oven and allow it to cool for 10 minutes.

8. While the tarte cools, make the Cheddar mascarpone. Place both ingredients in a food processor or blender and blitz for 30 seconds until you have a thick, smooth cream.

9. To finish the tarte, run a small knife around the inside of the pan to ease away the caramelised pastry. Place a large serving dish on top of the pan then quickly turn the pan upside down, releasing the tarte (this needs to be done swiftly to prevent any liquid running out). Cut the tarte into portions and divide among serving plates, and serve with a spoon of the Cheddar mascarpone on top.

Pumpernickel and Cranberry Loaf

MAKES: 1 LOAF
PREPARATION TIME: 20 MINUTES, PLUS 1¼ HOURS RISING AND PROVING
COOKING TIME: 35–40 MINUTES

vegetable oil, for greasing
275g rye flour (light or dark), plus extra for dusting
2 tsp table salt
100g linseeds (flax seeds)
100g sunflower seeds
50g rolled oats, plus extra for sprinkling
200ml lukewarm milk
25g honey
25g black treacle
50g sour cream
7.5g dried active yeast (not instant, fast-action or easy bake) or 15g fresh yeast (page 275)
100g dried cranberries

Pumpernickel is a wonderful, dense German rye bread. The addition of the cranberry isn't traditional but it gives the loaf a slightly sweeter flavour than regular pumpernickel. Being heavier than other breads, it is rather filling, so slice it very thin, and bear in mind that the dough is quite tricky to knead by hand, so opt for a stand mixer which will make light work of it. It works well cut into thin slices or discs as a base for canapés, topped with the ingredient of your choice, such as cream cheese, smoked salmon, crab or caviar.

1. Grease a 900g loaf tin thoroughly with oil.

2. In the bowl of a stand mixer fitted with the dough hook, mix together the rye flour, salt, linseeds, sunflower seeds and oats until well combined.

3. In a jug, mix together the lukewarm milk, honey, treacle and sour cream, then sprinkle over the dried yeast or crumble in the fresh yeast. Stir and leave for a few minutes for the yeast to activate and the mixture to become bubbly.

4. Make a well in the centre of the flour mixture and pour in the liquid, then mix on a low speed until everything comes together to make a dough. Scrape down the sides every now and then to ensure all the flour is mixed in. Increase to a medium speed and knead for 5 minutes until you have a smooth dough. Add the dried cranberries and knead them through the dough for a further minute. Transfer the dough to a lightly oiled bowl, cover loosely with clingfilm and allow to rise for 45 minutes in a warm place.

5. Once proved, turn the dough out onto a lightly floured surface, shape it into a long loaf and place it in the greased loaf tin. Cover again with clingfilm and allow to prove for a further 30 minutes in a warm place. Preheat the oven to 190°C/170°C fan/gas 5.

7. Once the dough has proved, gently brush the top with water and sprinkle over about 1 tablespoon of rolled oats. Brush again with water, if necessary, to help the oats stick to the dough.

8. Bake the loaf in the centre of the hot oven for 35–40 minutes until golden and cooked through. Remove from the oven and tip the bread out of the loaf tin. Leave to cool completely on a wire rack before slicing.

English Muffins with Brown Crab and Miso Butter

MAKES: 10 MUFFINS
PREPARATION TIME: 35 MINUTES,
PLUS 1¼ HOURS RISING
COOKING TIME: 20 MINUTES

500g strong white bread flour, plus extra
  for dusting
1 tsp salt
2 tsp caster sugar
165ml tepid water
165ml lukewarm milk
15g fresh yeast or 7.5g dried active yeast
  (not instant, fast-action or easy bake)
  (page 275)
20g soft unsalted butter
100g semolina flour

**FOR THE BROWN CRAB AND MISO
BUTTER**
150g soft unsalted butter
75g pasteurised brown crab meat
1 tbsp miso paste
2 tbsp crème fraîche
salt
½ lemon

VARIATIONS

The muffins work with any butter – you
could serve them with cream cheese,
too. Or serve them with butter and jam
for a sweet variation.

GET AHEAD
You could make the muffins and the
butter the day before. Reheat the
muffins in a warm oven briefly, before
cutting and filling. Bring the butter to
room temperature and beat it before
serving.

This delicious fluffy risen bread is a really useful addition to
any cook's repertoire. I love it with the crab butter, flavoured
with miso and blended with crème fraîche for a light, creamy
texture. Serve with watercress or a peppery rocket salad.

1. Mix the flour, salt and sugar in a large bowl using a spoon or
whisk, or in a stand mixer fitted with the dough hook, until well
combined. In a jug, mix together the lukewarm water and milk,
then crumble in the fresh yeast or add the dried yeast.

2. Make a well in the flour and pour in the liquid. Add the
butter, then mix on slow until a dough has formed and comes
clean away from the sides of the bowl. Turn out onto a lightly
floured surface and knead by hand for 8–10 minutes, or knead
at medium speed in the stand mixer until smooth.

3. Transfer the dough to a clean mixing bowl, cover with
clingfilm and allow to rise for 45 minutes in a warm place until
doubled in size.

4. Turn the dough out onto the work surface that has been
dusted with flour or semolina. Dust the top of the dough with
flour, then flatten and pat down using the palms of your hands
(or roll) to a thickness of 2cm. Use a 7cm cutter to make 10
muffin rounds. Place the rounds on a semolina-dusted baking
tray, making sure they are evenly spaced. Cover loosely with
clingfilm and leave to prove for 20–30 minutes.

5. Just before the muffins have finished proving, heat a large
heavy-based frying pan over high heat for about 2 minutes.
Reduce the heat to the lowest setting and cook the muffins in
batches: gently place them directly into the hot pan and cook
for 5 minutes until a lightly golden crust forms, then gently flip
and cook for a further 5 minutes on the other side. Transfer to a
wire rack to cool slightly while you cook the remaining muffins.

6. To make the brown crab and miso butter, beat the butter in
a mixing bowl until well softened, then add the brown crab,
miso and crème fraîche and whisk until smooth. Season to
taste with a squeeze of lemon juice and salt to taste.

7. Cut the muffins in half and lightly toast, then serve with a
generous spreading of the whipped butter.

Red Onion and Kalamata Olive Focaccia

MAKES: 1 LOAF
PREP TIME: 20 MINUTES, PLUS
1 HOUR 25 MINUTES RISING AND
PROVING
COOKING TIME: 30 MINUTES

275g strong bread flour, plus extra for
    dusting
30g rolled oats
10g caster sugar
10g fine salt
7g sachet fast-action dried yeast or 21g
    crumbled fresh yeast (page 275)
190ml lukewarm water
50ml extra virgin olive oil
1 large red onion, thinly sliced
40g Kalamata olives, stones removed and
    olives cut in half
2 sprigs of rosemary, needles stripped and
    finely chopped
flaked sea salt, for sprinkling
olive oil, for greasing

GET AHEAD
Make the bread ahead of time and
reheat it in a hot oven when you are
ready to eat.

I think may have mentioned before that I love bread. This focaccia is very easy to make, and great if your kids like to get involved. I could happily eat this on its own straight from the oven, but you could serve it for lunch with feta crumbled on top, a little like a pizza.

1. Combine the flour, rolled oats, sugar and salt in a large mixing bowl.

2. Put the dried or crumbled fresh yeast in a jug, slowly add the lukewarm water and mix to a paste.

3. Make a well in the centre of the flour mixture and gradually pour in the yeast liquid, mixing until a dough has formed and starts to leave the sides of the bowl. Turn the dough out onto a lightly floured work surface and knead for 8–10 minutes until smooth and elastic. Alternatively, the dough can be made in a stand mixer fitted with the dough hook.

4. Transfer the dough to a clean mixing bowl, cover with clingfilm and allow to rise for 45 minutes in a warm place.

5. While the dough is rising, heat the olive oil in a frying pan over low heat, add the red onion and cook for 8–10 minutes until it has softened but still retains its colour. Remove from the heat, drain and reserve the oil. Add the chopped olives and rosemary to the red onion in a bowl and leave to cool.

6. Once the dough has risen, add the completely cooled onion, olive and rosemary mixture to the dough and knead through until evenly combined.

7. Lightly grease a 20 x 24cm baking tray, turn the dough out onto the greased baking tray and use your hands to flatten and stretch it to fill the tin. Cover loosely with an oiled sheet of clingfilm and leave to prove in a warm place for 30–40 minutes – this allows the stretched gluten to rest.

VARIATIONS

If you don't want to use onion, swap it for chopped garlic, fresh or dried herbs or even sundried tomatoes. Add them to the oil and allow them to infuse the oil before adding to the dough as above.

8. While the dough is proving, preheat the oven to 220°C/200°C fan/gas 7.

9. When the loaf has finished proving, drizzle the reserved oil you cooked the onions in over the top of the dough then, using your fingers, press into the dough to create little hollows for the oil to rest in. Sprinkle with flaked sea salt and bake in the oven for 20 minutes.

10. Remove from the oven and allow the focaccia to cool slightly before transferring it from the tray to a wire rack to cool further. Transfer to a tray to cool further for storage, though it is best served while slightly warm.

Fig and Cinnamon Rolls

MAKES: 10 ROLLS
PREP TIME: 40–50 MINUTES, PLUS
1¼ HOURS RISING AND PROVING
COOKING TIME: ABOUT 40
MINUTES

FOR THE FILLING
125g ready-to-eat dried figs, stalks removed
    and discarded, diced
100ml brandy
25ml balsamic vinegar
1 tsp ground cinnamon
½ tsp ground cardamom
125g fresh figs, chopped
50g soft light brown sugar

FOR THE DOUGH
150ml milk
150ml double cream
25g soft light brown sugar
30g soft unsalted butter
10g dried active yeast (not instant, fast-
    action or easy bake) or 20g fresh yeast,
    crumbled (page 275)
500g strong white bread flour, plus extra for
    dusting
5g table salt
1 tsp ground cinnamon
grated zest of 1 orange
1 egg, beaten
vegetable oil, for greasing

FOR THE ICING
50g icing sugar
½–1 tbsp orange juice

This is an impressive breakfast bread to serve to guests; it looks great and smells even better. It reminds me a little of Christmas with the aroma of fruit and spices.

1. First, make the filling. Put the figs in a saucepan, cover with 90ml water and the brandy, bring to the boil, then reduce the heat and cook over medium heat for 10 minutes until the figs have rehydrated and the liquid has almost all dissolved. Add the remaining ingredients and cook for 5 minutes until the mixture has a jam-like consistency. Remove from the heat and allow to cool slightly, then transfer to a food processor and lightly pulse to break up any large pieces of fig. Transfer to a bowl and leave to cool. It must be completely cold before you use it, or it will make the pastry wet and gooey.

2. To make the dough, warm the milk and cream in a saucepan over low heat for about 2 minutes until lukewarm to touch. Remove from the heat and whisk in the sugar, butter and yeast (the warm liquid activates the yeast so it mustn't be too hot).

3. In a mixing bowl, combine the flour, salt, cinnamon and orange zest, then make a well in the centre. Pour the lukewarm yeast mixture into the well, followed by the egg. Gradually stir the wet ingredients into the flour, starting from the centre and bringing the dry ingredients into the middle to avoid lumps forming until everything comes together to form a dough.

4. Transfer the dough to a floured work surface and knead for 5–8 minutes until the dough is smooth and elastic. The dough can be made using a stand mixer fitted with the dough hook if you prefer: follow the method above and knead the dough on medium speed for about 3 minutes until smooth.

5. Lightly grease a clean bowl with oil, add the dough and cover with greased clingfilm. Allow the dough to rise in a warm place for 45 minutes until it has doubled in size.

6. After the dough has risen, tip it onto a lightly floured work surface and flatten it out. Roll it into a large rectangle measuring about 30 x 20cm (about 1cm thick). Position the rectangle in front of you, with one of the longest sides lying horizontally towards you. Spread the cold filling evenly over the dough, leaving a 2.5cm border along the side closest to you uncovered. Working from the long edge furthest away from you, roll the dough tightly into a sausage shape, ensuring the dough is sealed along its length so that no filling escapes.

GET AHEAD

To get ahead, make the fig 'jam' the day before so it has cooled fully. Then it's just a matter of making the bread and putting it together.

If you want to get ahead for breakfast, prepare the loaf the night before, then chill before the final prove. In the morning, if cooking for breakfast, remove from the fridge and put in a warm place to prove for an hour before baking.

7. Slice the dough into 10 equal pieces with a serrated knife, using a ruler to ensure the pieces are even. Place the rolls in a lightly oiled baking tin (ideally a round cake tin) 1–2cm apart to allow them space to rise. Cover the buns loosely with a piece of lightly greased clingfilm and allow to prove in a warm place for 25–30 minutes, or until doubled in size.

8. Preheat the oven to 180°C/160°C fan/gas 4.

9. Once the rolls have proved, remove the clingfilm and bake for 30–35 minutes until golden. Remove from the oven and allow to cool in the tin for 10 minutes before transferring to a wire rack to cool completely.

10. Once cool, make the icing by combining the icing sugar and orange juice in a bowl. Drizzle the icing over the top of the rolls, then allow to set before serving.

11. The rolls will keep in an airtight container for up to 2–3 days. Warm them in a low oven to refresh before serving.

Almond Flour Cakes

MAKES: 12–14 CAKES
PREP TIME: 20 MINUTES, PLUS
30 MINUTES CHILLING
COOKING TIME: 15–18 MINUTES

130g self-raising flour, plus extra for dusting
100g cold unsalted butter, cubed, plus extra
   for frying
pinch of table salt
50g ground almonds
40g caster sugar, plus extra to serve
½ tsp ground cinnamon
a few gratings of nutmeg
40g raisins
2 eggs, well beaten

TO SERVE
golden syrup, for drizzling
strong Cheddar cheese

These take me right back to my childhood. On my way home from school as a boy, I would regularly stop off at my dad's warehouse. He was a fruit-and-veg merchant and supplied hotels, restaurants, corner shops and schools, working with his siblings. Nana Wareing lived right next door and used to keep them furnished with teas, sandwiches and flour cakes throughout the day, just as she did for my grandad when he ran the business. I believe these are similar to Welsh cakes. We used to eat them with sliced apple and Cheddar cheese. You will need a 6cm round cutter.

1. Sift the flour into a mixing bowl, add the cubed butter and rub it into the flour with your fingertips until the mixture resembles rough breadcrumbs (it shouldn't be too fine). Add all the other ingredients except the eggs and mix together, then stir in the beaten eggs, using a fork to bind the mixture together just until it forms a dough and trying not to handle it too much. Shape the dough into a ball, flatten it slightly to form a disc and wrap in clingfilm. Rest in the fridge for 30 minutes.

2. Dust a work surface lightly with flour, unwrap the dough and roll it out to a thickness of 1cm. Using a 6cm round cutter, cut out 12 cakes. Roll any trimmings to form two more cakes, handling the dough as little as possible.

3. To cook, heat a frying pan over medium heat, then add a knob of butter. When the butter is gently foaming, place four of the cakes in the pan (you need to cook them in batches). Cook for 2–3 minutes on each side until golden brown and slightly puffed up. If the butter looks like it's burnt after frying a batch, wipe out the pan with kitchen paper and add another knob of butter before frying the rest of the cakes – burnt butter in the mix will taint the flavour of the cake. Set each batch aside on a plate.

4. Serve the cakes while they are still warm, with a drizzle of golden syrup and a chunk of strong Cheddar.

Hummingbird Cake

**MAKES: 1 LARGE CAKE
(SERVES ABOUT 16)
PREP TIME: 45 MINUTES
COOKING TIME: 1 HOUR
15 MINUTES**

60g caster sugar
2 ripe bananas, thickly sliced (about 200g
    peeled weight)
150g drained tinned pineapple chunks
juice of 2 limes (grate the zest of 1 of the
    limes first, for the frosting)
300g butter, cubed, plus extra for greasing
200g soft light brown sugar
5 eggs, at room temperature
80g honey
275g self-raising flour
10g baking powder
2 tsp mixed spice
¼ tsp table salt
200g milk chocolate (100g melted, 100g
    chopped into small pieces)
75g pecans, chopped into small pieces, plus
    extra pecan halves to decorate

FOR THE FROSTING
120g soft salted butter
350g icing sugar, sifted
220g full-fat cream cheese, at room
    temperature
grated zest of 1 lime (see above)

Hummingbird cake, made with banana and pineapple, with the added richness of chocolate, hails from the Southern States of the US and is quite decadent. It reminds me of my school days and pineapple upside-down cake and my time in the US in the early nineties.

1. Put the caster sugar in a heavy-based saucepan over medium heat and cook until it has caramelised to a light golden brown colour. Add the sliced bananas, chopped pineapple and lime juice and cook for 2 minutes to soften the fruit, stirring to coat the ingredients in the caramel, then remove from the heat and leave to cool.

2. While the fruit is cooling, brown the butter for the sponge. Melt the butter in a medium heavy-based saucepan over low heat, then turn up the heat to cook it, whisking continuously until it is nut brown (this is called a 'beurre noisette'). Remove from the heat and leave to cool completely (you could transfer it to a cold bowl to speed up this process).

3. Preheat the oven to 200°C/180°C fan/gas 6 and grease and line three 20cm cake tins.

4. To make the cake batter, put the beurre noisette, caramelised fruit and light brown sugar in the bowl of a stand mixer fitted with the paddle attachment and mix on medium speed for 2–3 minutes to break up the fruit pieces. Gradually add the eggs and honey, with the paddle still turning, until fully incorporated. Sift the flour into a bowl and mix in the baking powder, mixed spice and salt, then add the mixture to the fruit and egg, continuing to mix until fully incorporated. (A stand mixer works best for this, due to the quantity of ingredients, but you could use an electric mixer and large bowl if you don't have one.) Finally, mix through the melted milk chocolate, chopped chocolate and pecans before dividing the mixture evenly between the prepared tins. Smooth the tops a little with the back of the spoon and wipe any excess from around the edges of the tins (to avoid it burning).

5. Place the tins in the centre of the hot oven and cook for 40–45 minutes. A skewer inserted into the middle of the cake should come out clean when it is cooked.

6. Remove from the oven and allow to cool for 10–15 minutes, then remove the sponges from the tins and leave to cool completely on a wire rack.

7. To make the cream cheese frosting, cream together the soft butter and half the icing sugar in a bowl with a spatula until light and fluffy, then add the cream cheese and remaining icing sugar and mix again with a whisk until fully incorporated and smooth.

8. To finish the cake, place one sponge on a cake stand and spread it with a third of the frosting. Cover with the second sponge, add another third of frosting. Then neatly spread the remaining frosting over the top of the cake. Decorate with pecan halves and sprinkle over the lime zest.

No-knead Doughnuts with Rosemary and Chocolate Sauce

MAKES: 20–24
PREP TIME: ABOUT 30 MINUTES
COOKING TIME: ABOUT 30 MINUTES

FOR THE ROSEMARY AND CHOCOLATE SAUCE
250ml double cream
2 tbsp honey
40g unsalted butter
2 sprigs of rosemary
100g dark chocolate (70% cocoa solid), finely chopped
pinch of sea salt

FOR THE DOUGHNUTS
330g plain flour, plus extra for dusting
11g baking powder
65g caster sugar
pinch of table salt
90g cold butter, cubed
215ml sour cream, at room temperature
500–750ml sunflower or vegetable oil, for deep-frying
icing sugar, for dusting

VARIATION

Swap the rosemary in the chocolate sauce for sprigs of lavender.

Doughnuts are always a treat. There are some well-known brands out there that occasionally appear in my house, but these are so much better, and the dough doesn't require any kneading. It's more of a cake recipe, with the addition of the sour cream and baking powder instead of yeast like the more modern bread style. The chocolate sauce is absolutely delicious: the rosemary fills the kitchen with the most wonderful aroma as it cooks. Dip the doughnuts in the sauce and eat by hand or serve them in a bowl as a dessert with the sauce on the side. I like them dusted with icing sugar, but you could mix caster sugar and ground cinnamon for a variation.

1. First, make the rosemary and chocolate sauce. Pour the cream into a small saucepan, add the honey, butter and rosemary, and heat until it's just about to boil. Remove from the heat and allow to infuse for 10 minutes.

2. Put the chocolate in a large heatproof bowl. Pour the hot infused cream through a sieve into the bowl and allow the cream to melt the chocolate for 2 minutes before whisking until smooth, adding the pinch of salt. Set aside.

3. To make the doughnuts, combine the flour, baking powder, caster sugar and salt in a large bowl. Add the cubed butter and, using your fingertips, rub the butter into the flour until the mixture resembles breadcrumbs. Make a well in the middle of the butter and flour mixture and use a knife to mix through the sour cream. Bring the mixture together with your hands to form a soft dough, adding a touch of milk (or more sour cream) if it is a little dry.

4. Turn the dough out onto a floured work surface and roll it out to a thickness of 1.5cm. Using a floured 4.5cm pastry cutter, cut out about 15 small rounds, then place them to one side. Re-roll the leftover dough to a thickness of 1.5cm and cut about 8 more rounds.

RECIPE CONTINUES OVER THE PAGE

TIP
You can re-use frying oil two or three times before discarding it, but just remember that if you are frying something with a strong flavour, such as fish, the oil will take on that flavour.

5. Pour vegetable oil in a deep-fat fryer or a large, deep saucepan. If using a deep-fat fryer or if you have a thermometer, heat the oil to 180°C. If not, to check the oil is at the right temperature, drop a 2–3cm cube of bread into the hot oil – it should turn golden and crisp in 30 seconds. Remember the heat will drop each time you add things to the oil so keep an eye on the temperature through the cooking process.

6. Line a large plate or tray with kitchen paper.

7. Once the oil is hot, cook the doughnuts in batches for 3–4 minutes per batch, turning them halfway through so they cook until golden brown on each side. (It's important to cook them in batches as they expand while cooking and lower the temperature of the oil.) Remove from the oil with a slotted spoon and drain well on the kitchen paper to remove any excess oil.

8. Warm the chocolate sauce through over low heat.

9. To serve, transfer the hot doughnuts to a large bowl or plate and dust lightly with icing sugar, then enjoy alongside the warm rosemary and chocolate sauce.

Lamington Tray Bake

MAKES: 1 TRAY (ABOUT 15 PIECES)
PREP TIME: 40 MINUTES
COOKING TIME: 30 MINUTES, PLUS
2–3 HOURS SETTING

180g soft unsalted butter
180g caster sugar
1 tbsp vanilla bean paste
4 eggs, beaten
200g self-raising flour
1 tbsp milk
1 small punnet of raspberries (about 125g)
75g raspberry jam
100g desiccated coconut

FOR THE CHOCOLATE GANACHE
100ml full-fat coconut milk
200g good-quality dark chocolate (minimum
    60– 70% cocoa solids), broken into pieces
55g soft unsalted butter

I am told this cake is an iconic and traditional Australian- or perhaps New Zealand-born, bake. I have had it a few times and find it quite delicious – the chocolate, coconut and jam combination reminds me of my childhood. You will need a 30 x 22cm baking tray. Serve a piece of this with a cup of tea.

1. Preheat the oven to 180°C/160°C fan/gas 4 and line a 30 x 22cm baking tray with a silicone baking mat or baking parchment.

2. Beat together the soft butter with the caster sugar and vanilla paste in a large mixing bowl with an electric whisk for 2–3 minutes until pale and fluffy. Gradually add the beaten eggs, a little at a time, mixing between each addition until fully incorporated. Whisk in a tablespoon of the flour if it looks like the mixture is starting to curdle. Alternatively, use a stand mixer fitted with the whisk attachment. Sift in the flour and gently fold it through with the milk until you have a smooth batter. Finally, gently fold the fresh raspberries through the batter.

3. Spoon the cake mixture into the lined baking tray and spread it into the corners of the tin so it lies in an even layer. Bake in the oven for about 25 minutes until golden brown – a skewer inserted into the middle of the sponge should come out clean. Remove from the oven and leave to cool completely in the tin.

4. While the cooled sponge is still in the tin, spoon the raspberry jam on top and use the back of the spoon to spread it all over the sponge.

5. Now, make the chocolate ganache. Warm the coconut milk gently until it's hand hot. Melt the chocolate in a heatproof bowl placed over a pan of simmering water, making sure the base of the bowl doesn't touch the water. Once melted, whisk in the warmed coconut milk, followed by the butter, to make a thick and glossy ganache.

6. While the ganache is still pourable, tip it over the raspberry sponge and spread it out flat. Sprinkle generously and evenly with the desiccated coconut. Allow the ganache to set for 2–3 hours.

7. Once set, remove from the baking tin and portion into 15 pieces.

8. The tray bake will keep in an airtight container for up to 3 days.

Strawberry, Rose and Fennel Seed Slice

MAKES: 8–12 SLICES
PREP TIME: 1 HOUR
COOKING TIME: ABOUT 30 MINUTES

1 x 320g sheet of ready-rolled all-butter puff pastry (almost at room temperature)
1 egg, beaten
¼ bunch of mint, leaves picked
250ml double cream, lightly whipped

FOR THE PASTRY CREAM
2 tsp ground fennel seeds
240ml milk
60ml double cream
35g cornflour
5 egg yolks (see Tip on page 106)
70g caster sugar
1 tbsp vanilla bean paste
125ml double cream, lightly whipped

FOR THE STRAWBERRIES
600–800g strawberries, hulled and halved
50g icing sugar, plus extra for dusting
2 tsp rose water
grated zest of 1 lemon
splash of vodka or gin

VARIATION

If you want to make this slice in winter, replace the strawberries with the poached pears on page 184 and flavour the pastry cream with cinnamon by dropping a cinnamon stick into the cream during the cooking process. Sprinkle the slice with demerara sugar.

Mille-feuille has always been one of my favourite pastries, and this much simpler version is just divine. Fennel seeds have a subtle anise flavour that beautifully complements strawberry and rose. Some people aren't so keen on the taste of fennel, however the seeds don't taste strong and, all together, the flavours are an English summer garden on a plate. The pastry cream requires a large number of egg yolks, which means you have a large number of whites remaining – see pages 276–7 for ideas to use them up.

1. Preheat the oven to 220°C/200°C fan/gas 7.

2. Unroll the puff pastry onto a baking sheet or silicone sheet, then glaze it all over with the beaten egg. Gently score a 2cm border around the edge of the pastry with a small knife, being careful not to cut all the way through. This will form the rim. Place in the oven, then reduce the temperature to 180°C/160°C fan/gas 4 and bake for 25–35 minutes until crisp and golden. Remove from the oven, place the tray on a wire rack and leave to cool.

3. Once cool, gently transfer the pastry to a serving plate (it will be very difficult to move when it has a filling and likely to break). Run a table knife around the scored border to loosen, then gently push down the pastry within this line to create a central space for the filling, leaving the raised rim around. Imagine it is like a large, rectangular vol-au-vent.

4. To make the pastry cream, put the ground fennel seeds, milk and double cream in a heavy-based saucepan and heat over medium heat. While the cream is warming up, mix together the cornflour, egg yolks, sugar and vanilla paste in a separate heatproof bowl. Just before the cream starts boiling, pour a third of it over the egg yolk mixture, whisking continuously and slowing down or stopping adding the cream for a moment if required, as you do not want to cook the egg yolk. Continue until all the cream is incorporated into the egg mixture. It's important to stir well at this stage to ensure that all the sugar dissolves into the liquid.

RECIPE CONTINUES OVER THE PAGE

GET AHEAD
**Make the custard and bake the pastry
the day before you want to serve
the slice (whipping the cream and
marinating the strawberries on the day).**

5. Rinse out the pan, pour the mixture back and return to a low heat. Cook gently until it thickens, whisking constantly to ensure you have a smooth mix with no lumps, and it doesn't stick to the bottom. You will know the pastry cream is thick enough when you coat the back of the spatula or spoon and run your finger down through the mixture. If it's thick enough, the line you've made should remain.

6. Remove the pastry cream from the heat and pour it through a fine sieve into a heatproof bowl. Cover the surface of the pastry cream with greaseproof paper or clingfilm, pressing it onto the surface to avoid a skin forming. Allow the mixture to cool then transfer to the fridge until completely cool.

7. While the pastry cream is cooling, prepare the strawberries. Combine all the ingredients in a bowl and stir to coat the strawberries in the sugar mixture. Marinate in the fridge for 30 minutes.

8. Once cool, beat the pastry cream lightly to loosen it, then gently fold through the whipped double cream until evenly combined.

9. To assemble the tart, fill the inside of the pastry with the pastry cream, then arrange the marinated strawberries over the top. Garnish with the freshly picked mint leaves and a dusting of icing sugar then portion into 8–12 slices, or serve whole and cut at the table. Serve with lightly whipped cream.

* Make it perfect
When you're making a custard, it is important to 'temper' the cold ingredients with a little of the hot ingredients before mixing them both fully – this increases the temperature of the egg mixture gradually. If you add hot liquid to cold liquid too quickly, then the mixture will split (and therefore not properly combine).

St Clement's Treacle Tart

SERVES: 8
PREP TIME: 25 MINUTES, PLUS 50 MINUTES RESTING
COOKING TIME: 1 HOUR 10 MINUTES

FOR THE PASTRY
160g plain flour, plus extra for dusting
60g icing sugar
30g ground almonds
90g cold butter, cubed
4 egg yolks (see Tip on page 106)
grated zest of 1 orange

St Clement's is a classic non-alcoholic cocktail made with a mix of bitter lemon and orange. In this tart the combination of the two fruits brings a light citrus flavour to the filling to cut through the rich, sweet syrup. I would certainly make this to impress – it's not something I could possibly eat every day. As a chef, I am very keen to not let anything go to waste – even stale bread. To make your own breadcrumbs, blitz old bread and keep it in the freezer until you need it. You will need a 22cm deep, loose-bottomed tart tin. Photographed overleaf.

1. To make the pastry, rub together the flour, icing sugar, ground almonds and cold butter in a bowl with your fingertips until the mixture resembles breadcrumbs and all the butter has been rubbed in, with no lumps remaining. (Alternatively, blitz in a food processor.) Stir in two of the egg yolks along with the orange zest and mix to form a soft dough. Shape the dough into a ball, then flatten it slightly to form a disc and wrap in clingfilm. Rest in the fridge for 30 minutes.

2. Dust a work surface lightly with flour, unwrap the pastry and roll it out into a 4mm-thick circle, then use it to line a 22cm deep, loose-bottomed tart tin, leaving a little excess pastry hanging over the edges (to allow for shrinkage). Return to the fridge and allow to rest for a further 20 minutes.

3. Preheat the oven to 180°C/160°C fan/gas 4.

4. Line the pastry case with baking parchment and fill with baking beans or dried rice. Sit the tart case on a baking tray and bake for 25 minutes. Beat the remaining two eggs yolks together. Remove the parchment and baking beans, brush the pastry all over with the beaten egg yolks and return to the oven for a further 5 minutes until evenly golden. This process forms a sealed base to ensure the filling doesn't leak.

FOR THE FILLING
325g golden syrup
50g black treacle
75g butter
3 eggs
120ml double cream
grated zest and juice of 2 lemons
grated zest of 1 orange
120g fine dried breadcrumbs

crème fraîche, to serve

* Make it perfect
Working with pastry requires a light touch to avoid overheating the mix – the gluten in the pastry will tighten and the pastry will become tough when cooked if overworked. Resting the pastry dough makes it easier to handle and roll out and helps it relax before it's used to line a case.

5. While the pastry shell is baking, make the filling. Heat the golden syrup, treacle and butter in a saucepan until hot. In a separate bowl, whisk together the eggs, double cream and citrus zest and juice. Add the dried breadcrumbs and whisk in until smooth. Once the syrup is hot, gradually pour it into the egg mixture in small quantities while whisking continuously to ensure the eggs don't scramble.

6. After the case has baked for 30 minutes, reduce the oven temperature to 140°C/120°C fan/gas 1 (while the case is still in the oven). It's very difficult to carry a pastry case full of filling without spilling it, so instead, fill the case while it's in the oven (I had to do this with the egg custard tart I made for the Queens 80th birthday banquet). Gently slide the tray forward, ensuring the tart case remains halfway in the oven, then slowly pour the filling into the case, filling to a level 2mm from the top of the case. Gently slide the tart back into the oven.

7. Bake the tart for 35–40 minutes until there is just a slight wobble in the centre of the filling. Carefully remove the tart from the oven and, once it's cool enough to handle, trim away the excess pastry with a sharp knife. When the tart is completely cool you can remove it from the tin.

8. Serve with crème fraîche.

Lavender Frangipane Tart with Tonka Bean Poached Pears

SERVES: 8
PREP TIME: 45 MINUTES, PLUS 50 MINUTES RESTING AND CHILLING
COOKING TIME: 15 MINUTES FOR THE FRUIT, 1 HOUR 10 MINUTES FOR THE TART

FOR THE TONKA BEAN POACHED PEARS
4 firm Conference pears (or seasonal pears of choice)
200g soft light brown sugar
pared peel of 1 orange
pared peel of 1 lemon
3 tonka beans

FOR THE PASTRY
250g plain flour, plus extra for dusting
125g icing sugar
1 tsp sea salt
125g cold unsalted butter, cubed
1 egg, beaten
1 tsp vanilla extract

FOR THE FRANGIPANE
150g soft unsalted butter
150g caster sugar
150g ground almonds
3 eggs
35g plain flour
1 tbsp Amaretto
3 tsp lavender extract (or to taste)
50g flaked almonds, for sprinkling

VARIATION

Swap the pears for firm apples such as Braeburn or Pink Lady and poach them for the same time as the pears.

When I eat out, if I have a dessert, I can guarantee it will be a traditional tart of some sort just like this one – flavoured fruit and a frangipane filling. The pears, cooked like this, would make a delicious dessert all on their own with a blob of cream. Under-ripe work best as they are easier to peel. Do try and use the tonka beans, we use them at the restaurant and they bring an unusual, complex flavour of vanilla, coconut and spices to the dish. You can buy them online or at a health food shop, but if you can't source them a good replacement would be a vanilla pod and its seeds. You will need a 22cm deep, loose-bottomed tart tin. Serve the tart with whipped cream for a more refined dessert, or custard for a winter warmer. See photo on previous page.

1. To prepare the pears for poaching, peel and halve them lengthways, then use a melon baller to scoop out the seeds and core from each half.

2. To make the poaching syrup, put the brown sugar, citrus peels, tonka beans and 350ml water in a large saucepan. Bring to the boil over medium heat, then add the pear halves, cover, and reduce the heat to a low simmer. Cook the pears for 10–15 minutes until they are just tender enough that they can be pierced easily with a knife. Remove from the heat, leaving the lid on to allow the pears to continue cooking in the residual heat.

3. To make the pastry, rub the flour, icing sugar, salt and cold butter together in a bowl with your fingertips until the mixture resembles breadcrumbs and all the butter has been rubbed in, with no lumps remaining. (Alternatively, blitz in a food processor.) Add the beaten egg and vanilla extract and mix to form a soft dough. Shape the dough into a ball, then flatten it slightly to form a disc and wrap in clingfilm. Rest in the fridge for 30 minutes.

GET AHEAD
Poach the pears the day before making the tart and keep them in the fridge, or make them further in advance, putting the hot pears and liquor in a sterilised jar where they will keep for a few weeks in the fridge. Double up the quantities if you like, so you have some pears left over for other dishes.

* Make it perfect

Beware that flavourings are available in different forms and strengths and, although they are interchangeable, 'flavourings' usually have a weaker taste than a more concentrated 'extract'. If you are unsure how much lavender extract to use, add the amount in the recipe in small drops. When you can smell the lavender in the mix then it will be enough.

4. Dust a work surface lightly with flour, unwrap the pastry and roll it out into a 3mm-thick circle. Use it to line a 22cm deep, loose-bottomed tart tin, leaving a little excess pastry hanging over the edges to allow for shrinkage. Return the lined tin to the fridge for 20 minutes.

5. Preheat the oven to 180°C/160°C fan/gas 4.

6. Line the pastry case with baking parchment and fill with baking beans or dried rice. Sit the tart case on a baking sheet and bake for 25 minutes. Remove from the oven, remove the baking beans and parchment, then return the case to the oven for a further 5 minutes and bake until evenly golden. Remove from the oven and allow to cool slightly. Reduce the oven temperature to 160°C/140°C fan/gas 3.

7. While the pastry is baking, make the frangipane.

8. Beat the butter and sugar in a bowl until pale and fluffy, by hand with a wooden spoon or using an electric whisk or stand mixer, then stir in the ground almonds. Add the eggs one at a time, beating well after each addition until fully incorporated. Sift the flour into the frangipane mix and fold through quickly, then stir through the Amaretto and the lavender extract. Fill the baked tart case with the frangipane mix, ensuring it is level. Arrange the 8 poached pear halves evenly in a circle on top of the frangipane, with the tops of the pears pointing towards the centre of the tart. Sprinkle the flaked almonds over the top, place it in the centre of the oven and bake for 30–35 minutes until evenly golden. Remove from the oven and, once cool enough to handle, trim away the excess pastry with a sharp knife. When the tart is completely cool, remove it from the tin. If you like, you can reduce the pear poaching liquor down to form a glaze, then – while the liquor is hot – brush the top of the cooled tart to give it an extra-shiny finish.

Marmalade and Whisky Steamed Pudding

SERVES: 6
PREP TIME: 30 MINUTES
COOKING TIME: 55 MINUTES

175g soft unsalted butter, plus extra for greasing
175g light brown muscovado sugar
1 tbsp golden syrup
3 large eggs, lightly beaten
175g self-raising flour
1 tsp ground ginger
200g orange marmalade

FOR THE WHISKY SAUCE
35g butter
150g light brown muscovado sugar
100g orange marmalade
3 tbsp whisky
150ml double cream
juice of ½ lemon

GET AHEAD
Make the pudding mixture and place it in the moulds, then cover with foil, place in freezer bags, tie and seal. Freeze, then defrost to cook.

Who doesn't love a steamed pudding? It's a classic English dessert. Here they are made in individual dariole moulds. If you don't have these, you could use a pudding basin to make one large one, or ramekins to make slightly smaller ones. If you have all the ingredients, it's a quick and easy pudding. Serve with a blob of crème fraîche or vanilla ice cream, or omit the whisky sauce and serve with plain custard.

1. Cream the butter and sugar together in a bowl with an electric whisk (or use a stand mixer fitted with the whisk attachment) until light and fluffy. Add the syrup, then slowly add the eggs, a little at a time, whisking continuously. You can add a little flour with the egg to avoid the mixture splitting, if necessary. Combine the flour and ginger, then fold them into the dry ingredients using a large metal spoon to retain the air.

2. Preheat the oven to 180°C/160°C fan/gas 4 and grease six small pudding basins (dariole moulds). Put a small disc of baking parchment in the base of each one.

3. Divide the marmalade evenly among the greased moulds. This will be on the top once the puddings are tipped out. Divide the pudding mixture among the moulds and smooth the tops with a knife. Cover the top of each mould with a piece of tightly fitting foil.

4. Place a wire rack or trivet on the bottom of a large roasting tray (a tray that is big enough for six moulds and the rack/trivet – the recipe will work without a trivet, but I prefer it for more even cooking). Place the moulds on top of the rack and pour boiling water into the tray until it comes halfway up the sides of the puddings. Cover the top of the tray with a large piece of foil and fold it tightly to seal. The aim is to steam the puddings, so you need to keep all the steam in the tray.

VARIATION

Instead of the ground ginger, use the same amount of ground cinnamon or mace.

TIP

If you want to cook the sponge as a large pudding rather than in individual moulds, increase the cooking time to 1½ hours.

5. Steam the puddings in the oven for about 45–55 minutes. To test if they are cooked, push a skewer into them through the foil lid. If the skewer comes out clean, the puddings are cooked. If not, return to the oven for another 10 minutes. Check the water level, adding more to the tray if necessary. If you prefer, you can steam them in a steamer on the hob, using a similar cooking time.

6. While the puddings are in the oven, prepare the sauce. Gently heat the butter, sugar, marmalade and whisky in a saucepan over low heat, stirring occasionally until everything has dissolved. Do not have the heat too high as it will burn. Add the cream and the lemon juice, then remove from the heat.

7. Once the puddings are cooked, remove from the oven and let them rest (still sitting in their water bath, covered with foil). When you're ready to serve, gently loosen the edges of the puddings with the tip of a knife. Put a plate on the top of a pudding, turn the pudding upside down over the plate and it should easily release onto the plate. Serve with the whisky sauce.

Worth the Wait

Sautéed Potato Gnocchi with Broccoli, Rocket and Parmesan

SERVES: 4
PREP TIME: 30 MINUTES
COOKING TIME: 55 MINUTES

2 tbsp vegetable oil, plus extra for drizzling
100g unsalted butter
1 head of broccoli, cut into small florets
100ml good-quality vegetable stock
100g rocket
50g Parmesan cheese, finely grated
nutmeg, for grating
sea salt and freshly ground black pepper

FOR THE GNOCCHI

2 large red-skinned potatoes (about 655g total weight)
100g plain flour, plus extra for dusting
2 large egg yolks

GET AHEAD

Cook the gnocchi, then cool, spread over an oiled tray, and drizzle with oil to stop them sticking together. Cover with oiled clingfilm and chill for up to 24 hours. Cook from room temperature. Freeze the uncooked gnocchi on a tray lined with baking parchment. Once solid, transfer to a freezable container and freeze for up to 1 month. Cook from frozen in boiling water for 2–3 minutes (don't thaw, or they'll stick together).

VARIATIONS

For a quick supper, serve the cooked gnocchi with a simple, smooth tomato sauce and some chopped basil. Or simply top the cooked gnocchi with extra virgin olive oil, grated Parmesan cheese and toasted pine nuts.

This is a great meat-free dish for midweek and the perfect 'fits all' option when feeding vegetarian friends and you want a dish everyone can eat. Gnocchi is a dumpling made from potato that's similar to pasta. You can buy ready-made gnocchi, but I find making it yourself is tastier and lots of fun, and it's a brilliant introduction to cooking for children who like a bit of a mess. The potato pillows are delicious with the fresh, vibrant greens of broccoli and rocket. You can make the gnocchi with a metal sieve, but a potato ricer is faster and easier to create smooth potato for the dough.

1. First, make the gnocchi. Put the whole unpeeled potatoes in a saucepan and cover with cold water. Add a pinch of salt, place over medium heat and bring to the boil. When it starts to boil lower the heat and simmer for 35–45 minutes until the potatoes are soft when pierced with a knife. Drain and steam dry for 5 minutes. While still hot, peel the skin then push the flesh through a potato ricer into a large mixing bowl (or press them through a fine metal sieve using the back of a large kitchen spoon). Mix the flour, egg yolks and ¾ teaspoon of salt into the potato until the mixture comes together as a dough.

2. Transfer the dough to a floured work surface and divide into 4 pieces about 150g each. Using both hands, roll each into a long sausage about 38cm long and 2cm in diameter, then cut into 2.5cm pieces. You should have 15 pieces per sausage.

3. Bring a saucepan of water to the boil over medium heat, then poach the gnocchi in batches; once they rise to the surface, let them cook for 1 minute. They will look like little parcels. After 1 minute, use a slotted spoon to transfer the gnocchi to an oiled tray in a single layer. Leave to cool. You can drizzle the gnocchi with oil to prevent them drying out and sticking together.

4. Once all the gnocchi is cooked, heat the oil in a large sauté pan over high heat. Cook the gnocchi for 1–2 minutes on each side until golden. Once coloured, melt the butter in the pan; when it begins to foam, add the broccoli and stock with a pinch of salt. Cover with a lid and steam the broccoli for 2 minutes, then remove the lid, stir through the rocket and allow it to wilt. Remove from the heat and finish the gnocchi with the grated Parmesan, pepper and a grating of nutmeg before serving.

Soy-cured Trout with Wasabi Yoghurt and Lime Pickle

SERVES: 4–6 AS A STARTER
PREP TIME: 20 MINUTES,
PLUS 8 HOURS CURING AND
CHILLING

200ml dark soy sauce
200ml light soy sauce
200g black treacle
pared zest of 1 lime
pared zest of 1 lemon
1 tbsp coriander seeds, toasted
1 large fillet of trout (600–800g), skinned
    and trimmed
1 tbsp toasted sesame oil
20g black sesame seeds

FOR THE LIME PICKLE
2 shallots, peeled and sliced into thin rings
juice of 2 limes
2 tbsp rice wine vinegar
pinch of salt

FOR THE WASABI YOGHURT
200g Greek yoghurt
50g wasabi paste

VARIATION

Swap the trout for a fillet of salmon.

SHORTCUT
**The cured fish will keep in the fridge for
up to 3 days.**

Salmon is the fish most commonly cured with soy, but I rather like using trout. This is a really tasty and simple dish, and although it does take a little planning as the fish needs to cure for about 6 hours – it's not a dish that can be rushed – at the last minute, once you have followed the steps, it's fairly easy to bring it together to serve to guests. The wasabi yoghurt is a lovely touch, adding some fiery heat to a creamy dressing.

1. Combine the soy sauces, treacle, citrus peels and toasted coriander seeds in a large mixing bowl and whisk until the treacle has dissolved evenly.

2. Put the trout in a shallow dish that will allow the fish to be submerged in the cure, then pour the liquid over it. Cover with clingfilm and marinate in the fridge for 6 hours.

3. After 6 hours, drain the marinade from the fish and discard, then pat both sides of the fish dry with kitchen paper. Return the cured trout to the fridge for a further 2 hours, uncovered, to allow it to dry and firm up.

4. An hour before serving, make the lime pickle and wasabi yoghurt. Dress the sliced shallots in a bowl with the lime juice and rice wine vinegar and salt. Cover and allow the shallots to pickle for 1 hour at room temperature. To make the wasabi yoghurt, whisk the yoghurt and wasabi paste in a mixing bowl until fully combined.

5. To serve, thinly slice the cured trout, brush the slices with a little sesame oil, then sprinkle with the sesame seeds.

6. Place a spoonful of the wasabi yoghurt beside the slices of the cured trout. Then drain the pickled shallots andd place some of the shallot rings across the trout.

* Make it perfect
To slice the fish, use a long, sharp cook's knife with a smooth blade. Rather than carving the fish at an angle like classical smoked salmon, carve it in thin tranches, so you get the flavour on the outside of the fish in a thin layer.

Rosemary and Malt-glazed Lamb Belly with Salsa Verde

SERVES: 6
PREP TIME: 15 MINUTES
COOKING TIME: 2 HOURS 20 MINUTES

2 lamb breasts (bone in)
about 100ml olive oil
2 garlic cloves, skin on and smashed
2 sprigs of rosemary
sea salt

FOR THE MALT GLAZE
200ml malt vinegar
2 tbsp malt syrup
100g soft light or dark brown sugar
1 tbsp freshly chopped rosemary

FOR THE SALSA VERDE
1 bunch of flat-leaf parsley
½ bunch of mint
leaves from 1 sprig of rosemary
15g capers
30g tinned anchovies
1 garlic clove, peeled
grated zest and juice of 1 lemon
1 slice of white bread, crusts removed
150ml extra virgin rapeseed oil

GET AHEAD
Cook the lamb belly and make the salsa verde several hours in advance, then reheat the meat when you want it. Leave the slow-cooked lamb on the side after its 2 hours of cooking, covered in its tray, then put in a hot oven and follow the glazing steps above as it comes back to temperature before serving.

VARIATION
Swap the lamb belly for lamb shoulder, which is a little less fatty than the belly.

In the past, cuts like lamb belly were known as 'the butcher's cut' – cuts taken home by the butcher as they were cheap and didn't sell. Lamb belly, also known as lamb breast, is still not a particularly common cut, but restaurants have begun to make it fashionable, and it makes a great sharing meal as everyone gets to pull some meat from the belly on the serving plate. Don't be put off by the anchovies in the sauce, they add a great depth of flavour and can't even be seen when the sauce is whizzed up. This would be delicious with couscous (see page 198) or parmentier potatoes, or even in wraps with salad, and the salsa verde drizzled over.

1. Preheat the oven to 160°C/140°C fan/gas 3.

2. Place the lamb in a large roasting tray, season generously with salt and rub in the oil followed by the garlic and rosemary. Cover with foil and cook in the oven for 2 hours. Once cooked, you should be able to pull the meat away from the bone.

3. While the lamb is cooking, prepare the malt glaze. Combine all the ingredients in a saucepan, then bring to the boil over medium heat and cook for 8–10 minutes until reduced to a syrupy consistency.

4. Once the lamb has been cooking for 2 hours, remove it from the oven and increase the temperature to 190°C/170°C fan/gas 5. Remove the foil and glaze the meat with one-third of the malt syrup using a pastry brush. Return to the oven for 5 minutes until the glaze starts to lightly caramelise and become golden, then remove from the oven and repeat this process twice more using the remaining glaze. After the final glaze the lamb belly should be sticky and caramelised with the malt syrup.

5. Allow to rest for 10 minutes before serving.

6. To make the salsa verde, put all the ingredients in a food processor and blitz until smooth. Adjust the seasoning if required.

7. Serve the rested lamb belly with the salsa verde, family style, letting everyone help themselves to the piece they like. It doesn't need to be carved, the meat will be very tender and will just pull apart.

Lockdown Caraway and Coriander Rye Bread

MAKES: 1 SMALL LOAF
PREP TIME: 20 MINUTES, PLUS 6
DAYS FERMENTING THE STARTER
AND 1½ DAYS FERMENTING AND
PROVING THE BREAD
COOKING TIME: 40 MINUTES

FOR THE STARTER (NEEDS TO BE
MADE A WEEK IN ADVANCE)
50g wholemeal rye flour, plus extra for
  feeding
50ml cold water, plus extra for feeding

BREAD DAY ONE
75g of the starter
140ml cold water
100g wholemeal rye flour

BREAD DAY TWO
175g rye flour, plus extra for dusting
6g fine sea salt
10g caraway seeds
10g coriander seeds
1 tsp molasses or black treacle
130ml cold water
neutral oil, for greasing

This rye bread has the lovely addition of coriander and caraway seeds, the latter bringing a subtle hint of anise to the dough. Don't be daunted by the stages below; the recipe doesn't involve masses of time in the kitchen, just some organised, forward planning. Make it in a holiday when you have plenty of time (we made it in lockdown – hence the name). The starter has to be made a week in advance and nurtured, and the bread takes a couple of days to make with resting time included. The starter is the natural raising agent in the loaf, taking the role of the yeast in normal bread-baking, and it gives the bread a wonderful texture and flavour. Once you have a starter under way you can keep making bread with it as long as you continue to feed it. Show it off on a rustic breadboard to make it the centrepiece and serve it thinly sliced. I like it with butter, smoked salmon, sour cream and capers and gherkins. It's lovely with cold meats and pickles, too, or just toasted and served with butter.

AT LEAST SIX DAYS BEFORE YOU WANT TO MAKE THE BREAD, MAKE THE STARTER
Mix the 50g of flour and 50ml water in a medium bowl and beat until it is a creamy, sticky mix. Put the bowl in a plastic bag, seal the bag and leave in a warm place. Every day, mix 1 tablespoon of rye flour and 1 tablespoon of cold water into the starter mix, then return it to a warm place. After five days you will notice bubbles on the surface of the mixture. You have now made your own raising agent and your starter is ready to use. It can be stored in the fridge in an airtight container, though you should use it at least once every 2 weeks. Each time you want to use some, add 75g rye flour and 75g water, mix and leave in a warm place for 8 hours until bubbles appear on the surface. It is live and needs to be looked after (fed); whenever you use some starter, feed it with flour and water and allow it to rise again or put it straight in the fridge.

* Make it perfect

Check your oven – many modern domestic ovens have useful settings, such as dough proving, or even 'cooking with moisture', which always helps with this bread (and would mean you don't need the tray of water at the bottom of the oven).

Write a schedule in advance: it's very easy to forget where you are at with this bread.

THE DAY BEFORE YOU WANT TO COOK YOUR BREAD, START THE FIRST STAGE OF MAKING THE LOAF

This is the pre-fermentation part of the process. Mix the 75g starter (that was fed the day before and is now bubbling) with the water in a bowl (one that's large enough to allow the mixture to rise). Add the rye flour and bring it all together to form a loose mixture. Cover the bowl with a tea towel and leave at room temperature for 12–24 hours until risen and bubbly. The length of time it takes to become bubbly will depend on the time of year and temperature in the kitchen.

ON THE FOLLOWING DAY

1. Uncover the pre-fermented mix. There will be lots of bubbles and it will have a pleasant aroma.

2. Put all the 'Day Two' ingredients in a bowl with the pre-fermented mixture and use your fingers to bring it all together. Mix for at least 2 minutes until everything is combined. It will be a thick, sticky paste.

3. Cover with clingfilm and leave to rest for 10 minutes.

4. Meanwhile, lightly grease a small loaf tin (about 18 x 8 x 6cm) with oil, using your fingers to ensure it's well coated, and line the base and sides with baking parchment.

5. To bring the dough together, dust a clean surface with rye flour. You don't have to knead the dough (it's a fairly dense bread that doesn't need the kneading that yeasted breads require) – just form it into a shape that will fit in the tin. The dough will be sticky but try not to add too much flour while you shape it – using floured hands helps. Place the dough in the tin, sprinkle a fine dusting of rye flour on the loaf and cover loosely with clingfilm. Leave in a warm place for 2–3 hours until it has doubled in size.

6. Preheat the oven to 230°C/210°C fan/gas 8 and place a baking tray on the bottom of the oven.

7. When the dough has risen, transfer it to the oven and just before you close the door, pour a cup of water onto the tray at the bottom of the oven and close the door. It will create a burst of steam. Bake for 40 minutes – it should sound hollow when tapped on the base.

8. Remove from the oven and allow the loaf to rest in the tin for 10 minutes before transferring it to a wire rack to cool fully (it's easier to slice when it is cold).

9. The bread will keep for up to 7 days, stored in an airtight container.

Cumin and Saffron-braised Lamb Shoulder with Apricot and Pistachio Couscous

SERVES: 6
PREP TIME: 30 MINUTES
COOKING TIME: 3¾ HOURS, PLUS
20 MINUTES RESTING

2 tbsp ground cumin
1 whole shoulder of lamb, on the bone
50ml vegetable oil
2 carrots, diced
3 celery sticks, diced
2 red onions, diced
2 garlic cloves, thinly sliced
pinch of saffron
2 tbsp tomato purée
1 litre good-quality chicken stock
500ml tomato passata
300ml whipping cream
½ bunch of flat-leaf parsley, chopped
sea salt

FOR THE COUSCOUS
450ml good-quality chicken stock
10 dried apricots, finely chopped
pinch of saffron
300g couscous
1 red onion, finely diced
50g shelled unsalted pistachios, roughly
   chopped

* Make it perfect

I am often asked about altering the serve numbers in my recipes. If you double the quantity of meat here, you need to double the rest of the ingredients, but not the time. If you double up, use a large roasting dish and cover it tightly with foil.

We eat a lot of lamb – it's always been a favourite of ours – particularly slow-cooked. Our local shepherd grazes his flock on our fields at Melfort House and we are lucky enough to enjoy his new-season lamb through the year with the benefit of our freezer. The cumin and saffron give a slightly Middle Eastern flavour to the meat. You could put it in the oven and go for a long walk before sitting down to eat. Alternatively, cook it on a Friday and reheat for Sunday lunch. It's a great sharing dish. We serve this with sour cream or crème fraîche, a green vegetable and pickled red cabbage.

1. Preheat the oven to 150°C/130°C fan/gas 2.

2. Mix 1 teaspoon of sea salt in a small bowl with 1 heaped tablespoon of the cumin. Using a sharp knife, roughly score the skin and fat of the lamb, press in the mix and set aside.

3. Heat the oil in a casserole over medium heat. Once hot, sear the lamb all over until golden but not cooked through. Transfer to a plate, leaving the oil in the dish. Add the vegetables to the dish and cook over medium heat for 3–5 minutes until lightly coloured. Add the remaining cumin, saffron and tomato purée. Cook for 1 minute, add the stock, passata, cream and some salt. Submerge the lamb in the liquid, bring to the boil and cover with a tight-fitting lid or foil to stop moisture escaping.

4. Cook in the oven for 3½ hours. Baste occasionally with the liquid, adding water if it becomes too dry. When cooked, the meat should pull away from the bone easily. If not, cook for another 15 minutes. Remove from the oven and rest, covered, for 20 minutes, so the meat relaxes, absorbing more flavour.

5. While the meat rests, prepare the couscous. Put the stock, apricots and saffron in a pan with a pinch of salt and bring to the boil. Put the couscous in a heatproof bowl, pour over the stock, cover with clingfilm and leave for 20 minutes. Once all the liquid has been absorbed, use a fork to separate the grains. Stir through the onion and pistachios. Season if required.

6. Sprinkle the lamb with the parsley and serve with the couscous and the lamb cooking juices for pouring over.

VARIATION

This recipe would work well with lamb leg instead of lamb shoulder (with the same cooking times).

Ham Hock Terrine with Gribiche Sauce

**SERVES: 12 AS A STARTER OR
LIGHT LUNCH
PREP TIME: ABOUT 2 HOURS, PLUS
1 HOUR COOLING AND 24 HOURS
CHILLING
COOKING TIME: ABOUT 3 HOURS**

3 smoked ham hocks (about 3.6kg total
   weight)
2 bay leaves
1 celery stick, halved
1 onion, halved (skin on)
1 tbsp black peppercorns
1 star anise
50g capers, chopped
½ bunch of tarragon, leaves chopped
1 tbsp wholegrain mustard
2 tbsp sherry vinegar
sea salt and freshly ground black pepper
toasted sourdough, to serve

FOR THE GRIBICHE SAUCE
6 eggs
50g capers, chopped
100g cornichons, chopped
1 shallot, finely diced
½ bunch of chives, chopped
½ bunch of tarragon, chopped
grated zest and juice of 1 lemon
1 tsp Dijon mustard
75ml extra virgin olive oil

I learnt how to make gribiche sauce at college. It's a classic French cold mayonnaise made with boiled eggs, capers and cornichons and served with a boiled meat which is why it works so well with this delicious ham hock terrine. The ham hock is the joint where the leg meets the foot – don't be put off by the size of the raw hock, as there is quite a lot you can't use. Cooking the hocks slowly in stock ensures the meat is tender and that the fat dissolves and adds to the flavour of the terrine. This dish is great for lunch, or served in smaller portions as a starter, with sourdough and some green salad. Keep the terrine in the fridge to cut a slice as required. Any leftover terrine would work well with the Apple, Mustard and Honey Dressing on page 268.

1. Double-line a 900g loaf tin with clingfilm.

2. Place the ham hocks in a very large pan or stock pot, cover with cold water, place over high heat and bring to the boil. Once the water has reached boiling point, carefully remove the hocks and drain the water (this first boil is to remove some of the salt). Place the ham hocks back in the pan or pot, add the bay leaves, celery, onion, peppercorns and star anise, cover with fresh cold water and bring to the boil again over high heat. Once the water reaches boiling point, reduce to low-medium heat and simmer for 2–3 hours, occasionally skimming any scum that forms on the surface of the water, until the meat is tender and flakes away from the bone.

3. Remove from the heat and allow the hocks to cool in the stock for 1 hour.

4. Once the hocks have cooled, gently remove them from the stock and set aside. Strain the stock through a fine sieve into a clean pan. Place the stock over medium heat and let it boil until it has reduced by three-quarters, to concentrate the flavour for the terrine (it will become gelatinous once it's cold).

5. To make the terrine, carefully pick the meat away from the bones and reserve in a clean bowl, being careful to remove any small pieces of bone or gelatinous sinew or gristle. Mix the picked meat with the capers, tarragon, mustard and sherry vinegar, and season with black pepper. Spoon the meat

GET AHEAD
Make the terrine a few days in advance. It will keep in the fridge for up to 10 days. Let it come to room temperature before serving.

mixture into the lined tin and press down so it's even. Ladle the hot stock over the terrine, allowing the liquid to sink into it before adding more and until it rests at the same level as the meat. Leave the meat and stock in the lined tin for a minute or two to allow it to drip through, shaking it very gently if needed, then top up if necessary. Cover with clingfilm and allow to set in the fridge overnight.

6. The following day, make the gribiche sauce. Bring a medium saucepan of water to the boil and carefully lower the eggs into it. Reduce the heat and simmer for 10 minutes. Transfer the eggs to a bowl and cover with very cold water. Allow 5 minutes to cool quickly, then peel. Using the fine side of a box grater, grate all of the hard-boiled eggs into a bowl. Add the capers, cornichons, shallot, herbs, lemon zest and juice and Dijon mustard and mix until evenly combined. Trickle in the extra virgin olive oil, mixing the sauce slowly, until all the oil is fully incorporated. Season with salt and pepper.

7. To finish, remove the clingfilm from the top of the loaf tin and upturn the terrine onto a board. Carefully remove the remaining clingfilm and cut the terrine into 1.5cm-thick slices. Serve the slices alongside the gribiche sauce and some toasted sourdough.

Cured, Barbecued Duck with Sweet and Sour Peppers

SERVES: 2–3
PREP TIME: 30 MINUTES, PLUS
MINIMUM 12 HOURS MARINATING
COOKING TIME: 20 MINUTES, PLUS
5 MINUTES RESTING

2 duck breasts (about 425g total weight)
olive oil, for cooking

FOR THE DUCK CURE
1 tbsp fennel seeds
1 tbsp coriander seeds
1 tsp Chinese five-spice powder
100g demerara sugar
80g rock salt
grated zest of 1 orange

FOR THE SWEET AND SOUR PEPPERS
2 tbsp olive oil
1 red pepper, deseeded and thinly sliced
1 yellow pepper, deseeded and thinly sliced
1 red chilli, deseeded and thinly sliced
1 tbsp caster sugar
2 tbsp red wine vinegar
2 tbsp light soy sauce

Duck lends itself beautifully to the spices in this recipe and the final cooking on the barbecue (though I've included a hob-top method, too). Taking the time to cure the duck in advance – overnight is best – is well worth it as the flavour really penetrates the meat. Serve the duck and peppers with noodles or plain boiled basmati rice to accompany the rich flavours.

1. To make the cure for the duck, gently toast the fennel and coriander seeds in a dry frying pan over low heat for 30 seconds–1 minute, stirring, then add the five-spice powder and toast for a further 30 seconds, keeping the spices moving to avoid them burning. Remove from the heat and leave to cool. Place the toasted spices in a food processor with the sugar, salt and orange zest and blitz briefly to break up the spices. Alternatively, grind them in a spice grinder or in a mortar with a pestle.

2. Gently score the duck skin in a criss-cross pattern using a sharp knife, making sure you don't cut all the way through the fat and into the flesh.

3. In a small tray, make a 'bed' with a third of the cure mix and lay the duck breasts on it skin side down, then top with the remaining cure mix. Cover with clingfilm and place in the fridge for at least 12 hours (or overnight). Once the duck has finished curing, rinse the breasts well in a bowl of cold water, then pat them dry with kitchen paper and set aside. The meat will be a little firmer at this stage.

4. Heat the barbecue until hot (the coals should be white).

5. Now, prepare the sweet and sour peppers. Heat the olive oil in a large frying pan over high heat until the pan is smoking hot. Add the sliced peppers and chilli and sauté for 2–3 minutes until softened, then sprinkle with the sugar and cook for at least 5 minutes until caramelised. Deglaze the pan with the vinegar and soy sauce and reduce for 1–2 minutes until the peppers are coated in a sweet, sticky dressing.

RECIPE CONTINUES OVER THE PAGE

6. Before you start cooking the meat, make sure the duck breasts are at room temperature (this will take about an hour, after removing them from the fridge). Drizzle both sides of each breast with olive oil and cook the duck, skin side down on the grill over the hot coals for 2 minutes until the skin is golden and lightly charred.

7. Turn the duck and cook for a further 2–3 minutes; it should still be quite rare – cured duck cooks faster than uncured meat, and is nice and tender when rare. The breasts should feel spongy to the touch – test them with a skewer if you like, to check that the meat is warm in the middle. Remove from the grill and allow the duck to rest on a board for 5 minutes.

8. To cook the duck in a frying pan or on a griddle pan, heat the pan over high heat and cook the duck skin side down, then drain the fat from the pan, turn the duck breasts over and continue to cook on the other side – it may take a little longer to cook them in a pan than it will on the barbecue. Rest on a board as above.

9. To serve, thinly slice the barbecued duck breasts across the grain and serve on a bed of the sweet and sour peppers.

* Make it perfect

Duck is a lean meat with a great layer of fat that adds flavour to it, which must be scored. Try to marinate it for as long as you can to infuse the spices. Duck also has a layer of sinew, so if the heat is too high it will curl up. I suggest using a cooler part of the barbecue if you can and always start skin side down, as you want to render the fat and crisp the skin. The resting stage is important, too, so that the juices don't just run out on cutting; you want the meat to be succulent.

Liquorice-braised Ox Cheek with Champ Potatoes

SERVES: 6
PREP TIME: 15 MINUTES, PLUS
MINIMUM 6 HOURS MARINATING
COOKING TIME: 4 HOURS

3 large ox/beef cheeks, trimmed of tough
    sinew and each cut in half
drizzle of vegetable oil
sea salt and freshly ground black pepper

FOR THE MARINADE
2 onions, finely diced
2 garlic cloves, crushed
1 litre good-quality beef stock
400ml stout
20g black treacle
2 bay leaves
2 star anise
1 liquorice root stick

FOR THE CHAMP
900g floury potatoes, peeled and cut into
    chunks
200g unsalted butter
200g crème fraîche
1 bunch of spring onions, trimmed and thinly
    sliced
½ bunch of chives, chopped

* Make it perfect
I was taught these rules at college: old
potatoes should be cooked starting in
cold water; new potatoes from boiling.
For perfect mash, you need to mash
the potatoes, then almost beat them
for a smooth, lump-free consistency.

GET AHEAD
Prepare in advance and chill or freeze,
then reheat in the oven and serve with
a chunk of bread instead of potato.

This recipe evokes memories of beef stew when I was a
child growing up in Southport. My dad was a fruit-and-veg
merchant so we had lots of potatoes, and they were ideal for
this dish – I am pretty sure he would love the combination
of beef and mash. Who wouldn't? It's the perfect comfort
food: warm, hearty and melt in the mouth, and great as bowl
food for friends. The crème fraîche adds a nice tang to the
potatoes. I know liquorice is a love/hate flavour, but I find in
this dish it enhances the rich and thick beef-cheek sauce, so
give it a try. You can find liquorice root online or in health-
food shops. Buy it in bulk and store in an airtight container.
It works well in desserts such as ice creams, or even in a BBQ
marinade. Serve the ox cheeks with some simply cooked,
well-seasoned cabbage or pickled red cabbage.

1. Put all the marinade ingredients in a vessel large enough to
fit the meat, add the cheeks, cover with clingfilm or a lid and
chill in the fridge for a minimum of 6 hours (ideally overnight).

2. The next day, preheat the oven to 150°C/130°C fan/gas 2.

3. Remove the cheeks from the marinade and transfer to a
plate. Pat dry and season, reserving the marinade.

4. Heat the oil in a casserole dish over medium heat and
sear the cheeks on all sides until golden brown (in batches if
necessary). Add all the reserved marinade to the casserole
with all the cheeks; increase the heat and bring to the boil,
then cover with a lid and place in the oven. Cook for 3½ hours
until the meat is tender and the sauce has reduced. The meat
should be so soft you can eat it without needing a knife.

5. To make the champ, put the potatoes in a saucepan, cover
with cold water and season well. Place over medium-high heat
and bring to the boil, then reduce the heat and simmer for
15–20 minutes until soft. Drain well, then allow to steam dry for
2–3 minutes. Meanwhile, melt the butter in the saucepan over
low heat. Once melted, add the potatoes and mash well until
smooth. Add the crème fraîche, spring onions and chives and
beat briefly over low heat to combine. Season if required.

6. To serve, divide the potatoes among serving bowls, place a
piece of cheek on top and ladle over the braising juices.

Pork Neck Casserole with Cider and Ras el Hanout

SERVES: 4
PREP TIME: 15 MINUTES
COOKING TIME: 3 HOURS, PLUS RESTING

4 tbsp vegetable oil
2 onions, diced
2 carrots, diced
2 bay leaves
3 garlic cloves, crushed
50g plain flour
600g diced pork neck
2 tbsp ras el hanout
1 tsp ground white pepper
½ tsp ground fennel seeds
300ml dry cider
50ml cider vinegar
600ml good-quality chicken stock
100ml whipping cream
1 green apple, grated (peel on)
½ bunch of tarragon, leaves chopped
grated zest of ½ lemon
sea salt and freshly ground black pepper

* Make it perfect

Deglazing the pan ensures that all the flavour stuck to the bottom of the pan during the browning process is retained. When you have just cooked and removed meat or vegetables from a pan, ensure it's hot then pour in the liquid. The heat generated will cause the remnants of the ingredients stuck on the bottom of the pan to come clean, meaning you keep the flavour in your sauce. Remove any bits of ingredients that are burnt, however, before adding liquid – this would not make a good base flavour.

Most people tend to opt for belly, loin or chops when cooking pork, as these are more widely available, but it's worth keeping an eye out for less common cuts, such as pork neck. I find it's full of flavour and, when cooked for a long time, is just as tender. Pork is traditionally served with apple, and here this flavour pairing takes the form of cider and grated apple, with the ras el hanout spice blend adding a Moroccan feel. I serve this with mash, parmentier potatoes or couscous (see page 198), and a green vegetable.

1. Preheat the oven to 160°C/140°C fan/gas 3.

2. Heat 2 tablespoons of the vegetable oil in a large casserole dish over high heat, add the diced onions, carrots, bay leaves and crushed garlic, season with salt and pepper and cook for 6–10 minutes until golden brown. Transfer to a bowl with a spoon and set aside, retaining the oil in the dish.

3. Put the flour on a plate or in a bowl, coat the diced pork neck in the flour and season well with salt and pepper.

4. Heat another tablespoon of oil in the casserole dish over high heat. Add half the pork and cook for 5–10 minutes until well browned all over (it doesn't need to be cooked through), then set aside with the reserved vegetables and brown the remaining pork in the remaining oil. Cooking in batches enables the meat to take on colour and not steam (each piece needs to touch the bottom of the dish – a pile will not brown).

5. Reduce the heat under the casserole to medium. Add the spices with 2 tablespoons of water and cook for 1 minute, then deglaze the pan with 250ml of the cider and all the vinegar.

6. Cook for about 5 minutes until the liquid has reduced by half, then add the stock, cream and apple and bring to the boil. Return the pork and vegetables to the dish and season with salt. Cover with a lid and cook in the oven for 2½ hours.

7. Remove the casserole from the oven and allow the pork to rest (with the lid on) for 10 minutes.

8. Finish by stirring through the chopped tarragon, lemon zest and the remaining 50ml of cider, then serve.

Truffle, Mushroom and Chestnut Tortellini with Jerusalem Artichoke Sauce

SERVES: 2 AS A MAIN DISH, 4 AS A STARTER (MAKES 44 SMALL TORTELLINI)
PREP TIME: 45 MINUTES, PLUS 30 MINUTES RESTING
COOKING TIME: 35 MINUTES

FOR THE PASTA DOUGH
250g '00' pasta flour
8 egg yolks (see Tip on page 106)
2 tsp olive oil, plus extra for drizzling
2 tsp milk
semolina, for dusting

FOR THE TRUFFLE, MUSHROOM AND CHESTNUT FILLING
2 tbsp olive oil
1 shallot, finely diced
2 portobello mushrooms, finely chopped
75g cooked chestnuts, finely chopped
30g Parmesan cheese, finely grated
50g mascarpone
1 tbsp truffle oil

FOR THE JERUSALEM ARTICHOKE SAUCE
50g unsalted butter
200g Jerusalem artichokes, peeled and thinly sliced
salt
250ml milk
½ tsp sherry vinegar

Making pasta is time-consuming, and can take practice to perfect, but it can be extremely therapeutic – you just need to give yourself plenty of time during the process. I think a pasta machine is essential, too. The filling and sauce here are a match made in heaven. Every year at Melfort House we have a huge crop of Jerusalem artichokes: their stalks are the tallest in the garden all summer, and the artichokes are the most wonderful treat in autumn, just as the cold weather is upon us. Serve small tortellini for a starter or larger ones for a main course. A scattering of truffle shavings on top would be amazing, as would some fresh herbs or very thinly sliced mushrooms. You must have some fresh bread to mop up the sauce.

1. To make the pasta dough, put the flour, egg yolks, oil and milk in a food processor and blitz until the mixture resembles breadcrumbs. Bring it together and transfer to a work surface and knead for 4–5 minutes until the dough is smooth and elastic. It will feel very firm when you knead it but will soften when rested. Wrap the dough in clingfilm and leave to rest in the fridge for at least 30 minutes (or up to 2 days).

2. To make the filling, heat the olive oil in a large frying pan over medium-high heat, add the diced shallot and sweat for 2–3 minutes until softened, then increase the heat and add the chopped mushrooms. Fry for 2–3 minutes until the mushrooms have released their water and it has evaporated. Transfer to a large mixing bowl and put in the fridge to cool completely (it can be made up to 24 hours in advance). Once cold, bind together with the rest of the ingredients and season to taste.

3. To make the artichoke sauce, melt the butter in a saucepan over medium heat. Add the artichokes with a pinch of salt and sweat for 4–5 minutes until they begin to soften, then cover with the milk, reduce the heat and simmer for 15–20 minutes until completely soft. Transfer the artichokes and liquid to a

RECIPE CONTINUES OVER THE PAGE

SHORTCUT

If you don't have a pasta machine, or don't fancy making pasta from scratch, use wonton wrappers instead (page 126).

blender and blend for 1–2 minutes until silky smooth. Adjust the seasoning with the sherry vinegar (the vinegar should complement the sauce – the sauce shouldn't taste of vinegar – so you only need a little), then season to taste with salt. Set aside until the tortellini are made.

4. To make the tortellini, remove the pasta dough from the fridge. Unwrap it, dust with semolina flour and flatten it enough so that it will fit through your pasta machine. Start working the dough through the machine, initially at the thickest setting, working your way down through the settings right to the thinnest and dusting generously with semolina flour as you go (don't be tempted to force the dough through the machine as it will roll it unevenly and break at the edges). Roll until you have a long 1–2mm-thick sheet of pasta.

5. Cut out circles of dough using a 6–7cm cutter (or an 8cm cutter if making larger tortellini for a main course), then cover the discs with a clean, lightly dampened kitchen towel to prevent them drying out. Place just under 1 teaspoon of the filling mix on the centre of each pasta disc (or more if making larger tortellini), then dampen a pastry brush with water and wet the edges of the discs slightly. Fold the pasta over the filling to seal, pressing together along the edges while trying to remove any air from the filling. The shapes must be properly sealed to avoid water leaking into the filling, or the filling leaking out. For the classic tortellini shape, bring the edges together around your little finger, then seal by pressing them together. Place the shaped tortellini on a tray dusted with semolina, then repeat the process with the rest of the pasta and filling.

6. To cook the tortellini, bring a large saucepan of salted water to the boil. Once it's boiling, drop in the pasta and cook for 3–4 minutes. Meanwhile, gently reheat the sauce in a separate pan. Remove the pasta from the pan with a slotted spoon and drizzle with olive oil.

7. To serve, ladle the Jerusalem artichoke sauce onto serving plates then place the cooked tortellini on the sauce, finishing with another drizzle of olive oil.

Brown Sauce-glazed Ham with Onion Gravy

SERVES: 8
PREP TIME: 15 MINUTES, PLUS
1 HOUR COOLING
COOKING TIME: 3¼ HOURS

2kg boneless smoked gammon joint
2 bay leaves
4 garlic cloves, skin on
3 cloves
10 black peppercorns

FOR THE BROWN SAUCE GLAZE
150g brown sauce
150g date molasses
2 sprigs of thyme, leaves picked
150ml malt vinegar

FOR THE ONION GRAVY
50g butter
3 red onions, halved and thinly sliced
1 garlic clove, thinly sliced
2 tbsp plain flour
100ml white wine
500ml good-quality chicken stock
1 tbsp Dijon mustard
2 tbsp Worcestershire sauce
sea salt

Brown sauce is my condiment of choice with a bacon sandwich, so this baked ham dish is a natural progression. I use brown sauce to add a tang to some sauces, but only in moderation as it is quite sweet. Cabbage, lightly steamed and seasoned, or some plain boiled new potatoes, make great accompaniments. Once the ham is cool, it will keep in the fridge for up to 3 days. Served cold, it works really well with the Apple, Mustard and Honey Dressing on page 268.

1. Place the gammon in a large saucepan with the bay, garlic, cloves and peppercorns (the meat is salty, so there's no need to add salt). Add enough water to cover the joint, then bring to the boil over high heat. Once boiling, reduce the heat to low and simmer for 2 hours. When cooked, a knife inserted should meet no resistance. Add more water to the pan while the gammon cooks if it evaporates too much, to ensure the meat is still covered. Once cooked, switch off the heat, remove the pan from the hob and allow to cool for 1 hour in the braising liquid.

2. Preheat the oven to 200°C/180°C fan/gas 6 and line a large baking tray with baking parchment.

3. Once the ham is cool, drain, then carefully peel away the skin, keeping a thin layer of fat attached. Transfer to the lined baking tray and use a sharp knife to score only the fat (not the meat) in a shallow criss-cross pattern.

4. Combine all the glaze ingredients in a saucepan and bring to the boil over high heat. Once hot, brush the ham with half the glaze. Place the ham in the oven and roast for 10 minutes, then remove and brush with the remaining glaze. Roast for 15–20 minutes until sticky and caramelised. Remove the ham and rest.

5. To make the onion gravy, melt the butter in a large saucepan over medium heat, add the onions and garlic with a pinch of salt and sweat for 10–15 minutes until soft and caramelised. Increase the heat, and stir the flour into the onions. Cook for 2–3 minutes, then deglaze the pan with the wine, stirring, and reduce by half over medium heat. Add the stock, bring to the boil and simmer for 10–15 minutes until thickened. Stir through the mustard and Worcestershire sauce, then add salt to taste.

6. Carve the rested ham and serve it with the onion gravy.

Gooseberry Crumble Soufflés with Elderflower Custard

SERVES: 6
PREP TIME: ABOUT 1 HOUR
COOKING TIME: ABOUT 25 MINUTES

FOR THE PASTRY CREAM
300ml milk
100ml double cream
1 vanilla pod, split lengthways and seeds removed
5 medium egg yolks (reserve the whites for the meringue)
50g caster sugar
20g custard powder
15g plain flour

FOR THE GOOSEBERRY COMPOTE
300g gooseberries, topped and tailed
75g caster sugar
grated zest of ½ lemon

FOR THE CRUMBLE TOPPING
25g plain flour
15g golden caster sugar
15g cold unsalted butter, cubed
½ tbsp rolled oats

FOR THE ELDERFLOWER CUSTARD
125ml milk
175ml double cream
3 medium egg yolks (reserve the whites for the meringue)
50g caster sugar
25ml elderflower cordial
grated zest of ¼ lemon

FOR THE MERINGUE, AND FINISHING THE SOUFFLÉS
25g soft unsalted butter, for brushing
25g rich tea biscuits, blitzed to fine crumbs
reserved egg whites (from the pastry cream)
120g caster sugar

I do love gooseberries. We have a few bushes hidden behind the shed in my kitchen garden – they're not much fun to pick, but they are so delicious. Last year we made jam with them, but this year I think a variety of desserts are in order and this is the ultimate show-off dessert. You do need to take your time with this recipe as there are several parts to it, though many of the components can be made in advance and just put together at the last minute. It's well worth practising first on your family, before inviting guests!

1. To make the pastry cream, heat the milk, cream and vanilla (pod and seeds) in a saucepan until hot but not boiling. Beat the egg yolks, sugar, custard powder and flour together in a heatproof bowl. Pour half of the hot milk onto the egg yolk mixture, whisking till smooth, then pour in the remaining hot milk mixture.

2. Transfer to a clean saucepan and cook gently over the lowest heat for 2–3 minutes, stirring constantly with a spatula, until the custard has thickened considerably. Transfer to a bowl, cover with clingfilm and leave to cool completely.

3. To prepare the gooseberry compote, heat a wide saucepan over medium heat, then add the gooseberries, followed by the sugar and lemon zest. Cook until the fruit starts to break down, then reduce the heat and cook until the liquid has reduced and the fruit has a rich, jammy consistency, mashing the fruit if necessary to help it break down. Transfer to a bowl, cover and leave to cool completely.

4. To make the crumble topping, rub together the flour, sugar and cold butter in a mixing bowl until the mixture resembles breadcrumbs, then stir through the oats.

5. To make the elderflower custard, combine the milk and cream in a saucepan and slowly bring to the boil over medium heat. Combine the egg yolks and sugar in a heatproof bowl and cream together, then pour over a third of the hot cream and milk mixture and stir to combine. Pour over the remaining

RECIPE CONTINUES OVER THE PAGE

GET AHEAD
You can make the pastry cream, compote, crumble topping, the rich-tea crumb for the ramekins (buttering the ramekins and coating them with the crumbs) and even the custard in advance, just leaving you with the preparation of the meringue and baking of the soufflés to do just before serving.

* Make it perfect
It's really important to crumb the ramekin in advance of filling and cooking the soufflé. It stops the egg mix from sticking to the side of the ramekin which would in turn prevent the soufflé from rising. You mustn't miss a spot, the tiniest speck will allow the soufflé mix to stick.

two-thirds of the hot cream and milk and whisk again. Transfer to a clean saucepan and cook gently over the lowest heat for 4–5 minutes, stirring constantly with a spatula until the custard is thick enough to coat the back of the spoon, being careful not to scramble the eggs. To be extra precise, you can check the mixture with a thermometer – it should reach exactly 82°C. Remove from the heat and stir through the elderflower cordial and lemon zest. Set aside.

6. Now prepare 6 x 175g ramekins. Brush a little of the soft butter inside the ramekins, brushing the sides with it vertically all the way round. Place the ramekins in the fridge for a few minutes to allow the butter to set. Remove from the fridge and repeat the buttering process, ensuring there are no unbuttered parts as this will affect the end result. Add the rich tea crumbs to the ramekins and roll them around to ensure the crumbs stick to all of the soft butter. Chill the lined ramekins until needed.

7. Preheat the oven to 200°C/180°C fan/gas 6 and put a large baking sheet in the oven to heat up.

8. To assemble the soufflés, whisk the egg whites in a clean bowl and, once they start to aerate, gradually add the caster sugar and continue whisking until all the sugar has dissolved and you have a thick, glossy meringue.

9. Beat the chilled pastry cream a little, to loosen it, then fold a quarter of the meringue through the pastry cream. Once it's completely incorporated, gently fold in the remaining meringue. Lastly, fold through the gooseberry compote.

10. Divide the soufflé batter between the four ramekins, then scrape the tops with a palette knife. Carefully run your thumb around the edge of the ramekins to remove any excess soufflé mix. Transfer the filled ramekins to the preheated baking tray, ensuring they are evenly spaced. Sprinkle the crumble mixture lightly over the tops of the soufflés, place to the centre shelf of the oven and bake for 12–14 minutes until well risen and still slightly gooey in the centre. Do not open the door while they are cooking – the only way to tell if they are ready is if they have risen well. While the soufflés are baking, heat the custard.

11. Serve the soufflés immediately, with a jug of the warm elderflower custard. To eat, make a small hole in the middle of the soufflé with a knife and pour the custard in.

Pumpkin Seed Parfait with Maple Granola

SERVES: 8
PREP TIME: 30 MINUTES, PLUS 30 MINUTES COOLING AND 12 HOURS FREEZING
COOKING TIME: 35 MINUTES

FOR THE PUMPKIN SEED NOUGATINE
125g pumpkin seeds
125g caster sugar

FOR THE PARFAIT MIX
75g caster sugar
20g liquid glucose
70g egg whites (if you're not using carton egg whites, this will be about 2 large egg whites)
500ml whipping cream, lightly whipped

This frozen dessert, a delicious nougatine with a granola top that cuts through the sweetness, takes some planning in terms of timings but is actually fairly easy to create. I would recommend using a sugar or jam thermometer when heating the sugar for the meringue to ensure it reaches the correct temperature. You will need a 900g loaf tin. Photographed overleaf.

1. Preheat the oven to 180°C/160°C fan/gas 4.

2. Put the pumpkin seeds on a baking tray and toast them in the oven for 8–10 minutes so they warm through and their oil is released – the colour won't change much. Occasionally agitate the seeds so they toast evenly. Remove from the oven and set aside.

3. To make the nougatine, place a medium saucepan over medium heat, cover the base of the pan with the sugar and cook for about 8 minutes, swirling it gently in the pan if necessary to encourage it to melt evenly, but not stirring, until it is amber in colour. Remove from the heat and stir through the toasted pumpkin seeds. Transfer the nougatine to a sheet of baking parchment and spread it out to cool. Once it's completely cool, blitz it in a food processor to a coarse crumb, then set aside for later.

4. To make the parfait mix, begin by making a meringue. Put a small saucepan on a set of scales, add the sugar and liquid glucose, then add 2 tablespoons of water and place the pan over medium heat. Cook the sugar until it reaches 121°C on a sugar thermometer.

5. As soon as you place the pan of sugar for the parfait on the heat, simultaneously start to whisk the egg whites in the clean, grease-free bowl of a stand mixer fitted with the whisk attachment.

6. Once the egg whites have soft peaks, gradually add the syrup that has reached 121°C, slowly dribbling it directly onto the egg whites while whisking. Continue to mix the meringue for 10–15 minutes until it is cool to touch. Once the meringue is completely cool, fold in the lightly whipped cream until smooth, using a large metal spoon to avoid losing the air from the meringue.

FOR THE GRANOLA
100g jumbo oats
100g pumpkin seeds
100ml maple syrup, plus extra to serve
2 tbsp vegetable oil
pinch of salt

GET AHEAD
The granola can be made in advance and stored in an airtight jar – it's also great for breakfast with yoghurt.

7. Finally, add the chopped pumpkin seed nougatine and fold it through to evenly distribute the seeds.

8. Line a 900g loaf tin with baking parchment. Transfer the parfait mix to the tin and level it out as much as you can. Transfer to a freezer for 12 hours to set (overnight is best). It should be set like ice cream.

9. Once the parfait is set, prepare the granola. Preheat the oven to 170°C/150°C fan/gas 4 and line a baking tray with a silicone baking mat or baking parchment. Combine all the ingredients in a bowl and mix until the seeds and oats are coated in the syrup and oil. Spread the mixture out on the lined baking tray and bake for 15–20 minutes until golden, stirring the granola on the tray every 5 minutes to ensure it bakes evenly. Remove from the oven and leave to cool.

10. To assemble the dish, remove the parfait from the freezer, take it out of its tin and peel away the baking parchment. Use a warmed serrated knife to cut the parfait into generous slices. Drizzle over a little maple syrup and sprinkle over the granola for extra crunch. Serve.

Bay Leaf Ice Cream with Apricot Ripple

SERVES: 6–8
PREP TIME: ABOUT 30 MINUTES, PLUS A FEW HOURS COOLING
COOKING TIME: 10–12 MINUTES, PLUS CHURNING AND FREEZING

960ml milk
450ml double cream
10 fresh bay leaves
6 egg yolks (see Tip on page 106)
240g caster sugar
pinch of salt

FOR THE APRICOT RIPPLE
250g apricots
2 tbsp clear honey

This year we finally got an ice-cream machine at home, which has given us the opportunity to try all sorts of flavour combinations. Once you master the art of making a custard, anything is possible. We have a few bay trees in the garden – they are a favourite as they taste good, look good in the garden, and are there all year round. I think many people consider bay leaves as a flavour for savoury dishes, but here it works a treat with summery, fragrant apricots. This ice cream is great in a cone, or if you want to present it as a dessert, serve in glass bowls with a drizzle of honey on top and a sablé biscuit. The recipe requires an ice-cream machine in order to get the best result. See photo on previous page.

1. Put the milk and cream in a medium heavy-based saucepan. Break the bay leaves in your hands and add them to the pan (breaking the leaves helps release their flavour), then place the pan over low heat. Heat until it is about to simmer, stirring frequently to avoid it sticking to the bottom of the pan – make sure it doesn't boil – then remove from the heat. This is just to infuse the milk and cream with the flavour of the leaf, like making tea. If you can't smell the bay in the pan, feel free to add more leaves. The leaves will not stay in the final ice cream, so the flavour has to come from infusion.

2. Whisk the egg yolks with the sugar and salt in a heatproof bowl to aerate the mixture (it should become a slightly paler colour), then pour in a third of the hot cream mixture, whisking continuously and slowing down or stopping adding the cream for a moment if required, as you do not want to cook the eggs. Continue until all the cream is incorporated into the egg mixture. It's important to stir well at this stage to ensure that all the sugar dissolves into the liquid.

3. Rinse out the pan, pour the custard mixture back into it and return to a low heat. Cook the custard, stirring constantly and gently with a spatula or spoon, for a further 5 minutes, until it thickens to make a smooth custard (the mixture mustn't boil or it will split or scramble the eggs). You will know the custard is thick enough when you test with the spoon or spatula – coat

SHORTCUTS

Swap the fresh apricots for tinned fruit (they won't need to be cooked for as long). Using 250g of a runny preserve would work well in place of the apricot 'jam'.

VARIATION

Swap the fresh apricots for other soft fruit such as peaches or raspberries.

the back of the spoon or spatula and run your finger down through the mixture. If it's thick enough, the line you've made should remain. To be extra precise, check the mixture with a thermometer – it should reach exactly 82°C.

4. Remove the custard from the heat and pour it into a clean heatproof bowl or jug. Cover it with a piece of greaseproof paper or clingfilm, pressing it onto the surface to avoid a skin forming. Allow the mixture to cool for a couple of hours, then transfer to the fridge until completely cool.

5. While the custard is in the fridge, prepare the apricot ripple. Remove the stones from the apricots and chop the flesh roughly. Put the chopped flesh in a small saucepan with the honey and 50ml water, partly cover with a lid, place over medium heat and simmer for about 5 minutes, stirring occasionally, until the fruit is completely soft, mashing it with the back of a spoon if necessary and adding a little more water to the pan if required. Once soft, transfer to a heatproof container and allow to cool before putting in the fridge to chill.

6. Switch on the ice-cream machine in advance to make sure the churning bowl is cold.

7. Strain the chilled custard to remove the bay leaves, transfer it to the churning chamber and churn following the manufacturer's instructions until thick but not fully frozen. Transfer the thick cream to a lidded container, then stir the apricot 'jam' through the ice cream to create a ripple effect. Freeze for at least 3 hours, or until required. I prefer to eat this freshly made, but it will keep well in the freezer for up to 2 weeks.

8. Remove from the freezer 10 minutes before you are ready to serve and scoop as required.

Something Special

Potted Salmon with Wholemeal Blinis

SERVES: 6 AS A STARTER OR LIGHT LUNCH
PREP TIME: 25 MINUTES, PLUS 2½ HOURS COOLING AND RESTING
COOKING TIME: 30 MINUTES

300g boneless raw salmon fillet
100g sliced smoked salmon
2 banana shallots, finely diced
extra virgin olive oil, for drizzling
100ml white wine
100g crème fraîche
15g dill, finely chopped, plus extra sprigs to serve
grated zest and juice of 1 lemon
sea salt and freshy ground black pepper

FOR THE WHOLEMEAL BLINIS
120g wholemeal flour
1 tsp table salt
20g caster sugar
190ml milk
4g fast-action dried yeast or 10g crumbled fresh yeast (page 275)
10g butter, melted and cooled
1 egg, separated
pinch of table salt
vegetable oil, for greasing

GET AHEAD
The blinis can be made up to 2 days in advance, stored in an airtight container in the fridge and reheated in a warm oven. Alternatively, freeze and defrost before reheating.

A blini is a small pancake of Russian origin made from buckwheat, and this is a delicious variation on the typical smoked-salmon topping. This light dish would be great for a summer brunch. You could even serve it with a poached egg for hungrier members of your household. Equally, you could make smaller blinis and serve them with pre-dinner drinks; they would work very well with a glass of champagne.

1. Preheat the oven to 180°C/160°C fan/gas 4.

2. Place the salmon fillet (skin down) and the smoked salmon on a baking tray with a lip (so the ingredients don't spill out). Sprinkle the fish with the diced shallots, drizzle with olive oil and season with salt and pepper. Put the baking tray in the oven then gently pour the white wine into it (this prevents spills as you walk across the kitchen). Bake for 12–20 minutes until the salmon fillet has lost its translucency and easily flakes, checking it frequently so it doesn't overcook (the time it takes to cook through will depend on the thickness of the fillet), then remove from the oven and leave to cool.

3. Once the salmon is cool, transfer the contents of the baking tray to a large mixing bowl, taking the flesh off the salmon skin as you do so and keeping the salmon in large flakes. Discard the skin and the remaining cooking liquid.

4. Add the crème fraîche, chopped dill, lemon zest and juice to the bowl and season with salt and pepper, then gently fold together until the salmon flakes apart and is coated in the crème fraîche mixture, being careful not to over-mix and break down the salmon too much.

5. Divide the salmon mixture between six serving pots, such as colourful ramekins, pressing it down with a spoon until the surface is flat. Drizzle over a little extra virgin olive oil to coat the surface and prevent the salmon from drying out and discolouring. Cover with clingfilm and store in the fridge until needed.

6. While the potted salmon is in the fridge, make the blinis. Combine the wholemeal flour, salt and sugar in a large bowl. In a jug, whisk together the milk, yeast, melted butter and the egg yolk.

RECIPE CONTINUES OVER THE PAGE

SHORTCUT

Buy ready-made blinis, heat them in the oven, then top with a teaspoon of the potted salmon to serve with pre-dinner drinks.

VARIATIONS

Serve the blinis with smoked salmon, a poached egg for breakfast or the Crab Butter or Dressed Crab on pages 160 and 82.

7. Make a well in the centre of the dry ingredients. Pour a small amount of the liquid mixture into the well and stir to gradually incorporate the dry ingredients into the liquid. Slowly incorporate the rest of the liquid while stirring – this should help prevent lumps forming and result in a smooth batter.

8. Whisk the egg white in a small bowl with the pinch of salt until stiff peaks form. Gently fold the egg white into the blini batter with a spatula, cover with clingfilm and leave to rest in a warm place for 30 minutes. It will become bubbly and aerated and small holes will appear.

9. To cook the blinis, lightly grease a large non-stick frying pan with vegetable oil and set over medium heat. Spoon in a tablespoon of the batter per blini and cook for 2 minutes on each side until golden brown. As they cook, the blinis will rise slightly and expand, and when the top is no longer wet/liquid it's time to flip them and cook the other side. Repeat until you have used all the blini mix.

10. Remove the potted salmon from the fridge at least 2 hours before serving, so it has time to soften. When ready to serve, top the salmon with few sprigs of dill and serve alongside the warm blinis.

Scotched Quail Eggs

MAKES: 10 SCOTCH EGGS (2 EACH FOR A STARTER, 3 FOR A LIGHT LUNCH, OR MORE WITH DRINKS, AS A SNACK)
PREP TIME: 45 MINUTES, PLUS 30 MINUTES CHILLING
COOKING TIME: 15 MINUTES

10 fresh, chilled quail eggs
250g good-quality sausage meat
250g pork mince
½ tsp sea salt
½ tsp cayenne pepper
50g plain flour, seasoned with ½ tsp salt
2 eggs, beaten
150g panko breadcrumbs
vegetable oil, for deep-frying

VARIATION

Add chopped fresh herbs to the sausage meat if you like – my favourites are rosemary or sage.

Scotch eggs were a source of amusement in the press during the 2020 Covid lockdowns. Do they count as a substantial meal or not? Well, these are tiny rather than substantial, but so tasty and such a treat. You may be aware that I am a number-one fan of LFC, so for me a couple of these eggs are perfect with a glass of beer while watching a match. I love them with piccalilli (shop-bought is fine) for dipping, or a chimichurri dipping sauce would work well, too; or try serving them as part of a cold-meat platter.

1. Prepare a bowl of iced water. Bring a saucepan of water to the boil, then drop in the quail eggs and cook for exactly 2½ minutes. Immediately transfer the eggs to the bowl of iced water. Cool for 5–10 minutes before peeling the shells. Cooling the eggs quickly like this avoids a grey sulphur ring.

2. To make the meat filling, mix the sausage meat, pork mince, salt and cayenne pepper in a bowl. Once mixed, weigh the meat into 10 individual 50g meatballs.

3. To assemble the Scotch eggs, take one meatball in the palm of your hand and flatten it into an oval-shaped patty. Take one peeled egg and gently shape the meat around it, moulding it in your palm until the egg is sealed in and fully encased. Repeat this process with the remaining eggs.

4. Put the flour, beaten eggs and breadcrumbs into three separate shallow dishes. Roll the meat-wrapped eggs in the flour, then coat in the beaten eggs and finish with a generous coating of breadcrumbs. Dip into the egg mixture and the panko again to give an extra crunchy outside to your Scotch eggs. Put them in the fridge to cool for 30 minutes.

5. Preheat the oven to 200°C/180°C fan/gas 6.

6. Pour enough oil into a deep saucepan or deep-fat fryer to come up to about 5cm and place over medium heat. If using a deep-fat fryer or you have a thermometer, heat the oil to 180°C. If not, check the oil temperature by dropping in a 2–3cm bread cube – it should turn golden and crisp in 30 seconds.

7. Remove the Scotch eggs from the fridge, then deep-fry in batches for 1–2 minutes, or until golden brown. Transfer to a wire rack over an oven tray, then cook in the oven for 6 minutes exactly. Remove, season lightly with sea salt and serve immediately while still hot and runny in the centre.

Devilled Mackerel with Cucumber Relish on Toasted Brioche

SERVES: 4
PREP TIME: 20 MINUTES, PLUS 30 MINUTES MARINATING
COOKING TIME: 10 MINUTES

4 slices of brioche loaf
extra virgin olive oil
4 whole mackerel, butterflied and pin bones removed
1 lemon

FOR THE CUCUMBER RELISH
1 cucumber, peeled, deseeded and diced
2 gherkins, thinly sliced
½ bunch of dill, chopped
1 shallot, thinly sliced
75ml white wine vinegar
30g caster sugar
1 tsp cornflour
¼ tsp sea salt

FOR THE DEVILLED BUTTER
100g soft butter
15g caster sugar
15g English mustard powder
15g cayenne pepper
15g sweet or hot smoked paprika
65ml red wine vinegar
15g fine sea salt
15g freshly ground black pepper

GET AHEAD
Make the devilled butter in advance and store it in the fridge until required. Let it come to room temperature before using, so you can spread it on the fish without tearing the skin.

I cooked a similar dish to this on *MasterChef: The Professionals* in 2020 and have been asked lots of questions about it. The term 'devilled' has a long history. In culinary terms it means to cook with a hot and spicy seasoning, though it is doubtlessly linked to the heat of the devil in days gone by. Here, the heat of the devilled butter complements the strong flavour of the mackerel and the soft brioche (though any bread would be delicious). The fabulous butter would work equally well with most meat or fish. If you order your fish in advance, ask the fishmonger to butterfly and pin-bone it for you. Serve with rice or salad to turn this into a main meal.

1. To make the relish, put the cucumber, gherkins, dill and shallot in a bowl. Mix the vinegar, sugar, cornflour and salt in a small saucepan until smooth, then bring to the boil over medium heat. Once boiling, remove from the heat and cool for 5 minutes, then pour it over the cucumber mixture. Stir and marinate for 30 minutes, then adjust the seasoning if required.

2. While the relish is marinating, make the devilled butter. Combine all the ingredients in a mixing bowl and beat until smooth and the spices are evenly mixed. Set aside.

3. Preheat a large griddle pan over high heat. Drizzle the brioche slices with olive oil and grill on both sides on the hot griddle – resist moving the slices, you want them to have grill lines. Set aside and reheat the griddle until almost smoking (the high heat will help stop the fish sticking to the pan).

4. Spread a thick layer of devilled butter on the skin side of the mackerel. Place the mackerel skin side down on the griddle pan by holding the tail end and slowly putting it into the pan head end first, lowering it away from you. This avoids spitting and keeps it in one place. Cook for 1½ minutes until charred with visible char marks (if you turn the fish too soon, the skin will stick to the griddle). Season the flesh side with the remaining devilled butter, then flip and cook for a further minute. When you turn the fish over, switch the heat off. Remove the fish from the griddle.

5. To assemble each plate, lay the grilled mackerel beside a brioche slice, with a spoonful of the relish on the side. Drizzle with olive oil and a fine grating of lemon zest.

Honey-glazed Poussin with Pear, Hazelnut and Endive Salad

SERVES: 4
PREP TIME: 20 MINUTES, PLUS
1 HOUR COOLING
COOKING TIME: 30 MINUTES

1.5 litres good-quality chicken stock
2 spatchcocked poussin
75g honey
1 tbsp freshly chopped thyme
Maldon salt

FOR THE SALAD
1 red endive, trimmed and leaves separated
1 white endive, trimmed and leaves
    separated
1 pear, cored, quartered and sliced
handful of pea shoots

FOR THE HAZELNUT DRESSING
1 tbsp white wine vinegar
1 tbsp Dijon mustard
75ml extra virgin rapeseed oil
75g roasted hazelnuts, finely chopped
½ bunch of chives, finely chopped

* Make it perfect
Spatchcocking a bird makes it a
more even size for cooking, and is a
technique used often for grilling the
birds. To spatchcock the poussin
yourself, place a bird breast side down
on a board and, using a strong, sharp
pair of kitchen scissors or poultry
shears, cut along both sides of the
backbone to remove it. Turn the bird
over again so it's breast side up and,
using the heel of your hand, push
down and flatten the bird on the work
surface. Lightly press it all over to
tenderise the meat and make it an even
thickness.

Here I have spatchcocked the poussin, this means it has been
butterflied and the backbone removed which allows the bird
to be flattened out for grilling. You can normally buy them
already prepared or ask your butcher to help. This dish has a
restaurant feel to it, it looks good and is very light and tasty.

1. Bring the stock to the boil in a large saucepan over medium
heat, then gently lower in the spatchcocked poussin. Reduce the
heat and simmer for 8–10 minutes until the poussin are cooked
but still slightly pink. Remove from the stock and place flat on
a wire rack over a baking tray to cool completely (uncovered),
allowing the skin to dry. This will take about an hour.

2. Preheat the oven to 210°C/190°C fan/gas 7.

3. Using a pastry brush, glaze the poussin generously with the
honey, then sprinkle with Maldon salt and the thyme. Keep on
the wire rack over the tray, place in the centre of the hot oven
and cook for 12–15 minutes until the honey caramelises and
the birds are golden brown. Remove from the oven and allow
to rest for 5 minutes. The double cooking process of braising
then a hot oven will cook the meat perfectly. If it starts to get
too dark, turn the oven down to 190°C/170°C fan/gas 5.

4. Now make the salad. Combine the endive and pear in a
bowl with the pea shoots.

5. To make the dressing, whisk together the vinegar and
mustard in a bowl, then slowly incorporate the oil. Season with
a pinch of salt, then add the chopped hazelnuts and chives.

6. To assemble the dish, cut each poussin in half, cutting
straight down the breastbone on the skin side using a sharp
knife. Dress the sliced pear, endive and pea shoots with the
hazelnut dressing and season lightly with a pinch of salt.

7. To plate, place a half poussin on the left of a serving plate
then arrange a pile of the dressed salad on the side.

VARIATION

**If you prefer, use skin-on, bone-in chicken thighs. Cook in the
stock for the same time as a poussin, but they may not need
the full 12–15 minutes in the oven.**

Lobster Thermidor 'Benedict'

SERVES: 4
PREP TIME: 30 MINUTES, PLUS 20 MINUTES FOR THE HOLLANDAISE
COOKING TIME: 30 MINUTES

1 whole lobster, bought from a reputable fishmonger (alive, its claws taped), a pre-cooked lobster or shop-bought cooked lobster meat
30g butter, plus extra for spreading
1 small carrot, peeled and grated
1 shallot, diced
1 garlic clove, crushed
1 tbsp tomato purée
50ml brandy
4 eggs (as fresh as possible)
75g crème fraîche
50g mature Cheddar cheese, grated
¼ bunch of tarragon, leaves chopped
juice of ½ lemon
4 English muffins, halved and toasted
small block of Parmesan cheese, for grating
sea salt and freshly ground black pepper
1 quantity of Hollandaise Sauce (page 269), to serve

I have made a variety of Benedicts over the years, and it is always a rich, decadent dish, but this lobster one is particularly special. I can imagine it as a celebration brunch or supper. The dish isn't difficult but there are plenty of elements that need to come together at the last moment so weighing everything out in advance and having your equipment ready will make it easier. You can buy cooked lobster meat or have a go at cooking it yourself.

1. If using pre-cooked lobster, skip to number 6.

2. Bring a large saucepan of water to the boil – it needs to be deep and wide enough to cover the lobster completely.

3. Lay the lobster on a board. As you look down on it you will see the large taped claws. You will also see the head (there is a curve on the shell protecting the head). Place the tip of a large knife on the start of the curve, press down firmly and move the knife in a straight line towards the claws along the short distance, until you can remove the knife cleanly. Remove the tape from the claws.

4. Plunge the lobster in the boiling water, then bring the water back to the boil. You will know the lobster is almost cooked when the shell has turned from black to red. A 450g lobster will take about 6 minutes (it doesn't need cooking for longer, as the meat is cooked again). Once cooked, remove the lobster from the water with tongs. Allow it to drain and cool slightly before removing the meat.

5. Once the lobster is cool enough for you to hold it comfortably, remove the meat. Hold the tail firmly and twist it sharply to remove it from the body. Turn it over and, using a pair of kitchen scissors, cut the underside to reveal the meat. Remove the meat by pulling the two sides of the shell apart. Sharply crack the claw shells with shell-crackers or a small hammer (be careful not to damage the meat inside). Peel away the shell and gently pull out the meat. Discard any membranes. Ideally, take the meat out of the claws in large pieces. Dice all the lobster meat.

RECIPE CONTINUES OVER THE PAGE

VARIATION

Swap the lobster meat for crab meat.

6. To prepare the lobster filling, melt the butter in a frying pan over medium heat, add the carrot, shallot and garlic with a pinch of salt and sweat for 3–5 minutes until softened, without letting them colour. Stir in the tomato purée and cook for 1 minute, then deglaze the pan with the brandy and let it reduce to burn off the alcohol. Remove from the heat.

7. For the poached eggs, bring a large saucepan of salted water to the boil. When the bubbles are consistent, stir vigorously to create a whirlpool, then crack the eggs into small cups and drop them into the boiling water one by one. Poach the eggs for 2–3 minutes for soft yolks.

8. While the eggs are poaching place the frying pan with the carrot, shallot and garlic back over low heat and add the diced lobster meat along with the crème fraîche. Gently warm through.

9. Remove the eggs from the pan carefully with a slotted spoon and transfer to kitchen paper to drain. Season with salt and pepper.

10. Finish the lobster filling by stirring through the grated Cheddar and chopped tarragon. Adjust the seasoning with the lemon juice and salt and pepper.

11. Warm through the hollandaise sauce.

12. Assemble the Benedict by topping 4 toasted muffin halves with a good spoonful of the lobster filling and spreading them flat. Place a poached egg on top of each and ladle over the warm hollandaise sauce to generously cover them. Grate Parmesan over the top of each Benedict, butter the remaining half muffins and serve on the side of each plate.

Jerusalem Artichoke and Barley 'Risotto' with Grated Bottarga

---

SERVES: 4
PREP TIME: 30 MINUTES
COOKING TIME: 45 MINUTES

300g Jerusalem artichokes
3 sprigs of thyme
2 tbsp olive oil, plus extra for drizzling
1 onion, finely diced
200g pearl barley, rinsed and drained
150ml white wine
700ml good-quality hot vegetable stock
100g mascarpone
50g pecorino, grated
juice of 1 lemon
½ bunch of tarragon, chopped
sea salt and freshly ground black pepper
bottarga, to serve

This is similar to a traditional risotto in texture and appearance, but is made with pearl barley instead of rice. It is easier to make because you don't have to stand over the barley as it cooks, unlike a rice risotto, which involves stirring. The delicious Jerusalem artichokes, available in winter months, give this dish an earthy flavour, though when they're out of season you can cook the barley in the same way with other vegetables, or funghi such as sautéed mushrooms. Bottarga is the salted and dried roe sac of fish and is a unique delicacy with a big flavour – the dish will still work well without the bottarga but do give it a try if you can find some. The addition of fresh thyme, rosemary, marjoram or oregano would all complement the barley and add a layer of flavour, too. Photographed overleaf.

1. Put the artichokes, unpeeled, in a saucepan with the sprigs of thyme and a teaspoon of salt. Cover with cold water, place over high heat and bring to the boil, then reduce the heat slightly and cook for 15– 20 minutes until they are soft when pierced with a knife.

2. Meanwhile, start the risotto. Heat the olive oil in a large saucepan over low-medium heat, add the diced onion and sweat for 8–10 minutes until soft and translucent, stirring every now and then. Add the wet barley and a pinch of salt and toast the grains in the oil for 1 minute, then add the white wine, turn up the heat a little, and reduce until almost all the wine has evaporated. Add the vegetable stock, season with black pepper and cook over medium heat for about 25 minutes until the barley is soft but still retains a slight bite.

3. Preheat the oven to 170°C/150°C fan/gas 4.

4. While the barley is simmering, drain the artichokes through a sieve, then sit the sieve in a bowl and allow them to air-dry as they cool. Once cool enough to handle, cut the artichokes in half. Using a fork, scoop out the soft flesh and put it in a bowl then crush with the back of the fork. Set the crushed flesh aside for later and retain the skins.

5. Scatter the artichoke skins on a baking tray and dress with a little olive oil. Arrange them on the tray so they lie in a single even layer. Place in the oven and roast for about 15 minutes until crisp. Remove from the oven and season the crispy skins with a pinch of salt.

6. When the barley is ready, and still over low heat, add the reserved crushed artichokes and stir everything together gently to warm the artichokes through in the risotto (keeping a bit of the texture as you mix), then remove from the heat.

7. To finish, stir through the mascarpone, grated pecorino, lemon juice and chopped tarragon. Stir well to encourage the mascarpone to melt, then season with salt and pepper to taste. The risotto should be thick but loose enough to be pourable.

8. Divide the risotto among four serving bowls, top each with a few of the crispy artichoke skins, and finely grate over some bottarga for an extra layer of flavour.

Prawns with a Bisque and Tomato Fregola

SERVES: 6
PREP TIME: 2–2½ HOURS, PLUS COOLING
COOKING TIME: ABOUT 1½ HOURS

500g raw tiger prawns, in their shells
120ml olive oil
2 banana shallots, diced
6 plum tomatoes, diced
½ fennel bulb, diced
2 sprigs of rosemary, needles picked
2 garlic cloves, sliced
1 tsp coriander seeds
1 tsp fennel seeds
1 tbsp tomato purée
4 tbsp tomato ketchup
100ml white wine
1 litre tomato juice
1 litre good-quality fish stock
500g fregola
50–100g crème fraîche
sea salt and freshly ground black pepper

TO SERVE
½ bunch of tarragon, leaves chopped
extra virgin olive oil, for drizzling

Fregola is a semolina-based pasta from Sardinia that looks a lot like couscous. Here it adds texture to a classical bisque and makes the dish a little more substantial. This is a fabulous, impressive supper for friends and the key to the flavour is the cooking and seasoning of each stage of the dish. The first step gives you a perfect bisque if you just want a soup (and you could use the prawns for something else). Serve with chunky bread if you like, though it's not essential as there's the pasta in the dish. A blob of sour cream or crème fraîche on top of each serving will cut through the rich sauce. See photo on previous page.

1. Peel the prawns from their shells and remove the heads. Set the heads and the shells aside to be used later. Using a small knife, cut along the back of each prawn, then gently pull away the dark veins and discard. Put the prepared prawns in the fridge.

2. Heat a large, deep stockpot or heavy-based, deep-sided saucepan over high heat and add 100ml of the olive oil, the reserved prawn heads and the shells. Generously season with salt and pepper then reduce the heat to medium and cook for 3–4 minutes, stirring every now and then, until lightly roasted. They'll turn from grey to a glorious orange colour. Add the shallots, tomatoes, fennel, rosemary, garlic, coriander seeds and fennel seeds and cook for a further 5–6 minutes until the vegetables are starting to caramelise. Once the vegetables have started to colour, stir through the tomato purée and tomato ketchup and cook for a further 2 minutes. Deglaze the pan with the white wine, bring to a simmer and cook for about 1 hour until reduced by half, then pour in the tomato juice and fish stock and bring to the boil before reducing the heat to a simmer and covering the pan with a lid. Simmer the bisque for 30 minutes.

3. Remove the bisque from the heat and allow to cool slightly, with the lid off, for 20–30 minutes.

GET AHEAD
Make the bisque in advance of cooking the final dish, either earlier in the day or the day before, storing it in the fridge once it has been passed through the sieve and cooled. Bring to a simmer in a casserole dish when you're ready to finish cooking the dish, adding the fregola before baking.

4. Ladle around a quarter of the bisque into a high-powered blender or Thermomix and blitz for 30 seconds to break up the shells. Pass the bisque through a fine sieve into a clean pan, using the back of the ladle to press through as much liquid as possible and leaving behind the thick paste of blitzed shells and vegetables. Repeat these steps for the remaining bisque. Discard any thick paste that remains in the sieve and season the bisque to taste with salt and pepper.

5. Preheat the oven to 180°C/160°C fan/gas 4.

6. Place the fregola in a large casserole dish then pour over the seasoned bisque. Cover with foil or a tight-fitting lid, then transfer to the oven and cook for 25 minutes.

7. Remove the prepared prawns from the fridge, season and dress with the remaining olive oil.

8. Remove the casserole dish from the oven, remove the foil or lid and stir in crème fraîche to taste (this will tone down the richness of the bisque and thicken it a little) then arrange the dressed prawns over the surface of the baked fregola. Return to the oven and cook for a further 10 minutes, uncovered, to allow the prawns to roast. Remove from the oven once the prawns are cooked through and the fregola has absorbed most of the bisque. Sprinkle over the chopped tarragon and drizzle with a little extra virgin olive oil.

Rump Cap with Beef-fat Béarnaise and Potato Terrine

SERVES: 6
PREP TIME: 40 MINUTES, PLUS OVERNIGHT CHILLING
COOKING TIME: 2 HOURS 10 MINUTES, PLUS RESTING

beef rump cap joint (800g–1kg)
2 tbsp vegetable oil
50g butter
2 sprigs of thyme
2 sprigs of rosemary
1 garlic bulb, cut in half
sea salt and freshly ground black pepper

FOR THE POTATO TERRINE
10 Maris Piper potatoes, peeled
2 sprigs of thyme, leaves picked
100g butter, melted, plus extra for greasing
25g cornflour

FOR THE BÉARNAISE
75ml madeira
3 tbsp sherry vinegar
1 sprig of rosemary, leaves picked
1 shallot, sliced
3 egg yolks (see Tip on page 106)
1 tbsp Dijon mustard
pinch of salt
100g unsalted butter, melted
75g roasted beef dripping, melted
¼ bunch of tarragon, leaves finely chopped

This really is a delicious combination – a fabulous cut of meat served with potato terrine and a rich béarnaise sauce. For me, it's the perfect steak. The dish does involve some advance preparation but it is well worth the effort. Rump cap, called 'picanha' in Brazil, is a beautiful triangle-shaped cut of meat located on the top of the rump. 'Cap' refers to the large piece of fat that sits on top of the meat like a cap, and adds great flavour to the meat when cooked. Buy the best meat you can, from your butcher.

DAY 1
1. The day before you want to serve, prepare the potato terrine.

2. Preheat the oven to 180°C/160°C fan/gas 4. Grease a 900g loaf tin and line the base with baking parchment (you will also need a second loaf tin of the same size for pressing the terrine).

3. Thinly slice the potatoes to a thickness of about 2mm using a mandoline. Arrange an even layer of sliced potatoes in the base of the greased and lined tin, season the potatoes lightly with salt, add a sprinkling of the picked thyme leaves, then dust lightly with a little of the cornflour. Brush with plenty of the melted butter to moisten the potatoes (this is the only moisture for the cooking, apart from the water in the potatoes). Repeat this layering process until all the potato slices have been used, then cover the top with a rectangle of baking parchment and wrap with foil over the top. Place in the centre of the oven and bake for 1½–2 hours, until the potatoes are tender all the way through when you lift the foil and check with a skewer in a couple of places.

4. Remove from the oven, remove the foil and allow to cool for 20–30 minutes, then place the second loaf tin on top of the layers to press the terrine (weigh down the second loaf tin with a couple of full tins to add extra pressure if you like). Place in the fridge to set overnight (with the upper tin on top).

RECIPE CONTINUES OVER THE PAGE

Make it perfect

– If you have a probe thermometer and want to test the meat for doneness, a guideline for the temperature should be 50°C for rare, 60°C for medium and 70°C for well done.

– When cooking a piece of meat, it's important to always let it rest. As it rests, the meat relaxes, takes on the flavours (if a sauce is used during cooking) and doesn't 'bleed' when cut.

– Only season meat just before cooking it. Salt cures the meat and draws out the water, so if you put it on the meat too soon it will sizzle in the pan and steam rather than fry.

DAY 2

1. Remove the beef cap from the fridge at least 2 hours before using, to allow it to reach room temperature.

2. Preheat the oven to 200°C/180°C fan/gas 6.

3. Place a large roasting tray over medium heat and add the 2 tablespoons of vegetable oil to the tray. Just before cooking, season both sides of the meat with salt and pepper. Lay the beef in the tray fat side down and cook for 3–5 minutes until the fat has rendered slightly and is starting to caramelise. Add the butter, herbs and garlic and heat until the butter begins to foam.

4. Place the roasting tray of beef in the hot oven and cook for 20–30 minutes, turning the beef halfway through cooking and adjusting the cooking time depending on how you prefer your beef to be cooked. Remove from the oven and rest for 15–20 minutes, covered loosely with foil, on a large plate.

5. To make the beef-fat béarnaise, first combine the madeira, 2 tablespoons of the sherry vinegar and the picked rosemary leaves and sliced shallot in a small saucepan. Cook over medium heat for 5–10 minutes until reduced to a third of its original volume, then allow to cool for 5 minutes. Combine the Dijon mustard, egg yolks and salt in a bowl, then pass the reduced liquid into the bowl through a sieve, stirring continuously. Place the bowl on top of a saucepan of simmering water, making sure the bottom of the bowl doesn't touch the water, and whisk continuously for 3–5 minutes, until the sauce has thickened and reached a ribbon stage, leaving lines in the mixture when the whisk is lifted. Turn off the heat and slowly whisk in the warm melted butter a little at a time, followed by the warm melted beef fat, until thick and emulsified. Finish the béarnaise with the chopped tarragon, taste and season with the remaining sherry vinegar and salt, if needed. Cover and keep in a warm place until required.

6. Just before serving, remove the potato terrine from the tin by turning the tin upside down and trim the edges to neaten. Slice into 6 square portions, then cook in a non-stick pan over medium heat for 2–3 minutes on each side until golden and crisp, and season with a little sea salt before serving.

7. Carve the rested beef into thick slices and serve alongside the crispy potato terrine and the beef-fat béarnaise.

Barbecued Pork Burgers

SERVES: 6
PREP TIME: 20 MINUTES, PLUS
MINIMUM 1 HOUR CHILLING
COOKING TIME: 15 MINUTES

FOR THE BURGERS

300g good-quality pork mince
200g good-quality sausage meat
50g smoked pancetta, finely chopped
2 garlic cloves, crushed
2 tsp hot or sweet smoked paprika
1 tsp English mustard powder
2 tsp onion powder
½ tsp salt
1 tbsp tomato purée
25g soft dark brown sugar
50g dried breadcrumbs
1 large egg, lightly beaten
1 tbsp Marmite
vegetable oil, for frying

TO SERVE

100g American mustard
6 buns (we like brioche buns)
sliced cheese of choice
2 large tomatoes, ideally on-the-vine for
    flavour, thinly sliced and seasoned with
    salt and pepper
2 iceberg lettuce leaves, broken into large
    pieces (keeps its crunch)
1 white onion, thinly sliced
pickled cucumbers or gherkins
salt, to taste

* Make it perfect

This recipe uses sausage meat and mince
to offer varying textures in the patties
(the sausage meat is seasoned and the
mince is like sausage meat without
seasoning). Try to buy good-quality meat
for this. The fat provides flavour, so go
for minimum 5% fat, and free-range if
you can. Go for meat without anything
added, such as breadcrumbs, though you
may not be able to avoid seasoning.

Who doesn't love a burger? In our house, burger night
means break-from-the-kitchen night, as the kids tend to take
over. This is the classic hamburger, made using pork and
given a twist with the addition of Marmite, the heat of the
smoky paprika, mustard and pancetta. For the best flavour,
use a barbecue to cook the patties. Serve with a relish of
your preference. I like a spicy tomato relish but it would work
well with the Roasted Garlic and Buttermilk Dressing on
page 268, the Caesar Mayo on page 267, or the Blue Cheese
Dressing on page 52, too.

1. Combine all the burger ingredients, except the oil, in a
large mixing bowl and use your hands to scrunch everything
together until evenly combined. Divide into 6 and shape into
patties. Place on a tray and chill and firm up in the fridge for at
least 1 hour.

2. To cook the patties, rub them with oil and season lightly with
salt on both sides.

3. If you are using a barbecue, make sure the coals are hot
before grilling. Cook the patties on the grill over hot coals for
1 minute on each side to form a crust. Once a crust has
formed, brush one side with the American mustard, flip and
cook for 1 minute and brush the other side. Once the mustard
has caramelised, repeat this process once more on each side,
so you cook the patties for a total of 6 minutes each.

4. If the outsides of the patties are cooking too quickly, move
them to a cooler part of the grill.

5. Alternatively, cook the patties in batches in a griddle pan or
wide-based frying pan. If you want to melt the cheese, pop it
on the patties 1 minute before they're ready, put the lid on for
1 minute, then serve.

6. Toast the buns, then add the patties, cheese, tomatoes,
lettuce, onion and cucumbers or gherkins, seasoning with salt
to taste. Serve.

GET AHEAD
Make the burgers up to a couple of days in advance and chill
or freeze them, separated by sheets of greaseproof paper
until you want to cook them. If freezing, defrost fully before
cooking.

Red-wine-braised Cuttlefish with Parmesan Polenta

SERVES: 6
PREP TIME: ABOUT 45 MINUTES
COOKING TIME: 1½–2 HOURS

50ml olive oil
1kg large, cleaned cuttlefish (ink sac removed), chopped into 2–3cm pieces (you will need an approx. 1.75kg cuttlefish if you're prepping it yourself)
1 large red onion, diced
2 garlic cloves, sliced
2 sprigs of rosemary, leaves picked
100g small button mushrooms (halved if large)
1 carrot, diced
2 celery sticks, diced
2 tbsp tomato purée
200ml red wine
750ml good-quality beef stock
sea salt and freshly ground black pepper

FOR THE PARMESAN POLENTA
250ml milk
500ml good-quality vegetable stock
½ tsp salt
175g quick-cook polenta
100g unsalted butter, cubed
75g Parmesan cheese, grated

VARIATION

Swap the cuttlefish for squid. Cuttlefish is from the same family as octopus and squid with a flavour that sits somewhere between the two. It is slightly larger than squid, though is normally a cheaper alternative as it is used less in Britain.

Polenta is a corn carbohydrate commonly used in Italian cooking; we occasionally use it in the restaurant as it makes a great base on the plate with a sauce. In this dish, it absorbs the flavours of the cuttlefish and makes a soothing, warming dish. Cuttlefish is a member of the squid family, with a similar texture and taste, so the two could be interchanged (see Variation). Preparing either is a fairly messy job, so I suggest buying pre-cleaned cuttlefish, frozen or fresh.

1. Preheat the oven to 170°C/150°C fan/gas 4.

2. Heat the olive oil in a large casserole dish over medium heat, then add the chopped cuttlefish, season with salt and sauté for 2 minutes until lightly coloured. Use a slotted spoon to remove the cuttlefish and set aside on kitchen paper to drain.

3. In the dish, stir the onion, garlic, rosemary, button mushrooms, carrot, celery and a pinch of salt to combine the ingredients, then cook over medium heat for 4–5 minutes until starting to colour. Stir in the tomato purée and cook for a further 2 minutes, then deglaze the pan with the red wine and bring to the boil. Once boiling, pour in the beef stock and return the cuttlefish to the dish. Cover and bring to the boil.

4. Place the casserole dish in the oven and braise for 1½ hours until the cuttlefish is tender and the stock has reduced slightly (undercooked cuttlefish will be rubbery, so do ensure you cook it for long enough).

5. Remove from the oven and allow to cool for 10 minutes.

6. While the cuttlefish mixture is cooling, cook the polenta. Bring the milk and vegetable stock to the boil in a large saucepan with the salt. Tip in the polenta slowly, whisking constantly, and cook over medium heat for about 3 minutes until the grains have softened and the mixture has thickened. Remove from the heat and whisk in the butter and grated Parmesan until rich and glossy, loosening it with a little boiling water if it's too thick. Adjust the seasoning to taste, adding lots of freshly ground black pepper.

7. To serve, divide the Parmesan polenta among serving bowls and use the back of a spoon to make a well in the centre. Ladle in the braised cuttlefish along with the braising juices.

Chicken, Mushroom and Pancetta Wellington

SERVES: 6–8
PREPARATION TIME: 1 HOUR 40 MINUTES, PLUS 2 HOURS CHILLING
COOKING TIME: 1 HOUR 5 MINUTES

200g chestnut mushrooms, quartered
3 large skinless chicken breasts
5 egg yolks (see Tip on page 106)
1 tbsp finely chopped thyme, the leaves and tender stalk (remove woody ends)
1 tbsp finely chopped rosemary needles
1 small shallot, finely diced
1 garlic clove, crushed
75g fresh fine breadcrumbs
1 tbsp Dijon mustard
200g sliced pancetta (smoked or unsmoked)
1 sheet of ready-rolled all-butter puff pastry
olive oil
sea salt and freshly ground black pepper

GET AHEAD
Make the mushroom filling the day before and chill in the fridge until required. The chicken can also be prepared and rolled the day before, and kept in the fridge.

Though a Wellington is usually made with beef, it works beautifully with chicken, too. This is a real showstopper of a dish. Follow the instructions and you will avoid the dreaded soggy bottom and worry of raw meat. It's great served with steamed hispi cabbage and perhaps try it with the Black Garlic Barbecue Sauce on page 271.

1. Place the bowl and blade of a food processor in the fridge or freezer for 30 minutes (or longer) to cool. They need to be well chilled before use. Preheat the oven to 180°C/160°C fan/gas 4.

2. Lay the quartered mushrooms out on a baking tray and season with salt and pepper. Drizzle with olive oil and roast in the oven for 15–20 minutes until they are golden and have shrunk in size. Remove and leave to cool.

3. Square off the chicken breasts by trimming away the narrow bottom.

4. Remove the food processor bowl and blade from the fridge or freezer and blitz 130g of the chicken trimmings with 3 of the egg yolks and ½ teaspoon of salt for 1 minute until smooth. By using a cold blade and bowl you avoid cooking the chicken (the blade does become warm as it spins).

5. Remove the lid of the food processor and add the roasted mushrooms, chopped herbs, diced shallot, crushed garlic, breadcrumbs and mustard. Blitz for 30 seconds to break up the mushrooms and bring all the ingredients together. Lift out the blade from the bowl and scrape any of the mixture off it and back into the bowl. Transfer to a clean bowl and chill until required.

6. Carefully cut down the middle of each chicken breast to open it up – do not cut all the way through (you want to keep each breast in one piece). The effect is to make a thinner layer of chicken, though it will still be uneven in thickness at this point.

RECIPE CONTINUES OVER THE PAGE

NOTE

As you are handling raw chicken, read the recipe first and organise the double layers of clingfilm in advance, so you have exactly what you need to hand before you begin. It is important to chill everything as you go along.

7. Lay out a double layer of clingfilm on the work surface and place slices of pancetta into two long rows, ensuring the slices overlap as you arrange them. Set aside. Place another double layer of clingfilm on the work surface. Lay the butterflied chicken breasts flat on the clingfilm so they slightly overlap each another. Cover with another double layer of clingfilm and gently bash them with a rolling pin to make a large 20 x 25cm rectangle with an even thickness of 3–4mm. Remove the two top layers of clingfilm and evenly spread the chilled mushroom stuffing over the surface. Carefully roll the chicken, using the clingfilm to help you and making sure you roll it tightly enough to keep the filling enclosed. Place the roll on the pancetta close to one long edge, and roll again to encase the stuffed chicken in the pancetta, finishing with the seal at the bottom. Tightly wrap in clingfilm and chill in the fridge to firm up for 1–2 hours.

8. Preheat the oven to 220°C/200°C fan/gas 7. Put a baking tray in the oven to heat up – preheating it will help seal the base of the Wellington. Cut a piece of baking parchment to fit the tray which will be used during cooking (don't put the paper in the oven yet).

9. To finish the Wellington, brush the edges of the sheet of puff pastry lightly with some of the remaining egg yolk, remove the clingfilm from the rolled chicken and place it on top, with the part where the pancetta slices are sealed facing upwards – the longest edge of the chicken roll should be towards the edge of the longest edge of the pastry. Roll the chicken in the pastry, ensuring the seal is on the bottom of the Wellington. Press the two ends of the pastry together at each end of the roll and use the back of a fork to seal completely. Turn the roll over, then brush the Wellington with the remaining egg yolk and transfer to the baking parchment. Allow the Wellington to come to room temperature for 30 minutes.

10. Lift the parchment and Wellington and place it on the hot tray, then bake in the hot oven for 15 minutes. Turn the tray in the oven, reduce the heat to 190°C/170°C fan/gas 5 and bake for a further 20–25 minutes.

11. Once cooked, remove from the oven and allow to rest for a minimum of 10–15 minutes before carving.

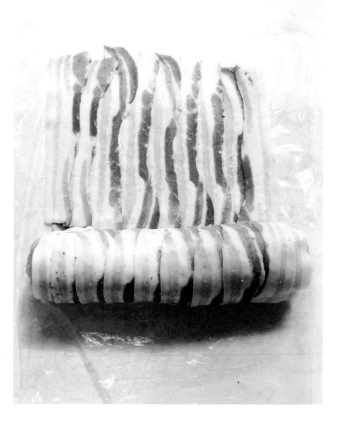

White Chocolate and Star Anise Ice Cream with Summer Peaches

SERVES: 6–8
PREP TIME: 20–30 MINUTES,
PLUS INFUSING AND COOLING
COOKING TIME: 5 MINUTES,
PLUS CHURNING AND FREEZING

250ml milk
250ml double cream
3 star anise
4 egg yolks (see Tip on page 106)
90g caster sugar
100g good-quality white chocolate,
    chopped
stems of fresh lavender, to serve

FOR THE PEACHES
4 ripe peaches
caster sugar, for sprinkling
splash of vodka

This beautiful, fresh dessert pairs ripe summer peaches with smooth, aromatic ice cream flavoured with star anise, and makes a super-easy dessert for any day of the week. The recipe requires an ice-cream machine in order to get the best result.

1. Put the milk, cream and star anise in a heavy-based saucepan over low heat, stirring frequently to avoid sticking. Once it begins to simmer, remove from the heat and cover with a lid. Allow the anise to infuse the milk for 1 hour.

2. Once infused, remove the star anise and reheat the milk and cream mixture, this time removing the pan from the heat just before it simmers.

3. Whisk the egg yolks and sugar in a heatproof bowl until smooth, then pour in a third of the hot cream mixture, whisking continuously and slowing down or stopping adding the cream for a moment if required, as you do not want to cook the eggs. Continue until all the cream is incorporated into the egg mixture. It's important to stir well at this stage to ensure that all the sugar dissolves into the liquid.

4. Rinse out the pan, pour the mixture back into the pan and return to a low heat. Cook the custard, stirring constantly and gently with a spatula or spoon for about 10 minutes. You will know the custard is thick enough when you coat the back of the spatula or spoon and run your finger down through the mixture. If it's thick enough, the line you've made should remain. To be extra precise, check the mixture with a thermometer – it should reach exactly 82°C.

5. Remove the custard from the heat and pour it through a fine sieve into a heatproof bowl containing the chopped white chocolate. Allow the chocolate to melt for 2 minutes, then mix until fully combined. Cover the hot custard with a piece of greaseproof paper or clingfilm, pressing it onto the surface to avoid a skin forming. Allow the mixture to cool for a couple of hours, then transfer to the fridge until completely cool.

VARIATION

Swap the peaches for ripe apricots or nectarines. Strawberries would also work, though they will not need to macerate for as long as the stone fruits.

6. Switch on the ice-cream machine in advance to make sure the churning bowl is cold. Once the custard is cool, transfer it to the churning chamber and churn following the manufacturer's instructions until frozen.

7. Put the ice cream in a lidded container. It will keep in the freezer for up to 2 weeks.

8. Before serving, cut the peaches into halves or quarters. Put them in a bowl with a sprinkle of sugar and a splash of vodka and leave to macerate for 35–40 minutes. Twenty minutes before serving, remove the ice cream from the freezer so it can soften slightly.

9. Place some of the peaches with the liquid in a glass bowl. Put a scoop of ice cream on the top and sprinkle with lavender flowers stripped from the stem.

Peanut Butter and Pretzel Cheesecake

SERVES: 12–14
PREP TIME: 25 MINUTES, PLUS AT LEAST 6½ HOURS CHILLING
COOKING TIME: 10 MINUTES

FOR THE BASE
100g digestive biscuits
200g salted pretzels
150g unsalted butter, melted and cooled
   slightly, plus extra for greasing

FOR THE CHEESECAKE MIX
500g full-fat cream cheese
150g smooth peanut butter
75g icing sugar
1 tbsp vanilla bean paste
250ml double cream

FOR THE PEANUT BRITTLE
100g caster sugar
25g golden syrup
½ tsp bicarbonate of soda
100g salted roasted peanuts

This is a real wow dessert. The cheesecake is made with a mix of cream cheese and peanut butter which results in a smooth, rich and almost salty layer, and a mix of digestives and pretzels for the base which cuts through the richness of the cheese layer with more salt. It's a really delicious combination. It is very simple to make – you just need to prepare it ahead, so it has time to chill. A sugar thermometer is useful for the peanut brittle, but it can be made without.

1. Line a 25cm loose-bottomed springform cake tin with greaseproof paper.

2. To make the cheesecake base, blitz the digestives and pretzels in a food processor to a fine crumb (or pound in a bag or between two sheets of clingfilm with a rolling pin). Transfer to a bowl and mix in the melted butter until the crumbs are fully coated. Transfer to the lined tin and press down with the back of a spoon to make a flat base. Place in the fridge for at least 30 minutes to set.

3. Now make the cheesecake mix. Beat the cream cheese, peanut butter, icing sugar and vanilla paste in a bowl with an electric whisk (or in the bowl of a stand mixer fitted with the whisk attachment) until smooth. Add the double cream and whisk again until fully incorporated and thickened.

4. Remove the biscuit base from the fridge and spoon the cream cheese mixture over the top; using the back of a spoon to spread the mixture level in the tin (you could shake the tin slightly to even the top). Cover with clingfilm and transfer to the fridge for at least 6 hours to set (preferably overnight).

5. To make the peanut brittle, first line a baking tray with a silicone baking mat or baking parchment. Put the caster sugar, golden syrup and 2 tablespoons of water in a medium heavy-based saucepan and cook over high heat for 5 minutes until the edges of the sugar syrup begin to caramelise and the temperature is 150°C on a sugar thermometer. Remove from the heat and whisk through the bicarbonate of soda until smooth, then add the peanuts. Carefully transfer the hot brittle mixture to the lined tray and leave to cool completely.

6. To finish the cheesecake, carefully remove from the tin and paper. Smash the set peanut brittle into pieces with a rolling pin, then cover the cheesecake with the broken brittle (you want to serve a piece of brittle with each piece of cake).

Prune and Armagnac Chocolate Torte

SERVES: 12
PREP TIME: 20 MINUTES, PLUS
OVERNIGHT SOAKING
COOKING TIME: 35 MINUTES

200g pitted prunes, chopped into small
    pieces
150ml Armagnac
300g dark chocolate (minimum 60% cocoa
    solids), broken into pieces
200g unsalted butter, plus extra for greasing
3 large eggs
90g caster sugar
85g ground almonds
20g self-raising flour
crème fraîche, to serve

Prunes have gone out of favour a little over the years but hopefully this grown-up dessert will remind you how wonderful they are. Prunes and brandy is a classic combination from the southwest of France, and the sweet, boozy fruit complements the bitter chocolate brilliantly to make a deliciously rich end to a meal. Get started the day before you want to serve the dessert, as the prunes need plenty of time to soak in the brandy.

1. Soak the prunes in a bowl with the Armagnac overnight.

2. The next day, preheat the oven to 150°C/130°C fan/gas 3 and line a 20cm springform cake tin with baking parchment.

3. Melt the chocolate and butter in a heatproof bowl over a pan of simmering water, making sure the base of the bowl doesn't touch the water (and being careful not to let any water get into the chocolate). Once the chocolate and butter mixture has melted, remove from the heat and allow to cool slightly.

4. In a stand mixer fitted with the whisk attachment, or using a bowl and an electric whisk, whisk the eggs with the caster sugar on high speed for 5–10 minutes until the mixture is thick and moussey, has increased in volume and falls in thick ribbons when the whisk is lifted.

5. Whisk the ground almonds and flour into the cooled chocolate mixture, then stir through half the soaked prunes (about 170g).

6. Gently fold a third of the egg and sugar mixture into the chocolate, then fold in the remaining two-thirds, being careful not to knock any air out of the mixture. Transfer to the lined tin, place in the middle of the oven and bake for 30–35 minutes, or until the torte has risen (almost like a soufflé) and a crust has formed on top. Do not open the oven door before it's cooked or it will sink.

7. Remove from the oven and leave to cool completely (to room temperature), then remove from the tin.

8. Slice the torte with a knife that has been warmed under a hot tap for a clean cut. Serve with a spoonful of the remaining soaked prunes on top and a blob of crème fraîche.

Hot Chocolate Mousse Pots

SERVES: 4
PREP TIME: 20 MINUTES
COOKING TIME: 20 MINUTES

200g dark chocolate (minimum 60% cocoa
    solids), broken into small pieces
40g unsalted butter, cubed
4 egg yolks
1 heaped tbsp cocoa powder
2 egg whites
50g caster sugar
100ml whipping cream

GET AHEAD
**You can prepare the pots up to 24 hours
in advance and set them aside in the
fridge until required. Allow them to
come up to room temperature during
the main course then pop them in the
oven before serving.**

This very decadent pudding uses similar ingredients to my cold Chocolate Mousse on page 46 but is made slightly differently, resulting in the most delicious hot baked mousse with a wobbly centre. It is very easy to make and looks great. Serve with a blob of whipped cream and raspberries or vanilla ice cream, or even a warm fruit compote.

1. Preheat the oven to 180°C/160°C fan/gas 4.

2. Put the chocolate and butter in a heatproof bowl, place over a pan of simmering water and slowly allow the chocolate to melt (making sure the water doesn't touch the bottom of the bowl, or get into it). Once melted, remove from the heat and allow to cool for 2–3 minutes before whisking in the egg yolks and cocoa powder until smooth.

3. Whisk the egg whites in a separate bowl with an electric whisk, or in the bowl of a stand mixer fitted with the whisk attachment, until they form stiff peaks, then gradually sprinkle in the sugar and continue to whisk until you have a thick, glossy meringue.

4. Lightly whisk the whipping cream in a bowl with a balloon whisk until it starts to thicken (if you tip the bowl it would fall, almost pour).

5. Fold the whipped cream into the chocolate mixture with a metal spoon until fully combined, then fold through half of the whisked egg whites to lighten the mix, then finally add the remaining egg whites, folding gently, so you keep the air in the mix. Divide the mixture among four ovenproof ramekins.

6. Place in the oven and bake for 15–20 minutes until the mousses have risen slightly but still wobble in the the centre.

7. Remove from the oven and allow to cool for a moment before serving in the ramekin on a dessert plate. If you're serving the mousse with whipped cream or vanilla ice cream on the side, serve it separately in a smaller bowl to avoid it melting.

Kitchen Foundations

Baked Apple Sauce

MAKES: 1.2KG
PREP TIME: 5 MINUTES
COOKING TIME: 25 MINUTES

4 Bramley apples, cored and quartered
4 Granny Smith apples, cored and quartered
100ml good-quality apple juice (or juice your own)

VARIATIONS

Bake the apples with cinnamon sticks or vanilla pods if you want to use the sauce as a dessert base. If you don't want to flavour all the apple sauce, add ground spices to a batch of the sauce as you heat it through before use instead. With added Asian spices such as cumin, saffron, even chilli, the sauce works well as an accompaniment to a curry (a bit like a chutney). As the spices need cooking through, they can be added at the oven-baking stage.

When we bought Melfort House we inherited a number of mature apple trees. We have two crops: the summer sweeter varieties and the autumn cookers. We collect them all and deliver them to a local fruit farm that juices and bottles them. This gives us a resource for the rest of the year, either as gifts, to drink or to cook with at The Berkeley. I'm always looking for ways to use up the apples and this sauce is great. For anyone with apple trees in their garden and a glut of apples, this is the perfect way to preserve them for the winter and bring back memories of warmer months. Baking apples with their skins on gives the purée an extra flavour dimension. The sauce is a classic addition to roast pork, but it also makes a fabulous base, for a crumble perhaps, or the delicious Apple Custard Pots on page 76. You can scale up the recipe based on how many apples you have.

1. Preheat the oven to 200°C/180°C fan/gas 6 and line a large baking tray with baking parchment (the tray should be at least a few centimetres deep, as the apples will foam up a little as they cook).

2. Place the prepared apples on the lined tray, making sure they are all skin side up, and bake in the oven for 20–25 minutes until the skins are dark in colour and the apples have shrunk in size. They shouldn't be burnt but will be dark.

3. Remove from the oven and leave for 10 minutes. While still warm, transfer the baked apples to a high-powered blender along with the apple juice and blitz for 2–3 minutes until smooth.

4. Store the apple sauce in airtight jars in the fridge for up to 1 week or freeze for 3 months.

*Make it perfect

The key to a good apple purée is concentration of flavour. The Bramleys used here contribute a tartness and the Granny Smith a sweet-and-sour flavour. You don't need to add sugar, as the Granny Smith is sweet enough. Be careful with the juice you choose to use: some shop-bought apple juices may be too sweet.

Avocado Dressing

MAKES: ABOUT 250ML
PREP TIME: 10 MINUTES

1 ripe avocado
100g natural yoghurt
juice of 1½ limes
2 tbsp olive oil
1 small garlic clove, finely chopped
½ bunch of dill
2 sprigs of tarragon
2 sprigs of chervil or curly parsley
sea salt and freshly ground black pepper

Though we always have a few jars of shop-bought dressings open in the fridge, we also enjoy making our own. Avocados make a great creamy dressing. It feels summery but, to be honest, we eat avocados all year round and always seem to have a straggler that needs using. Serve this dressing with a prawn cocktail in place of the classic Marie Rose sauce, on a green salad or a Caesar salad in place of the creamy Caesar dressing, or use it in sandwiches in place of salad cream. Chervil can be hard to find, so it's worth growing your own. Replace with parsley if you can't source it.

1. Cut open the avocado and remove the stone. Use a spoon to remove the flesh from the skin and drop the flesh into a blender or small food processor along with the other ingredients, except the salt. (Remember that the lime will prevent the avocado from browning so don't delay the combining of all the ingredients.) Blitz to a smooth consistency. If the dressing is a little thick, add a drop of cold water to loosen. Taste and season with salt and pepper.

2. The dressing will keep in the fridge in an airtight container for a day or so.

Basil and Green Olive Dressing

MAKES: 75ML
PREP TIME: 5 MINUTES

1 bunch of basil, leaves and stalks
50g green olives, pitted
75ml extra virgin olive oil

We eat plenty of pesto at home, and this dressing is very similar. It's so easy to whizz up whatever you might have in the fridge with some oil to make a fresh dressing. Green olives work so well with pasta, drizzled over mozzarella or just served as a dip. The dressing would also be a lovely addition to the Tomato and Fried Onion Salad on page 57 or perhaps stirred into some simply cooked fusilli pasta with some Parmesan cheese grated over the top.

1. Put all the ingredients in a small food processor and blitz until smooth. Add a splash of water if the dressing becomes too thick and re-blend to emulsify.

2. The dressing will keep in an airtight container in the fridge for up to 5 days. Add a layer of oil on top of the dressing to prevent it discolouring.

Caesar Mayonnaise

MAKES: 400ML
PREP TIME: 15 MINUTES

50g flat-leaf parsley leaves
50g tinned anchovies
1 garlic clove, crushed
150ml extra virgin olive oil
150ml extra virgin rapeseed oil
2 egg yolks
1 tbsp white wine vinegar
20g Dijon mustard
grated zest and juice of 1 lemon
20g Parmesan cheese, finely grated

A favourite salad at home is a classic Caesar salad, which we serve with seared tuna or grilled chicken. We tend to give the anchovies a miss, though we always include crisp lettuce leaves, lightly boiled green beans, homemade croutons and some soft-boiled eggs, drizzle everything with this dressing, then shave some Parmesan over the top. It's perfect for a summer's evening. It is also delicious with lightly poached asparagus.

1. Put the parsley, anchovies, garlic and oils in a small food processor and blitz until smooth.

2. Combine the egg yolks, vinegar, mustard and lemon zest and juice in a mixing bowl, then slowly pour the oil mixture onto the egg mix, whisking continuously until fully combined and emulsified. Finally, fold through the grated Parmesan.

3. The mayonnaise can be stored in an airtight container in the fridge for up to 3 days.

* Make it perfect

Mayonnaise, an emulsification of egg yolk and oil, is easy to make when you know how and if you follow a few rules.

- The ingredients should be at room temperature to help avoid curdling.
- Adding the oil too fast can also result in a curdled mix, so add it slowly while whisking continuously and at a constant, vigorous speed.
- If you feel you've added the oil too fast, stop adding it for a moment but keep whisking, then start adding again when the mix can take it.
- We used a mix of olive and rapeseed oils here, as too much olive oil will bring a strong olive flavour to the mayonnaise which you don't want for this recipe. You can also make 100 per cent rapeseed oil mayo.
- If the mixture is on the thin side, add more oil and keep whisking and it will thicken.
- If you have added too much oil and the mayonnaise is too thick, let it down by whisking in a drop of cold water.
- If the mayonnaise curdles during the process, add a drop of boiling water, whisk and it should come back together.
- You can make mayonnaise in a blender, just don't be put off by how it looks initially. It starts off looking like a thin liquid but the blades on the machine will do the work and it will come together very quickly – suddenly even, so keep a close eye on it as you add the oil very slowly.

Roasted Garlic and Buttermilk Dressing

MAKES: 250ML
PREP TIME: 15 MINUTES
COOKING TIME: 1–1½ HOURS,
PLUS 30 MINUTES COOLING

2 garlic bulbs
50ml olive oil
20g black onion seeds, toasted
200ml buttermilk
3 tbsp white wine vinegar
¼ bunch of chives, finely chopped
sea salt and freshly ground black pepper

This dressing works particularly well with grilled chicken served on mixed grains and salad leaves which absorb some of the fabulous flavours. By roasting the garlic, the dressing has a gentle hint of sweet garlic with none of the pungency of raw garlic. It would be a fabulous dipping sauce to accompany barbecued meat, perhaps chicken drumsticks or the Barbecued Pork Burgers on page 249.

1. Preheat the oven to 170°C/150°C fan/gas 4.

2. Cut the tops from each bulb of garlic to expose the cloves, while the bulbs remain intact, then place on a large square of foil and season with salt and pepper. Pour over the olive oil, scrunch in the sides of the foil to seal in the bulbs, place on a baking tray and roast in the oven for 1–1½ hours until the garlic is soft to touch. Remove from the oven, open the foil and allow to cool for 20–30 minutes.

3. Once cool, remove from the foil and squeeze the roasted garlic from the papery skins into a mixing bowl. Retain the foil for a moment, and – using the back of a fork – crush any larger pieces of garlic to a smooth pulp, using the oil that remains in the foil. Add the rest of the ingredients to the bowl, including some of the oil from the foil to add extra flavour to the dressing, and whisk until evenly incorporated. Season with salt and pepper to taste.

Apple, Mustard and Honey Dressing

MAKES: ABOUT 300ML
PREP TIME: 10 MINUTES

50g Baked Apple Sauce (page 264)
2 tbsp runny honey
50g wholegrain mustard
3 tbsp cider vinegar
150ml extra virgin rapeseed oil
1 Granny Smith apple, peeled, cored and
     grated
sea salt and freshly ground black pepper

I love using the apples from our orchard in dressings. Because this delicious fresh dressing has apple and cider flavours I think it will work really well with pork: perhaps the Ham Hock Terrine on page 200 or leftover Brown Sauce-glazed Ham on page 214.

1. Combine the apple sauce, honey, mustard and vinegar in a bowl. Pour in the rapeseed oil and whisk to emulsify.

2. Mix through the grated apple and season with salt and pepper to taste. The dressing will keep in an airtight container in the fridge for up to 2 days (after that, the apple will start to discolour).

Hollandaise

PREP TIME: 15 MINUTES
COOKING TIME: 5 MINUTES

3 egg yolks (see Tip on page 106)
2 tsp white wine vinegar
200g butter, melted
juice of ½ lemon
salt

A warm, creamy sauce made with egg yolks, vinegar and butter, this works well with so many things. At home we serve it with pan-fried salmon, new potatoes and green beans. As a treat we make eggs Benedict for a weekend brunch or for a light spring supper we serve it with English asparagus, Parmesan and softly boiled eggs. It is very simple to make, when you know how. Though you can buy hollandaise, the flavour of homemade is far better.

1. Combine the egg yolks, white wine vinegar and in a heatproof mixing bowl with 1 tablespoon of water. Place the bowl over a saucepan of simmering water, not allowing the base to touch the water, and whisk continuously for 3–5 minutes until thick and glossy.

2. Remove from the heat and slowly start pouring in the melted butter, ensuring it is fully incorporated before adding more; you want to thicken the sauce but not scramble the egg, so it's important not to rush this stage.

3. If the hollandaise curdles and starts to split, stir in an ice cube to bring it back together. Season with the lemon juice and salt to taste.

Harissa Romesco Sauce

**SERVES: 4–6, DEPENDING ON
WHAT YOU SERVE IT WITH
PREP TIME: 5 MINUTES
COOKING TIME: 10 MINUTES**

100g flaked almonds
80ml extra virgin olive oil
200g piquillo peppers from a jar, or fresh
   piquillo peppers (deseeded)
2 garlic cloves, sliced
1 red chilli, chopped (use less if you wish)
1 tsp hot smoked paprika
50g sundried tomatoes
50g rose harissa paste
1 tbsp sherry vinegar (or red wine vinegar)
grated zest and juice of 1 lemon
sea salt

SHORTCUT
**Use ready-toasted almonds, but still
heat them through as it releases the oils
and the flavour before you add them
to the sauce.**

VARIATION
Swap the almonds for pine nuts.

I make a lot of romesco sauce at home. I think I can confidently call it a family favourite – every time it is served there is a universal sigh of appreciation around the table. It is very adaptable and easy to whip up, especially if you have the base ingredients ready in the store cupboard, and has the ability to lift any dish, from a simple salad or a plate of mozzarella, to fish such as sea bass, roasted meat such as lamb, or flatbread. It can be used as a dip, as an accompaniment, as a pizza topping, or as a sauce with pasta such as the 'Nduja and Feta Ravioli on page 126. This is a delightful variation with an undertone of the rose harissa. Adapt the level of heat to suit your taste.

1. Toast the almonds in a dry frying pan over medium heat for about 5 minutes, tossing them in the pan so they cook evenly and don't burn. Once toasted, set aside.

2. If you're using fresh piquillo peppers, they need to be cooked before blitzing. Heat 30ml of the olive oil in a medium saucepan over medium-high heat, then add the fresh peppers. Cook for 5–6 minutes until the peppers start to colour and break down (avoid burning them, as this will make the sauce bitter). Once browned, add the sliced garlic, red chilli and smoked paprika and cook for a further minute, then remove from the heat. Allow to cool slightly before blending, along with the remaining oil and other ingredients.

3. If you're using jarred peppers, just put them straight in a food processor or blender along with the rest of the ingredients and blitz for 2 minutes, or until you have a smooth sauce. (We use a mini blender or a Nutribullet, which are simple to use and easy to clean. If you're using a Nutribullet, don't blend anything hot as the vacuum created can be dangerous and result in scalding.) Season with salt to taste.

4. This sauce is best served at room temperature, though it can be stored in the fridge for up to 5 days.

Black Garlic Barbecue Sauce

MAKES: 3 LITRES
**PREP TIME: 25 MINUTES, PLUS
15 MINUTES COOLING
COOKING TIME: 1 HOUR**

100ml smoked rapeseed oil
4 red onions, roughly chopped
2 cooking apples, cored, peeled and
    chopped
2 red chillies, chopped
2 black garlic bulbs, cloves separated and
    peeled
2 sprigs of rosemary
1 tbsp sweet or hot smoked paprika (you
    may want to adjust the fresh chilli if using
    hot paprika)
1 tbsp English mustard powder
1 tsp salt
150ml balsamic vinegar
100ml dark soy sauce
500ml apple juice
1.5 litres tomato passata
150g soft dark brown sugar
2 tbsp black treacle

This barbecue sauce made with garlic and tomato is really delicious. It adds something special to burgers, such as my pork burgers on page 249, can be served as a sauce and is also a great marinade for barbecue pork ribs or chicken legs (you can then brush the marinade over the meat as it cooks on the grill). It's worth making it in a large quantity, as I do here, as it keeps well in the cupboard and makes a wonderful flavouring to use through the year or give away as a gift. By the time everything is whizzed up I think anyone would find it difficult to name the single ingredients.

1. Heat the smoked oil in a large casserole dish over medium-high heat. Add the onions and fry for 5–6 minutes until well coloured, then add the chopped apples, chillies, peeled black garlic cloves and rosemary and fry for a further 5 minutes until the apples start to break down. Add the paprika, mustard and salt and cook for another 1–2 minutes. Deglaze the pan with the balsamic vinegar and soy sauce and simmer until reduced by half.

2. Add the apple juice and tomato passata to the dish and bring to the boil, then add the brown sugar and treacle and simmer over low heat for 30–40 minutes until the sauce has reduced and thickened, stirring it occasionally to avoid the mixture catching on the bottom of the pan.

3. Once reduced, remove from the heat and allow to cool for 10–15 minutes.

4. Once it has cooled slightly but is still hot (the heat will help the ingredients come together), remove the rosemary sprigs and blitz the sauce in batches in a high-powered blender or food processor for 2–3 minutes per batch until silky smooth.

5. Pass the blitzed sauce through a fine sieve into a bowl to remove any remaining lumps. Adjust the seasoning if required.

6. While it's still hot, pour the sauce into sterilised bottles or jars and seal. The barbecue sauce will keep well, unopened and stored in a cool, dark place, for up to 6 months. Once opened, store in the fridge for up to 2 weeks.

Cooking Perfect Rice

* Make it perfect

A lot of home cooks find cooking rice daunting. It's worth remembering that there are different types of rice that suit different dishes.

Long-/medium-/short-grain rice refers to the length of the grain. White or brown basmati and jasmine rice are all types of long-grain rice. The length of the grain affects the levels of starch that are exuded from the rice during cooking. If cooked at the same temperature and time, short-grain rice will exude more starch than long-grain, which will make it stickier. We tend to use short-grain rice for sushi or puddings, as the starchiness of the grains means they stick together when cooked, and medium-grain rice such as arborio for risottos, letting the starch gradually be released into the liquid as the risotto is stirred, and removing it from the heat while the grain still has a bite in the centre.

At home we cook with white or brown basmati rice. To cook white basmati rice, add rinsed rice to a pan, then cover with cold water so it sits 1.5cm above the level of rice (no salt added). Bring to the boil over medium heat, simmer for 2–3 minutes with the lid on, then switch off the heat, keeping the lid on. The residual heat in the pan keeps it warm. If you're using an induction hob, leave it on number 1 setting to retain some heat. After 10–15 minutes, remove the lid and stir the rice vigorously to agitate the starch and aerate the rice, then re-cover. It will be ready to serve after about 10 minutes. If you are cooking brown rice, then it needs to simmer for about 30 minutes, in a little more water. Stir through to fluff up the grains, then turn off the heat and leave the rice in pan, covered, for 10 minutes before serving.

Leftover rice should be cooled quickly and transferred to the fridge soon after cooking, then used within 24 hours. If you're reheating rice in the microwave, make sure it's piping hot throughout.

Goats' Milk Ricotta Cheese

MAKES: 185G
PREP TIME: 10 MINUTES
COOKING TIME: 20 MINUTES

1 litre full-fat goats' milk
juice of 1 lemon and zest of ½
1 tsp cider vinegar
1 tbsp extra virgin olive oil
sea salt and freshly ground black pepper

You can, of course, buy ricotta cheese but it's so easy to make and well worth a try. Originally it was just a by-product from cheese-making in Italy but now it's a fabulous cheese in its own right. This is a perfect addition to My Kitchen Garden Courgette Salad on page 50 or served at room temperature with some chunky bread. It would be easy to add more flavours along with lemon zest: you could finely chop a small bunch of chives and stir them in, or roast a garlic bulb for an hour before mashing the flesh and beating it into the cheese.

1. Slowly bring the milk to the boil in a heavy-based saucepan over low heat, stirring occasionally to prevent the milk from scorching on the bottom of the pan. Allow the milk to boil for 1 minute, then whisk in the lemon juice and the cider vinegar and stir gently. The acid helps break up the milk into solid curds and liquid whey. Reduce to the lowest possible heat and simmer for about 10 minutes, stirring occasionally until the curds have separated and are floating on the top. Pass the mixture through a fine sieve or muslin cloth over a heatproof bowl, reserving some of the whey that has separated.

2. Leave the curds to drain for 5 minutes, then transfer them to a mixing bowl and add the lemon zest, extra virgin olive oil and 1 tablespoon of the reserved whey. Season with salt and pepper to taste. The ricotta curds will be soft and crumbly. If you prefer your ricotta to be a little wetter, add another tablespoon of the whey.

3. Mix well, cool and store in the fridge for up to 2 days until required.

Flatbread

MAKES: 4 FLATBREADS
PREP TIME: 10 MINUTES, PLUS
30 MINUTES RESTING
COOKING TIME: 5 MINUTES

250g self-raising flour, plus extra for dusting
25g live plain yoghurt
5g fine sea salt
115ml lukewarm water
oil, for greasing

VARIATIONS

To make garlic flatbreads, cook crushed garlic in butter, then leave to infuse before brushing over the cooked breads. You could also infuse melted butter with rosemary.

Flatbreads are so easy to make and work well with many recipes. They make a quick and simple accompaniment to a pasta dish, or can be served with a dip such as Harissa Romesco Sauce (see page 270), and are delicious brushed with melted garlic butter and sprinkled with sea salt.

1. Combine the flour, yoghurt and salt in a mixing bowl, then slowly add the water and stir with a large spoon or whisk until all the ingredients come together to make a soft, slightly sticky dough. As it becomes more dough-like, swap the spoon or whisk for your hands. Turn the dough out onto a lightly floured work surface and knead for 2–3 minutes until it is smooth and elastic. Lightly grease a clean bowl, place the dough in the bowl and cover loosely with clingfilm. Allow the dough to rest at room temperature for 30 minutes.

2. Turn the rested dough onto a lightly floured work surface again and divide into 4 even balls. Gently roll out the balls to 12cm circles, about 5mm thick, with a rolling pin, and keep them on a piece of clingfilm or greaseproof paper as you heat a heavy-based frying pan over medium heat.

3. Once the pan is hot, cook the flatbreads, one by one, in the dry pan for 2 minutes on each side until lightly coloured and puffed up.

Baking with Yeast

* Make it perfect

We use yeast in baking to make the dough rise. It is a living organism that feeds off the sugars or carbohydrates in a mix to create carbon dioxide. This fermentation process forms bubbles in the dough, causing it to rise. There are three main options for the home baker: fresh, dried and fast-action dried.

FRESH YEAST

At the restaurant we mainly use fresh yeast. I think it gives a better flavour and it activates more quickly and for longer. In addition, we are continually baking so it keeps in the fridge and doesn't go to waste. Fresh yeast needs to be crumbled for use and mixed with a tepid liquid, usually water, to activate it. This could be alone or with other ingredients.

DRIED YEAST

At home we use dried yeast; this is dehydrated and looks like small granules. It has a longer shelf life and I think it does the job just as well. It works as a good option if you bake bread less often. Generally, you will need double the amount of fresh yeast to dried.

FAST-ACTION DRIED YEAST

I tend to use the fast activated yeast, also called instant or easy-bake yeast, when speed is more important, such as in bao buns (see page 130) and blinis (see page 228). If replacing fresh yeast in a recipe with fast-action, use 1g of fast-action to 3g of fresh.

In the bread recipes we have listed the quantities for both fresh and dried (not fast-acting) so you can use either (noting that they are different). But do follow the suggested option for yeast if you can as I think it works best, though I appreciate you may have your own preference. The recipes don't differ much as both types need to be activated with a tepid liquid.

Sourdough is made without adding extra yeast, the fermentation process being generated by mixing flour and water to create a pre-ferment. The slow fermentation process creates the bubbles needed to make the bread rise. Most bread recipes take time but this method also involves some planning, initially at least.

Garibaldi Biscuits

MAKES: ABOUT 20 BISCUITS
PREP TIME: 20 MINUTES, PLUS
1 HOUR RESTING TIME
COOKING TIME: 15–20 MINUTES

100g icing sugar, sifted
100g plain flour
100g butter, melted, then allowed to cool
  but not solidify
100g egg whites (about 3 medium egg
  whites)
200g currants
vegetable oil, for greasing

There are a few recipes in this book that use a number of egg yolks, such as the St Clement's Treacle Tart on page 180 and the Bay Leaf Ice Cream on page 224, which naturally leaves you with a lot of egg whites. This is a very quick and easy recipe to use them up. We used to make Garibaldi biscuits at the Berkeley and serve them with a cooked Earl Grey tea cream – it was a hugely popular dessert. They work well as a biscuit to serve with coffee or to accompany the Baked Apple Sauce on page 264.

1. First, make the biscuit batter. Stir together the icing sugar, flour and melted butter in a large mixing bowl with a wooden spoon until smooth.

2. Slowly stir the egg whites through the mix using a metal spoon until they are fully incorporated, then stir through the currants. The dough will be quite wet. Place it in a clean mixing bowl and put covered in the fridge for an hour to rest and firm up slightly.

3. Towards the end of the hour, preheat the oven to 190°C/170°C fan/gas 5 and line a 30 × 23cm baking tray with greaseproof paper.

4. Remove the chilled dough from the fridge. Take a heaped teaspoon of the mix and roll it into a ball in the palm of your hand. You may prefer to oil your hands to prevent it sticking. Place the balls on the tray and lightly press down to flatten, leaving enough space between each to allow for them roughly doubling in size during baking.

5. Bake in the oven for 15–20 minutes, or until golden brown (keep an eye on them towards the end of cooking, as the edges may start to catch). Remove from the oven and cool on a wire rack. Once completely cool they can be stored in an airtight container for up to a week.

Whisky Sour

SERVES: 1
PREP TIME: 5 MINUTES

50ml whisky
25ml lime juice
15ml grenadine
1 egg white
a handful of ice cubes
angostura bitters
a strip of lemon zest, to garnish

There are plenty of recipes in the book (particularly in Something Special or Worth the Wait) that use masses of egg yolks. It's nice to use the whites as well and you may not always want to make a meringue! Egg white won't affect the flavour of the cocktail, though it does add body and changes the appearance. This is a traditional whisky sour recipe but you can use a different spirit if you prefer. I raise my glass to The Gilbert Scott, 2011 to 2021. Cheers.

1. Put the whisky, lime juice, grenadine and egg white into a cocktail shaker. Shake until the mix is emulsified.

2. Add some ice cubes and a dash of angostura bitters and shake again before straining into a chilled glass (I like mine in a tumbler with fresh ice). Garnish with a strip of lemon zest and enjoy.

Mix-it-up Cookies

MAKES: 12
PREP TIME: 15 MINUTES
COOKING TIME: 18 MINUTES

100g soft unsalted butter
125g soft light brown sugar
1 egg yolk
2 tsp vanilla bean paste
160g plain flour
½ tsp salt
½ tsp baking powder

CHOCOLATE AND HAZELNUT
1 tsp cocoa powder
50g dark chocolate (70% cocoa solids),
   chopped
1 tbsp chocolate and hazelnut spread
50g toasted hazelnuts, crushed

BLUEBERRY AND COCONUT
80g frozen blueberries
50g rolled oats
30g desiccated coconut

GINGER AND WHITE CHOCOLATE
100g white chocolate, chopped
1 tsp ground ginger
4 pieces of stem ginger, grated
grated zest of 1 lemon

MINCEMEAT
4 tbsp mincemeat
70g ground almonds

GET AHEAD
Make a larger batch of dough and
freeze the extra mixture in a sausage
shape, wrapped in clingfilm. Defrost,
then slice and bake. Alternatively,
freeze cookie-sized balls of the dough
and bake straight from frozen.

My daughter makes all the cookies in our house. She used to spend ages trawling through recipes to find one she liked, but now she's mastered the perfect cookie base and the possibilities are endless. Here you have them all with a base that works. There's a really great mix of flavours.

1. Preheat the oven to 170°C/150°C fan/gas 4 and line two baking trays with a silicone baking mat or baking parchment.

2. To make the cookie dough base, beat the butter and sugar in a bowl until light and fluffy, by hand with a wooden spoon or using an electric whisk or stand mixer, then beat in the egg yolk and vanilla bean paste. Combine the flour, salt and baking powder in a separate bowl then stir into the butter and sugar mix until everything comes together as a soft dough.

3. Once you have the cookie dough base prepared, fold through the remaining ingredients to make your cookie flavour of choice.

4. Divide the flavoured cookie dough into 12 equal pieces and roll into balls. Place the balls on the lined baking trays, ensuring you leave some space between each cookie as they will increase in size a little while they bake, then lightly flatten them.

5. Place the trays in the oven and bake for 15–18 minutes until the edges begin to crisp but the cookies are still slightly soft in the middle.

6. Remove from the oven, allow to cool for a few minutes on the tray, then transfer to a wire rack to cool completely.

The Ultimate Fruit and Nut Granola

MAKES: 10–12 SERVINGS
PREP TIME: 20 MINUTES
COOKING TIME: 40–45 MINUTES

300g jumbo rolled oats
50g desiccated coconut
100g pumpkin seeds
100g sunflower seeds
75g flaked almonds
100g pitted dates, chopped
75g dried apricots, chopped
50g candied orange peel, diced
1 tsp salt
1 tsp mixed spice
120g soft light brown sugar
90ml vegetable oil
120g golden syrup

I like to eat a quick and easy breakfast as I head out to work, but I don't like to eat anything too sweet. Since this granola is homemade you are in full control of the sweetness. Enjoy it with yoghurt, milk, on top of porridge, or as a crumble on poached fruit or my Baked Apple Sauce on page 264 as a dessert. This makes a batch that can last you a couple of weeks (though it probably won't – it is that good).

1. Preheat the oven to 160°C/140°C fan/gas 3 and line a large baking tray with baking parchment.

2. Put the oats, coconut, seeds and almonds in a large bowl with half the measured and chopped dates, apricots and candied orange peel, and mix together. Add the salt and mixed spice and mix again.

3. Put the brown sugar, oil and golden syrup in a saucepan, place over low heat and cook gently until melted. Once fully melted, pour it over the dry mixture and use a spoon to mix until all the dried ingredients are evenly coated. Some of the mixture may look a bit dry, but it will all mix in once it starts to bake in the oven.

4. Transfer the granola to the lined baking tray and spread it out evenly, then bake in the oven for 40–45 minutes, stirring every 8–10 minutes to ensure it bakes evenly (you don't want it to burn as it will give the granola an unpleasant tang). Once golden, remove from the oven and leave to cool before adding the remaining dried and candied fruit.

5. Once cool, transfer to airtight jars or containers.

6. The granola will keep in an airtight container for up to 2–3 weeks.

INDEX

Acknowledgements

I am really delighted with this book. It will always be a reminder of a very strange and difficult year. I was delighted to have something positive to focus on, which also gave me the opportunity to work with a wonderful team of people again who made the process so easy.

Firstly, thanks to the book people:

It was great to work with Katya Shipster again, who initiated the discussions with her usual energy (and the quince tree is looking splendid, thank you!). Also Adam Humphrey, a very welcome addition to the team, so positive at all times and really easy to work with. Thanks to rest of the HarperCollins team including Oli, Hattie, Jessie, Tom, Alice and Caroline who put their faith in me before they even see the book.

I have worked with art director James Empringham four times now and each time we drop right into an easy routine. Despite this book having a very different look, it still sits comfortably on the shelf beside my others. Great job, really refreshing!

I am hugely impressed by project editor Sarah Hammond, who calmly and simply guided us through the complex book-writing process, pulling everything together at the right moment. This time she was working with my 'book novice' wife, Jane, as they both tried to encourage information out of a couple of chefs. Never an easy task!

I think the photographs are stunning. Susan Bell is hugely professional and wonderful to have around. Again, nothing was too much effort, even the 5am starts to get the sunrise shots of Melfort. Thanks also to Aloha Shaw, a photographer in her own right and very able assistant to Susan.

'Food styling' is a slightly misleading term because these dishes really do taste as good as they look in the photo on shoot day. This is down to Becks Wilkinson and her very able assistant Charlotte Whatcott (Jessie's inspiration). Becks is always 100 per cent focused on ensuring the dish stays looking good until the best photo has been captured. Thanks also for the wild garlic that is now growing at Melfort.

It is always interesting to watch Susan at work with Tabitha Hawkins, the props stylist. She seems to add things and remove things from the table at just the right moment for the right shot – every time.

Thank you to copyeditor Laura Nickoll and the three recipe testers, Pippa Leon, Katy Gilhooly and Emma Marsden. Each recipe has been tested to ensure it works at home, and I have come to learn that recipes written by chefs often have far less detail than is actually needed, so thanks to these guys who add the clarity and ask the right questions.

And to my own team who support me:

Thanks to my agent Richard Thompson at M&C Saatchi Merlin who, along with his expert team, has brought some clarity to my working life. Also Max Dundas, and in particular Ros Clarence-Smith, who handles my media queries perfectly.

Craig Johnston, co-author, joined my team at Marcus following his 2017 win of *Masterchef: The Professionals*, and he now forms part of the core team. I hope you enjoyed the book process, Craig. Although you are quiet I know you have taken everything in – your creative talent is clear to see.

The kitchen garden at Melfort House that you see through the book continues to develop and it's mostly down to Anatoliy Onischenko. I have enjoyed being your apprentice in the garden over the last year. I am so excited to see what each season will bring.

Thanks as ever to my family: Archie and Jessie who appear in some of the images and Jake (who is sadly missing from the images as he had got himself a holiday job!); our spaniel, Esme, who appears in the photos because she has a knack of running into shot at just the right moment; and thanks to Jane – we have always made a great team.

Last, but never least, thanks to the amazing team at Marcus led by my partners Mark and Shauna Froydenlund and supported by Lise Mabon, Ieva Grigaliunaite and Emily Jacobs, and not forgetting good friend Michael Deschamps. Through their support I know I can step away from the kitchen leaving Restaurant Marcus in their very capable hands.

HarperCollins*Publishers*
1 London Bridge Street
London SE1 9GF

www.harpercollins.co.uk

HarperCollins*Publishers*
1st Floor, Watermarque Building, Ringsend Road
Dublin 4, Ireland

First published by HarperCollins*Publishers* 2021

10 9 8 7 6 5 4 3 2 1

ISBN 978-0-00-846096-9

Food styling: Becks Wilkinson
Prop styling: Tabitha Hawkins

Printed and bound by GPS Group

MIX
Paper from
responsible sources
FSC™ C007454

FSC
www.fsc.org

This book is produced from independently certified FSC™ paper to
ensure responsible forest management.

For more information visit: www.harpercollins.co.uk/green

WHEN USING KITCHEN APPLIANCES PLEASE ALWAYS FOLLOW
THE MANUFACTURER'S INSTRUCTIONS